TOKEN TITANS

Tugan Bara & Niko Apollo

Token Titan Rights

Legal Disclaimer

The information provided in this book is for general informational purposes only and should not be construed as legal advice. The regulatory landscape surrounding Web3, blockchain technologies, and tokens varies from country to country and is subject to frequent changes. The authors of this book are not legal professionals, and the content herein should not be considered a substitute for consulting with qualified legal counsel.

"THE OLD WORLD IS DIYING, AND THE NEW WORLD STRUGGLES TO BE BORN:
NOW IS THE TIME OF MONSTERS"

ANTONIO GRAMSCI

Contents

Why This Book Exists

This book has been designed for Web3 builders, entrepreneurs, marketers, and developers.

Our mission is to make the best Web3 marketing education available for anyone. We believe that most of the problems, crashes, and failed projects in Web3 are caused not by bad intentions but by a lack of knowledge about what it means to build in Web3.

Bringing this knowledge to many will enable the creation of more and longer-lasting projects.

That's why this book exists.

How to Use This Book

This book is divided into five key sections. Each section is independent from the others. You can start with what you need the most. You don't have to read all the sections and chapters in a specific order.

SECTION 1—The Rule of the Game. Builders and marketers need to understand the context and the rules of the game when they innovate in Web3—what the power structures are and how to interact with opinion leaders and key communities.

SECTION 2—The Project. A project has to be designed and well thought out. From the positioning to the tokenomics. Without a proper foundation, Web3 ventures are too fragile. We will discuss token utilities, transparency, and even scarcity management.

SECTION 3—The Team. As a founder, you'll create a semipublic figure. You're the leader of the project. We will teach you how to create your own *Minimum Viable Guru* while being able to protect your privacy and stay alive. We will also talk about how you can build team structures that don't break with scale and ways to recruit and pay team members.

SECTION 4—The Crowd. The big difference between Web3 and Web2 marketing is that you talk to a crowd. The bigger the crowd, the more irrational it gets. Members of the crowd (or *"degens,"* as they like to call themselves) are not all similar. Some are beneficial for the project while others have a negative impact. Here you will learn how to handle an irrational crowd.

SECTION 5—The Growth. In the last section, we will talk about the best-performing growth strategies for Web3 projects. To make things super easy, for each method, we will give you a number of steps to follow and *"real-life"* examples.

Illustrations, WIIFM, Key Takeaways, and Definitions

Every time we use a technical concept, you will find a definition below the paragraph. A summary of all Web3 terms and definitions can be found at the end of the book.

Every chapter starts with a WIIFM section, which stands for *"What's in It for Me?"* It will give you a glance of the chapter's content and how you can get the most out of it.

At the end of every chapter, you will find a list of Key Takeaways that summarizes the chapter and its main components.

Besides that, Tugan spent dozens of hours drawing illustrations inspired by Web3 culture.

Bored Ape Monkeys, Little Penguins, and many other animals are adaptations from popular NFT collections. You will also see a lot of *"Pepe the Frog"* as it embodies the crazy side of Web3 holders.

Code of Conduct

The moral code of conduct in Web3 is very simple: Always act in the best interest of holders, stakeholders, and the community in general. That's it.

Crazy things will happen. Your token can go to the moon before collapsing violently. Projects might get hacked. Roadmaps might have to change and adapt to a new reality. And people make mistakes.

You'll do your best, and yet people will be angry at you. That's part of the job. One hundred percent of builders, founders, and marketers have been and will be accused by random people of random things.

And that's okay. Because you know that you always did your best for the project and for the holders. This book will help you build and navigate this nascent space.

Be a force for good.

Philosophical Foreword by Tugan

With Web3, you own.

—*Nicole Muniz.*
Former CEO of Yuga Labs

Crypto is *not* about currency and finance.

It's not about speculation and weird monkey JPEG files on the blockchain (others also call them *"NFTs"*).

It's about something much more important.

Something that changes everything if you have it.

And something that condemns you to poverty and misery if you lack it.

Something Cool Happened 161 Years Ago . . .

A hundred and sixty-one years ago, the Homestead Act was passed in the USA. It has nothing to do with Web3 . . . and yet relates to everything about Web3.

Let me explain, and everything will make sense.

The Homestead Act granted private property over 160 acres to any adult citizen willing to live on and improve the land for five years.

The act was passed to encourage people to settle in and inhabit the Western United States and promote economic development.

It significantly impacted the nature of property in the United States. Before the act, most land was owned by the government or major landowners.

The Homestead Act allowed individuals to own land, which gave them a stake in the country's future. This led to increased investment in land and improvements, which then led to growth. The Homestead Act also had a democratizing effect on American society. It allowed people from all walks of life to own land, regardless of their social status or wealth.

Cool stuff, right?

Now think about this:

You're a farmer in the 1860s in the United States. Thanks to this new law, you can have ownership over your field. It's the same for the three other farmers that settled next to you. Now, the son of one of the farmers has some spare time, so you get him a revolver. He will patrol around the field to protect them against Native Americans (whom the Homestead Act forgot about).

Thanks to the presence of this sheriff, more settlers are coming to the area and are sharing the cost of the sheriff's salary. The growing presence of farmers and their families makes it profitable to open a saloon. Now this area is protected by a sheriff and offers leisure. The land is getting more valuable around this area, and more people are coming.

It's now interesting for someone to open a bank and for the community to petition to be included in railroad and telegraph infrastructure developments. If successful, it will make the land more valuable and attract more settlers and service providers.

This drew the attention of two economists who later got a Nobel Prize in Economics for their work: Douglass North and Robert Fogel. According to their work, private property was a key factor in the economic growth of the United States in the nineteenth century and, generally speaking, around the world.

Private property has unleashed a wave of economic development. **Private property changes the nature of things and kicks off prosperity**. It can provide incentives to invest, improve security, and promote innovation.

Fast-forward to today's world.

For most of humanity and most countries, private property is *not* secured. **Things you own might be taken away by corrupt government officials, warlords, or gangsters.** In this context, people don't invest, don't innovate, don't get patents, don't improve their real estate, don't raise funds for a venture, etc.

Consequently, these areas don't experience economic growth and social development.

Think about it: **the only thing in common that all the malfunctioning, violent, and poor areas in the world have is the lack of private property**. They don't have the same political systems, religions, climate, culture, etc. But they have *one* and *only one* thing in common: private property is *not* secured.

This is where Web3 comes in . . .

Web3 Is Private Property for Everyone, Everywhere

Web3, blockchain, and crypto are about private property. **It's about owning stuff.** It's about having private property as long as you have the internet.

"With Web3, you own," said Nicole Muniz (former CEO of Yuga Labs)

It has been summarized the following way by venture capital firm Andreessen Horowitz (a16z) in their *"2023 State of Crypto"* report:

The Web1 era was about providing information and mostly static websites. Web2, with centralized products like Instagram and YouTube, made it possible for anyone to publish things and communicate without borders or limits. However, the economic value generated by these users was captured by the owners of these platforms. In Web3, people will use tokens to own and govern platforms.

Anyone interested in participating in Web3 will own and take part in the benefits of the infrastructure on which value will be built in the coming decades.

Speaking of taking part . . .

Building in Web3

Most people interested in Web3 take part as gamblers or investors. Very few are building because of the technical barriers (something that no-code platforms like Side.xyz are solving).

The real Web3 opportunity is to build, contribute, and market in this space. Web3 is a wild world. A week you spend building in Web3 is like a year in *"real life."* Web3 is faster entrepreneurship. Stakes are higher, perspectives are higher, and chances to contribute to a better world are also higher. Of course, profit opportunities are much higher than in Web2, but so are the risks.

Projects grow rapidly to hundreds of millions, if not billions, in market capitalization before crashing among conspiracies and suspicions of crime or malevolent activities. It's not uncommon to read about Web3 founders and innovators dying suddenly while their fortunes become impossible to find.

On a more positive note, new blockchains, technologies, and trends emerge every month, sometimes (but only sometimes) making previous notions obsolete.

Writing such a book was challenging in a constantly changing world, with marketing techniques and strategies changing quickly.

After working years in the shadow, Apollo and I concentrated on teaching you the secrets behind building successful projects in Web3. **This book is about what works and stays true independent of the trends, market mood swings, and incoming technological revolutions**.

It's your companion to build and innovate in this space.

Tugan Bara
October 2023, Dubai, UAE

PS. Wondering if we are interested in building your idea together with you? The answer is most likely, *"Hell yes!"* So please get in touch with us. Web3 is being built as we speak. And we want to build it with you. If that's something for you, go to www.tokentitans.com/go, and apply to become a portfolio company that we invest in or work with.

www.tuganapollo.com/go

SECTION 1
THE GAME

The 300: An Introduction to the Web3 Game

What important truth do very few people agree with you on?

—Peter Thiel

WIIFM

Web3 is a multitrillion-dollar industry, with little competition and huge potential . . . And the market hasn't priced it. We want to convince you that there is a strong contrarian bet to make.

If you get started in Web2 today, competition is overwhelming. The reasons are many: the markets are mature, demand is strong, and the barriers to entry are low thanks to *"no-code or low-code"* platforms.

Solutions like Shopify or ClickFunnels enable anyone to create a Web2 business. Stripe and PayPal allow you to bill customers. Meta, Snapchat, and TikTok let you run ads and attract thousands of customers. Thanks to TikTok or YouTube, developing an audience is cheap or free (if you're ready to put the time in).

But . . .

It's *saturated.*

You'll always have someone bigger, stronger, faster than you. Potential users and customers will always compare you to a more established brand and business. Competitors can spend more than you in ads and outprice you out of the market.

It's what's called a **red ocean**. Full of blood and sharks. What you want is a blue ocean, with less competition and blood spilled.

The Obvious (And Mostly Empty) Blue Ocean

Web3, in the meantime, is much less competitive. **It feels almost empty**. Solutions to build things without technical skills are few. The technical barrier to entry is still high for both founders and users.

The total addressable market is much lower than Web2 as only 420 million people own crypto worldwide as of 2023.* In comparison, 5.3 billion people are using the internet.

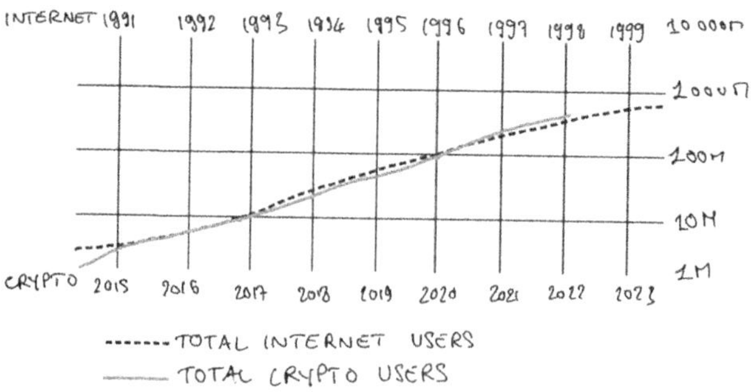

INTERNET VS. CRYPTO ADOPTION

We like to say that **it's a game of 300 builders.**

---

* https://triple-a.io/crypto-ownership-data/

Take the best Web3 developers, entrepreneurs, NFT influencers, and business angels. It's a group of a few hundred people.

In Web2, you have to compete against thousands, if not tens or hundreds of thousands, of people to become an insider and matter.

In Web3, you can become an insider if you work and focus. This book will teach you how. You'll learn about the codes, strategies, and secrets to build and matter in Web3.

In Web3, everything is in its infancy. Everything has to be built. As the meme says, *"You're early."*

YOU'RE SO EARLY!

Whether you want to become a builder, a marketer, or a business angel, there is plenty of room in Web3. Don't get us wrong: free space doesn't mean free lunch. You'll have to work, contribute, and fit into the culture. You'll have to build to prove your worth. Because people don't trust. They verify. But it's easier here than anywhere else.

In a matter of a couple of years, Web3 will be overcrowded with builders, big companies, and pure players worth tens of billions. **Some big brands like Gucci, Nike, and Starbucks are entering the space but are still very careful and shy.** As regulations will become more clear, many will come. Everyone will come to get their slice of the pie. All big consumer brands, entertainment franchises, or financial giants. Billions of people will own crypto and know how to use smart contracts and wallets. At this precise time, becoming one of the three hundred insiders will be almost impossible.

Definition: *smart contracts or contracts*
Smart contracts or *contracts* are like digital agreements or smart deals. It's a set of rules written in code that self-executes based on predefined conditions. Imagine a contract as a digital handshake, ensuring that specific actions occur automatically when certain conditions are met.

Definition: *wallet*
A *wallet* is like a digital bank account for the decentralized internet. It's a secure tool that lets you store, manage, and use cryptocurrencies and other digital assets. Imagine it as your personal digital wallet but for the blockchain world.

Right now it's possible. Maybe you are at the right time and place for the first time in your life. So keep reading, my friend.

The Important Truth That Builders Are Missing and the Market Hasn't Priced In

Entrepreneur and investor Peter Thiel likes to ask: *"What important truth do very few people agree with you on?"*

This question is often associated with Peter Thiel's book *Zero to One*, in which he explores the idea that innovative and successful businesses are often built on unique insights or contrarian beliefs that challenge conventional wisdom.

Our answer to this question lies with this book. **As an entrepreneur or aspiring entrepreneur, not building in Web3 is a mistake.** Same for a marketer, designer, and developer.

We're not in 2012 when Bitcoin was an under-the-radar weird thing that many cypherpunks adored. Crypto is going mainstream. All the big companies are coming. Institutional money is waiting to pour into Web3 technologies.

Michael Saylor is not exactly a supporter of Web3 as he is focused only on Bitcoin. Still, he made a very important point in 2020. Bitcoin was this obvious revolution that the market hadn't priced in yet. In 2010, Saylor believed that the GAFA companies (Google, Apple, Facebook, Amazon) were in a monopoly situation. They were about to rake in profit almost never seen since Rockefeller and Standard Oil. Yet the market hadn't priced it in as of 2010. It's the same for Bitcoin now.

This book's focus is broader as we build on Web3 and not Bitcoin alone. But this notion of Saylor is key to our understanding. Between 2010 and 2017, crypto was an exotic concept that still had a strong failure rate and was attracting mostly gamblers and zealots. **Crypto and Web3 today are in the *"obvious but not priced in, not saturated with builder"* phase.** Web3 tomorrow will be *"mainstream adoption, priced in and saturated with builders."*

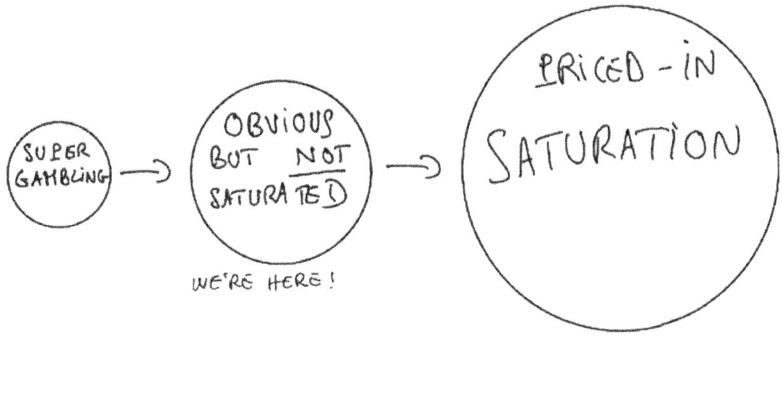

So you might ask . . .

Why Are So Many People Missing the Point?

For many reasons:

- *Obstacle 1: Volatility.* Things keep going up and down super violently. People panic and lose money.
- *Obstacle 2: Regulatory uncertainty.* You have no idea if the SEC will sue you tomorrow, and your lawyers don't know what to do.
- *Obstacle 3: Security concerns.* North Korea might hack you and leave you with nothing.
- *Obstacle 4: Lack of consumer protection.* You have no idea how to process a refund in Web3, as token ownership can change hands many times each day.
- *Obstacle 5: Technological complexity.* Web3 developers charge $30,000 per month. Technologies change all the time.
- *Obstacle 6: Market manipulation and rug pulls.* Some people are smarter than you and don't have your best interest in mind.
- *Obstacle 7: Lack of mainstream adoption.* Some people say that there are not enough people crazy enough to take part in this.
- *Obstacle 8: Environmental concerns.* You've heard that it's polluting, and you're worried your investors won't like it.
- *Obstacle 9: Legal and tax complexities.* Taxes are getting clearer, but there are still many legal obstacles in the way.
- *Obstacle 10: Innovation risk.* Things change quickly, and you might build something no one needs.
- *Obstacle 11: Assumption of limited use cases.* Do people really use wallets and Web3 for something other than gambling?
- *Obstacle 12: Difficulty in accessing funds.* Bringing money to crypto and bringing money back from crypto is challenging. Your bank might just shut down your account.

Definition: *rug pull*
A *rug pull*, derived from the phrase *"pulling the rug out,"* is a cryptocurrency scam in which fraudulent developers attract investors to what seems like a promising new opportunity, only to vanish with the invested money seconds later, leaving the investors with a valueless investment.

We could add another point:

- *Obstacle 13: Lack of courage and herd-like behavior.* People flock to an industry for an opportunity in a mimetic fashion. They wait for others to go first and show the way before moving.

The good news is that Web3 is experiencing its . . . *"Perestroika Moment."*

The Web3 Perestroika Moment

Let's get back to some AFK (*"away from keyboard"*) history. One of the authors of this book (Tugan) has an autistic focus on what happened in the Soviet Union and then Russia from 1985 to 1999.

It might sound unrelated to Web3, but let us explain.

In 1985, the Soviet Union's ultimate boss, Gorbachev, introduced two major reforms in a last attempt to revamp the Soviet economy. These reforms were called Perestroika and Glasnost.

Perestroika aimed to restructure the economy, allowing limited market reforms. It means a little bit less of communism and a little bit more of capitalism.

Glasnost promoted openness and free expression. While not designed for it, these changes indirectly influenced students by fostering a more open mindset and exposure to new ideas, which could inspire entrepreneurial ventures.

What happens after is fascinating.

A small group of bold entrepreneurs rushed into this loophole to create the first companies after decades of ruthless communism.

One of these entrepreneurs, Mikhail Khodorkovsky, even created his own bank. The concept originated in 1986, and Khodorkovsky then created the first privately owned banks in Russia in 1988 that later became the Menatep Bank.

Crazy, right?

(Keep in mind: it's still communism.)

Because these young entrepreneurs could provide goods and services to anyone, including key party members, they became very wealthy and politically connected.

They were the ones who would become the *"oligarchs"* a few years later when the Soviet Union collapsed. Thanks to the connection, capital, and experience they accumulated during communism, they could take over big chunks of the Russian economy in the '90s.

Somehow these young entrepreneurs knew an important truth that very few people in the Soviet days agreed with them. Because the risks were extremely high.

In his book *The Oligarchs: Wealth and Power in the New Russia*, author David Hoffman points out an interesting fact. He wonders why so few people seized the opportunity to join entrepreneurship during the Gorbachev reforms.

The answer is that **everyone assumed that sooner or later, the hard-liner communists would oust Gorbachev, take over the power, and throw all these minicapitalists to jail.**

"We were aware of the risks. We knew that the hard-liners could come back to power and punish us for what we were doing," said Leonid Nevzlin, Khodorkovsky's business partner.

This is the parallel with crypto and Web3.

Why are so few people and companies joining Web3? Because they fear or just assume that one day the government will wake up, ban crypto, make holding Bitcoin illegal, and throw anyone in jail who has built anything there.

In the same way communists could have stopped entrepreneurship overnight, the government could make Web3 simply illegal tomorrow.

This won't happen because the communists couldn't stop entrepreneurship in the late '80s. The reason is very simple: **in every layer of society, many people benefitted from it.**

In Communist Russia, working families could have an extra income thanks to the small student business of their sons. Anyone could now have access to more goods and services without waiting for the state to provide them. Even top party members were in the loop and enjoying the services provided by these entrepreneurs.

In any layer of society, a growing number of people started to like this freedom and these improvements.

It's the same for crypto. From low-income families to insider-trading-addicted Congress members to entrepreneurs going through Silicon Valley, **in every layer of today's society, a growing number**

of people, for many different reasons, want crypto to stay and to be successful.

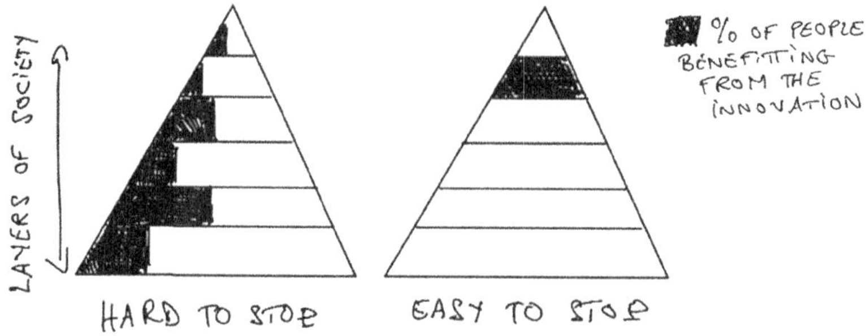

In the illustration above, you can see things that are easy to stop and things that are hard to stop. It would have been easy to cancel if it benefited only one layer of society and no one else. But if a growing number of people in any layer wanted this to stay, it's hard to stop.

Crypto is here to stay, and you can be part of it.

The Power Triangle

Power is power.

—Cersei Lannister

WIIFM

Any industry has codes, unwritten rules, players, and leverages. If you understand them, you thrive. If you don't understand them, you struggle. Let's uncover the secrets, rules, and power moves in Web3.

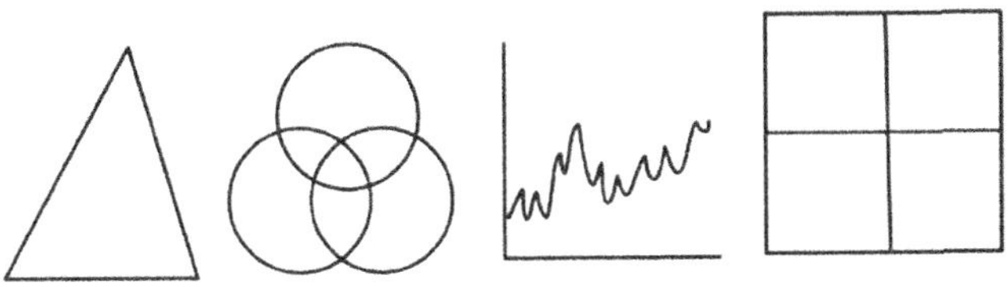

Introducing: The Web3 Power Triangle

Disclaimer: In the coming chapters, you'll see more and more little triangles, charts, circles, and matrices. That's our way of illustrating ideas.

The Web3 Power Triangle aims to map power structures and struggles in a growing yet nascent space where, overnight, autistic developers rub shoulders with crypto billionaire investors to launch a new token, create a FUD on a competing platform, or prepare the biggest ICO ever.

> Definition: *ICO*
> An *ICO* is a public fundraising event where a Web3 project sells its tokens to the general public.

> Definition: *FUD*
> *"Fear, uncertainty, and doubt" (FUD)* is used to put downward pressure on the price of a coin or NFT. *FUD* is often spread about new NFT projects, often unfairly to tank the floor price. This can be done to sweep up bargains if successful or as an act of sabotage.

It's a space where you can go from zero to hero in a matter of months or even weeks if you understand how to play the game.

Corner No. 1—Your PayPal Mafia

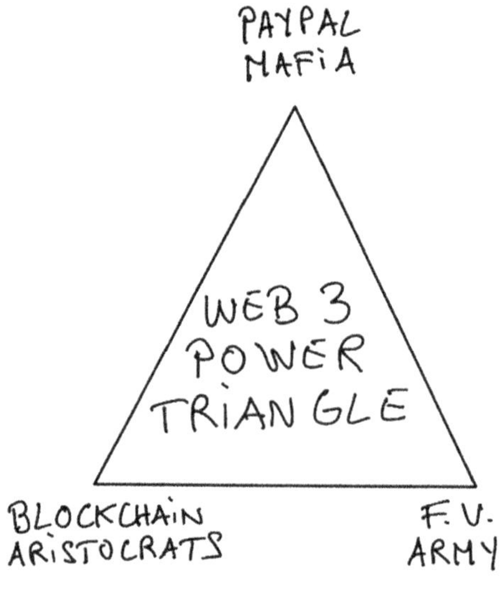

At this stage, the expression *"PayPal Mafia"* is well-known in Web2 entrepreneurship.

PayPal was founded in December 1998 as an online payment platform. It became quite successful and was eventually acquired by eBay in 2002. Many of the early employees and executives of PayPal went on to play influential roles in other prominent tech companies and start-ups. Think about Peter Thiel, Reid Hoffman, or Elon Musk. Together they are called the PayPal Mafia. As investors or entrepreneurs, they are behind companies like Facebook, Palantir, Stripe, Spotify, Airbnb, SpaceX, Tesla, Neuralink, The Boring Company, LinkedIn, YouTube, etc.

As Peter Thiel emphasized, the group had a very strong ideological (understand here: *libertarian*) homogeneity. He later explained that **the power of this group is the homogeneity in deviance from the social norm.**

In a class at Stanford in 2012, Thiel recalled:

> *PayPal's founding team was six people. Four of them were born outside of the United States. Five of them were 23 or younger. Four of them built bombs when they were in high school. (Your lecturer was not among them.) Two of these bomb makers did so in communist countries: Max in the Soviet Union and Yu Pan in China. This was not what people normally did in those countries at that time.*

Okay, what about Web3 here?

It means that to matter and grow in Web3, you need to create a circle of power around you. **You need to create your own PayPal Mafia.**

The best way to do it is to build something or join a group that builds something you believe in.

It's not about tweeting or going to networking events. It's about building. Builders recognize builders. As a consequence, the focus here is not to make money but to connect with like-minded builders.

PSY-OPS TIME—WHAT OTHER BUILDERS ARE LOOKING FOR

- *"If I build, they'll come."* Technical founders in Web3 are struggling to find talented marketers who understand the space and don't copy-paste sleazy Web2 strategies (while operating with little to no budget).
- *"I want something big."* Marketers are too often working on short-term cash-grab projects and wish to be part of a big project with either marketing impact (e.g., Yuga Labs) or technological breakthroughs (e.g., Uniswap).
- *Insight and insiders.* Builders want access and insight. How did they raise funds from this VC? How did they get a grant from this blockchain? Can someone make an intro? What works right now for NFT marketing?
- *Whitelisting and presale.* Can you get a whitelist for this project that mints next week? Could you keep a free slot in your presale for me?
- *The token-of-respect method.* When you launch a token or an NFT, give some supply for free to a few selected insiders and builders as a token of respect!
- *The status boost.* Everyone is thriving for status. Inviting other founders to become advisers for your project is a way to provide them with recognition and value.

Definition: *whitelisting*
Owning a *whitelist* is like having an exclusive guest list for a VIP event. It's a process where you register or get approval to participate in a specific activity, like a token sale or a restricted area. Only those on the list (whitelisted) are allowed access, adding an element of exclusivity and control to the event or platform.

Definition: *presale*
A *presale* is a limited-time sale before the official launch, where a project sells its tokens to a select group of early investors at a discounted price. It follows the same principles as an initial coin offering (ICO).

Definition: *mint*
A *mint* is usually used to describe the launch of an NFT collection in which users interact with the smart contract and receive a random NFT. In the previous NFT bull market, NFT mints were highly anticipated since users who were whitelisted were able to sell their minted NFTs only minutes later for thousands of dollars in profit.

Corner No. 2—The Blockchain Aristocrats

Let's address the obvious paradox here.

Aristocracy is about blood and birth. Yet we are in the first generation of people in blockchain technologies. The answer lies in the pace of evolution in Web3.

You have to consider each market cycle as a generation with key technical innovations and key platforms (centralized and decentralized).

2010–2011 BULL MARKET

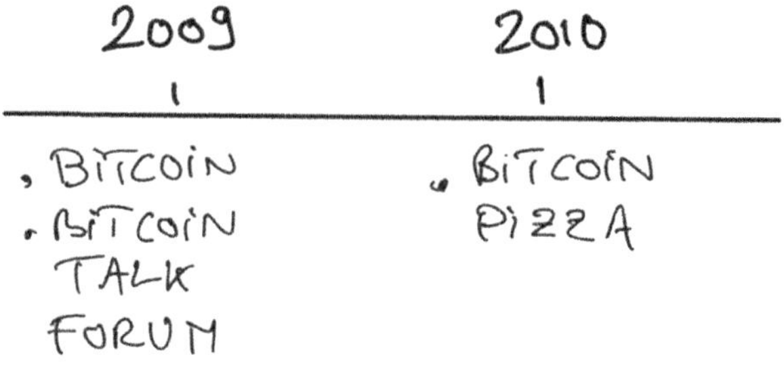

This is the *"early Bitcoin adoption"* period. We experience the first mythical events and milestones that kickstarted the Bitcoin journey.

Bitcoin first captured the interest of ideologically motivated early adopters. They saw its potential to reshape the financial world. The discussion happened on the BitcoinTalk forum.

It's also the time of the famous Bitcoin Pizza, when someone paid 10,000 BTC for two pizzas, marking one of the first commercial transactions using Bitcoin.

In February of 2011, we witnessed a significant milestone as Bitcoin's price reached parity with the US dollar, briefly trading at approximately $1 per BTC. During this period, BTC fluctuated from a few cents to over $30.

2013–2014 BULL MARKET

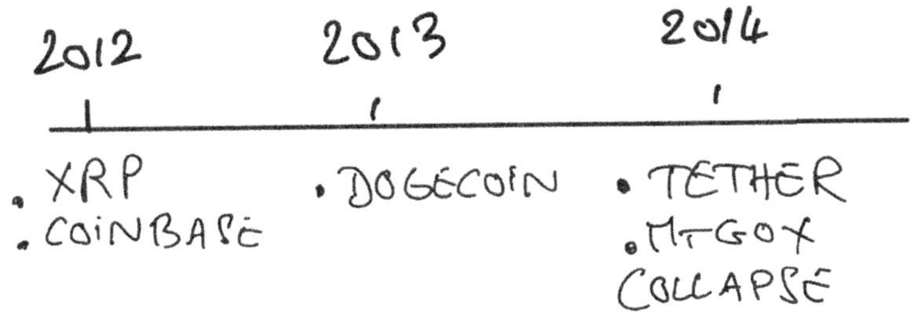

The period of the *"2013–2014 bull market"* in the crypto space marked a time of significant expansion and innovation. New cryptos joined the club with Litecoin, Ripple, and even Dogecoin.

These alternative cryptos offered different features and use cases. They captured the attention of both enthusiasts and investors. It's worth mentioning the announcement of Ethereum's development in late 2013 by Vitalik Buterin. He introduced the notion of smart contracts and decentralized applications.

From now on, crypto surpasses the notion of *"currencies"* and *"payment options."* The potential has become much larger, even though nobody is talking about *"Web3"* yet. This is the time for all future innovations to be made possible.

The bull market also brought a lot of mainstream media attention to Bitcoin. However, financial experts were still very critical of Bitcoin and crypto in general. Still, a growing number of people were aware of these innovations. Coinbase, which was launched in 2012, played a vital role in facilitating early adoption by offering an accessible platform for individuals to buy, sell, and store cryptocurrencies.

A big milestone of this period is the introduction of Tether (USDT), one of the first stablecoins, which sought to provide stability within the volatile crypto market by pegging its value to the US dollar.

Definition: *stablecoins*
Stablecoins are crypto tokens that have their value pegged to another asset like the USD ($). Crypto traders like to consolidate gains in stablecoins before going on a shopping spree when the market dips.

A large event of this period was the collapse of MtGox, the biggest crypto exchange in the world at the moment, with 70 percent of transactions.

2017–2018 BULL MARKET

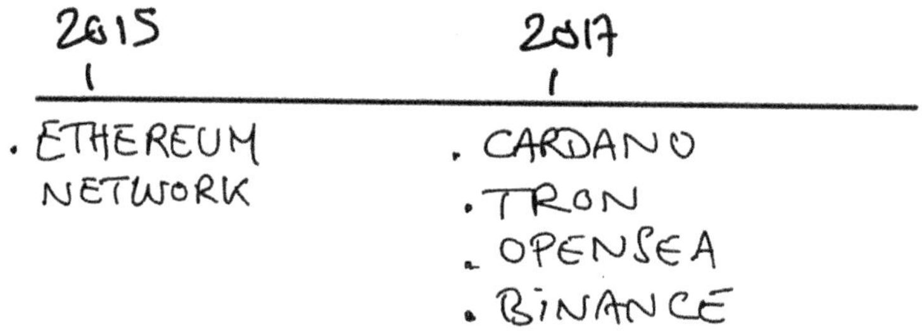

This bull run made Bitcoin and crypto mainstream. Maybe not mainstream in adoption, but mainstream in terms of awareness. Now everybody has heard of the term *cryptocurrency.*

Many people started trading and made fortunes (before losing it all during the crash of 2018). Financial experts were debating the utility of crypto on national television.

We also experienced a surge in fundraising through initial coin offerings (ICOs). These crowdfunding events allowed numerous projects to secure capital by issuing their tokens to backers.

Most of them turned out to be scams or simply bad ideas. But among them, notable projects emerged like Cardano, Tron, EOS, or XTZ.

Centralized exchange Binance was launched in 2017 by Changpeng Zhao. Within 180 days, it grew into the largest digital asset exchange in the world by trading volume.

Devin Finzer was inspired by CryptoKitties in 2017 and created the first NFT trading platform, OpenSea. Fast-forward to May 1, 2022, the platform recorded a record-breaking $2.7 billion in trading volume, which dropped by 99 percent only four months later.

> Definition: *CryptoKitties*
> *CryptoKitties* was one of the first blockchain games involving NFTs. Players were able to collect, breed, and trade digital cats. One CryptoKitty sold for over $100,000 in ETH, bringing the first wave of attention to NFTs and blockchain gaming.

2020–2021 BULL MARKET

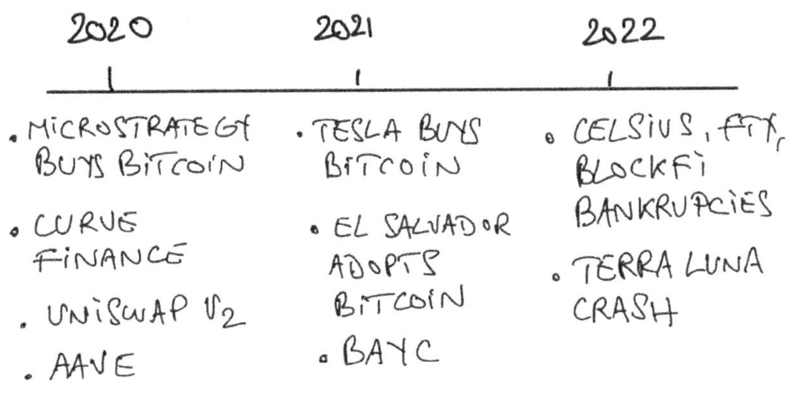

This bull market marked significance in both awareness and people's actual interaction with crypto.

The COVID and post-COVID money printing created a strong narrative around inflation hedges, and Bitcoin started to take (slowly) some market share from gold as a way to protect against inflation.

It was the first *"institutional interest"* in Bitcoin, with major companies such as MicroStrategy and Tesla making substantial purchases of Bitcoin.

This institutional adoption signaled growing recognition of Bitcoin's role in traditional finance. El Salvador's adoption of Bitcoin as a legal tender marked a milestone in the cryptocurrency's integration into national economies.

The *"DeFi (decentralized finance) boom"* was one of the key developments of this bull run. Protocols like Aave, Uniswap V2, and Curve lead the charge. These platforms use blockchain's capabilities to revolutionize traditional financial services by enabling decentralized lending, borrowing, and trading.

At the same time, the *"NFT (non-fungible token) craze"* brought digital ownership and creativity to millions of collectors and gamblers. People learned about OpenSea (created in 2017). NFT collections like the CryptoPunks and Bored Apes found buyers among international celebrities—Neymar and Jay-Z, just to name a few.

Of course, DeFi and NFT, like the wave of ICO in 2017, also brought a lot of scams and poorly designed products. We can mention the epic failure of Terra Luna.

Nevertheless, at the end of the bull market, the biggest failures came from centralized entities like Celsius Network, BlockFi, Voyager, and hedge fund Three Arrows Capital (3AC) and FTX. Remarkably, most big DeFi platforms like Aave and Curve stayed unaffected by the collapse of crypto assets.

HOW DO YOU BECOME A BLOCKCHAIN ARISTOCRAT?

Well . . . you start as a Web3 peasant. Then you start to build stuff. Now you're a builder . . .

But that's not enough.

You have to build something big. Something that will survive a bear market (at least one!) and stay in the space for the next bull. The longer you survive, the more you have a chance to become an aristocrat.

Blockchain Aristocrats nowadays are founders of blockchains, popular DeFi protocols (Aave, Curve, Uniswap), centralized exchange (Binance, Coinbase, Bitfinex), and successful tokens and NFTs (Yuga Labs, MakerDAO, Tether).

Very successful investors that had gone through boom and bust also got this aristocrat status. Think about Mike Novogratz. Some big VCs have also gotten this status.

Something you have to understand is that **reputation is extremely important for aristocrats.** Almost all of them have been at some point (rightly or falsely) accused of shady activities or other practices.

Having an odor of sanctity is primordial for them. Tron's founder, Justin Sun, even went as far as becoming an ambassador for the Grenada island. People had to call him *"Your Excellency."*

(Yes, this happened.)

The more the industry moves forward, the harder it gets to become an aristocrat.

Having made money in Web2 or TradFi (traditional finance) is not valuable in their eyes. Being a pure player, a believer, and an OG matters most.

Definition: *OG* *OGs* are referred to as *"original gangsters."* Being an *OG* means being there from the beginning.

They know who the early believers and risk-takers were and who came when it was easy to build and make money. Also, they see who is leaving the space during the bear market to only come back when there is *"easy"* money to make.

PSY-OPS TIME—WHAT ARISTOCRATS ARE LOOKING FOR

- *"Unghost the ghost chain, or ghost protocol."* Blockchain and platform founders need builders creating stuff, value to be invested on their chain (the total locked value, or TLV, is how you rank blockchain dominance), and awareness brought to their platform. Aristocrats are powerful but in competition against each other. Most products are lacking traction (hence the *"ghost chain"* expression).
- *"50–500x retail dumping."* VCs are looking for projects that can deliver 50x to 500x. They are not interested in equity in the company but in tokens. Haters would say, *"Tokens to dump on retail investors."*

- *"The next hot thing."* Aristocrats are looking to enter before anyone else in *"the next hot thing"* before it's hot. Access to a presale (angel investing) is interesting for them if the project's potential is big enough.

> Definition: *ghost chain*
> A *ghost chain* is defined as a blockchain that has nothing going on in its ecosystem.

Corner No. 3—The FU Army

I guess you know the notion of *"FU Money"*—money that can buy your freedom. With FU Money, you don't need to wake up and commute to work, you don't need to obey a boss, and you're free with your time and decisions. You can say FU if you wish.

Well . . .

When it comes to leverage and power in Web3, **having a crowd of holders, fans, or degens (they like to call themselves like this) is power.**

With hundreds of thousands of degens supporting your project and your mission, the following are possible:

- You *don't* need VC money. You can raise from them.
- You *don't* need to pay the influencer. You're the influencer.
- You *don't* need a blessing from anyone—you just do.
- You *don't* have to beg for talent to join you. They emerge from the community.
- You *don't* need to spend money on ads. The traction is already there.

But you have to understand the psychology of crowds and use it wisely (and ethically), or it might backfire.

Understand how all these people arrived there in the first place!

BITCOIN AND CRYPTO VOLATILITY IS NOT A BUG. IT'S A FEATURE

"It's a feature, not a bug" is a common joke in software development. It means that when something is broken or stupid, it actually might be useful or even on purpose.

So the Bitcoin volatility—its ATH (all-time-high) and epic crashes—is it a bug or a feature? Is it a problem to be solved or an opportunity?

It's an opportunity.

Bitcoin went up from $4,000 in March 2020 to $69,000 in November 2021 before crashing to $15,000 in June 2022, a marketing campaign for the whole space. **Shiba Inu, going 150,000,000 percent, is a PR agency for Web3**. An NFT going up in value before losing 90 percent of its value is creating a conversation about Web3.

This roller coaster has attracted tens of millions of eyeballs—some of whom became investors, influencers, and builders in the ecosystem. As we saw, hundreds of millions of people around the world own crypto, mostly thanks to this *"marketing"* feature.

Don't get us wrong: pretty much everyone came for the *"free money."* For the overnight generational wealth coming from a little under-the-radar token.

We saw the headlines about this kid making millions. We saw *Forbes* claiming Binance founder, *"CZ,"* is worth $100 billion and calling Sam Bankman-Fried *"the next J. P. Morgan"* before getting hit by the collapse of FTX.

People arrive with the FOMO before experiencing our first major FUD.

Definition: *FOMO*
"Fear of missing out" (FOMO) causes people to make hasty emotional decisions, generally near the top of a speculative mania. *FOMO* is the force behind Ponzi schemes, stock promotions, and simple legit bubbles.

Some people leave after getting burned. But most stay to become diamond hands or builders. Now they're *"here for the tech."*

Definition: *diamond hands*
A collector with *diamond hands* can resist panicking and hold onto an investment even when the price dips . . . believing that the price will rebound. Their hands are as strong and tough as diamonds and cannot be broken. The exact opposite of paper hands.

The madness of crypto is not a bug. It's a feature. If a company had to pay to get all these views and impressions, it would have cost tens of billions.

Here it comes for free. Or sort of.

The FU Army comes with waves of crypto adoption and crypto coverage in the media. But as a builder, you will have to create your community and following. We will go in-depth about this in *"The FU Army."*

PSY-OPS TIME—HOW TO GATHER PEOPLE IN AN FU ARMY

- *People want to follow a charismatic leade*r. Holders and investors will follow interesting and stimulating founders. Justin Sun from Tron is a perfect example. You love him or you hate him, but many follow and trust him. We will talk more about how you can create a charismatic leadership figure in the chapter *"Minimum Viable Guru."*
- *People want a project to believe in.* The project will become the vehicle to everything that they desire and want to achieve in life. It becomes part of their identity, and the other members become like family to them. The FU Army behind Cardano is a good example of this behavior.
- *People want to be part of a group.* They want to join something bigger than themselves. People need to identify with something and join a culture. Check the XRP army online if you want to see how this works in practice.
- *People want to make 100x.* They don't assume it, but one of their core motivations is to make money, become rich, and get a Lambo! They'll have a narrative about how, why, and when the token will go 10x, 50x, and 100x.
- *Not all degens are created equal.* In the chapter *"Typology of Degens,"* we will go through the different psychological profiles that will join your army and how to interact with them.

Three for the Price of Two

Good news! If you manage to have two corners of a triangle, the third one comes for free!

You have an FU Army and a PayPal Mafia. Being accepted by the aristocrats is just a matter of time. It was the case of Terra Luna's Do Kwon before his downfall.

You have a PayPal Mafia and a connection to the aristocrats. Sooner or later, a crowd will gather behind you. You can think about Chainlink, a very tech-oriented and technical project that has an army called the *"Chainlink Marines"* supporting everything that they do.

Now you are an aristocrat, and you have a crowd. From these connections and interactions, a PayPal Mafia will be built around your person or your team.

Key Takeaways

- To become an aristocrat, be.
- An FU Army gets you leverage. Leverage to raise money, act on your own will, and hire whomever you want.
- Owning two sides of the power triangle will automatically unlock the third.

Love. Hate. Web3.

Everything is awesome.

—The LEGO Movie

WIIFM

If you're new to Web3, you'll be surprised by the intensity of hate and distrust. Let's break it down so you know how to talk to whom.

Web3 is a cool space with a lot of innovation. It's easy to connect and gather communities around a mission (or a token!). A place full of fun and love but also madness, hate, and disdain.

Outside Web3 vs. Inside Web3

For people outside crypto, crypto is a very big Ponzi scheme, a *"tulip mania"* if you listen to *Black Swan* author Nassim Taleb or an *"index of money laundering,"* as BlackRock CEO Larry Fink used to say before becoming a big proponent of Bitcoin. Of course, for people in crypto, the fiat system is a giant, government-run Ponzi scheme too, which will explode anytime soon. The positive evolution here is to see, one by one, all the foes of crypto and Web3 become proponents of it after spending a few hours researching it.

Bitcoin Maximalists vs. Everyone Else Inside Crypto

Bitcoin minimalists believe that Bitcoin is not crypto and that all crypto and Web3 projects are *"centralized garbage," "unregistered securities,"* or *"shitcoins."* You get the idea. They especially hate Ethereum as it is slowly stealing market share and interest from Bitcoin. For the die-hard Ethereum supporters and so many people in crypto, Bitcoin is a dinosaur that doesn't innovate and is already obsolete.

Centralized Finance (CeFi) vs. Decentralized Finance (DeFi)

People in crypto want more people to enter crypto. Some wish for mass adoption, others just for stuff to go up, thanks to an increased demand for the stuff in question.

Well, to bring people to crypto, you need a centralized exchange (CEX) like Binance, Coinbase, or KuCoin, where people send their fiat currency to buy crypto. These places are centralized and are required to follow government regulations. This is the centralized finance (CeFi).

Against it, you have decentralized finance (DeFi) with decentralized exchanges (like Uniswap) and lending-borrowing platforms (like Aave). DeFi people hate CeFi people without really wondering how people should arrive in crypto firsthand.

To the credit of DeFi people, most big fuckups in crypto came from CeFi. Think about FTX, Celsius, BlockFi, etc.

Ethereum Diehards vs. Other Smart Contract Blockchains

When launched in 2014, Ethereum introduced the notion of smart contracts, and it paved the way for many copycats or adaptations of the concepts. Former members of the Ethereum foundations even launched some. For instance, Cardano (ADA) from Charles Hoskinson or Polkadot (DOT) from Gavin Wood.

Competitors of Ethereum are attacking its slow pace of updates and expense gas fees, making mass adoption a wet dream, while Ethereum maximalists point to the disloyalty of the former Ethereum core team that is ego-driven, greedy, and creating too centralized blockchains.

The fact that these competitors like to nickname themselves *"Ethereum killers"* is not helping.

> Definition: *gas fee*
> The *gas fee* is like a small charge you pay when doing something on a blockchain, such as sending cryptocurrency or using a smart contract. It's the cost you're willing to give to make sure your action gets processed on the blockchain quickly. The more you're willing to pay (higher gas fee), the faster your action gets done.

Blockchain Builders vs. People Building on Blockchain

The blockchain is the infrastructure on which people build stuff. By *stuff*, we mean smart contracts, tokens, and non-fungible tokens (NFTs). Here comes more fun. Most of the stuff created is very experimental, fails often, gets hacked, and gets rugged by unethical founders. So it usually doesn't end well.

Blockchain builders tend to have disdain for projects created on their blockchain (they call these projects *"shitcoins"* and *"cash grabs"*) without wondering, if these people don't build stuff, what is the purpose of the blockchain in question? Without builders, it's simply a *"ghost chain."* By the way, on most blockchains, nothing is going on.

People Building Stuff on the Blockchain vs. Other People Building Stuff on the Blockchain

Builders are competing for market shares and attention. Building in Web3, as we will see in the coming chapters, is a lot about relevance: how to get, and stay, in the spotlight.

Builders also have philosophical conflicts.

"Real" NFT artists who are here *"for the art"* are upset at very commercially successful NFT collections like the Bored Ape. These same artists, by the way, have no issue displaying their very expensive (and very commercial) Bored Ape NFT as a profile picture.

Established builders will often despise newcomers, especially if they come from Web2. They talk about decentralization but love to act as gatekeepers deciding who has the right to join the party and who doesn't.

Builders will also have conflicting views on the blockchain on which they should build their stuff. The positive aspect is that most people in the construction industry are generally kind to each other, except for a few who engage in dishonest practices.

People Building on the Blockchain vs. People Buying the Stuff Built on the Blockchain

We're not done yet! Now you have people building more, and less dubious, stuff on blockchains. And you have people who are buying them and/or using them (if it's a platform, a smart contract).

Well, usually, things are good at the beginning. You then have a phase of euphoria (it's called FOMO) and then a collective panic attack (it's called a FUD) leading to a crash.

A lot of people buying stuff built on the blockchain get burned and are very angry at people building stuff on the blockchain. Sometimes they have legitimate reasons to be angry. But sometimes they are just looking for a scapegoat.

People Buying the Stuff Built on the Blockchain vs. Other People Buying the Same or Different Stuff Built on the Blockchain

Most people who buy stuff on the blockchain want this stuff to go up in value so they can sell it, make *"generational wealth,"* spend the *"generational wealth"* on a yellow 640 hp Lamborghini Huracán, and say to everyone, *"I told you so."*

If many people sell before them, this beautiful scenario might not materialize. So they are upset at *"paper hands,"* who are selling without thinking about the fact that when they dump their bag, some other people might call them paper hands.

Suppose the project lacks real utility and technological development. In that case, it often ends up in a zero-sum game where some win what others lose.

If you turn $100 into $250,000, you sell at the ATH. Some other people buy at the ATH and lose. It's sadly very often players against players.

Most Governments vs. Logic

I said *"most"* governments. Not all of them. This point is maybe the most critical and hardest to grasp. Most governments pretend crypto doesn't exist, shouldn't exist, and is *"worth nothing"* (according to European Central Bank boss Christine Lagarde) while wanting to tax it (and creating their own digital currency).

So they want to tax worthless things . . .

Government regulation is also a big challenge. As a builder, it's almost impossible to know the exact rules, but in the meantime, anyone in Web3 can be sued for anything. Think about Coinbase.

Coinbase is a registered company in the United States. Their stock is listed on the New York Stock Exchange. The SEC (the financial police of the United States, if you prefer) gave the green light to Coinbase to be listed white, knowing their business model, but only a few years later sued them claiming their business model was illegal.

Thankfully, many government officials and elected representatives are working on comprehensive and transparent frameworks for crypto builders.

If you need to cheer up before going to the next chapter, head over to YouTube and listen to the *"Everything Is Awesome" The LEGO Movie* soundtrack.

Key Takeaways

- Web3 is complicated. Everybody seems to hate each other. Insiders and outsiders, CeFi vs. DeFi.
- Don't try to understand why people fight. Focus on cooperation over competition.
- Web3 is awesome! You're awesome! Everything is awesome!

Web2 vs. Web3 Marketing

I just talked to Mark Zuckerberg in an AMA . . .

—Nobody

WIIFM

Many of our readers are coming from Web2. You need to understand that what made you successful in Web2 will most likely prevent you from experiencing success in Web3.

Remember this sketch from the Foreword?

Web2 and Web3 refer to different generations of the internet, each with distinct characteristics and features. Marketing strategies have evolved alongside these technological shifts.

Here's how you can differentiate Web2 and Web3 marketing:

Web2 Marketing

Web2 is the era of the internet that is ruled by centralized platforms like Meta (Facebook, Instagram), Alphabet (Google, YouTube), or TikTok—just to name a few.

Users have the power to engage with each other and post things (blog posts, pictures, videos, etc.). However, users never fully own their content and data. They might get a fraction of the monetization, but the power lies in the hands of centralized platforms.

Marketing in Web2 relies heavily on traditional advertising and data-monetization methods.

Some key points about Web2 marketing include the following:

- *Centralized control.* Web2 platforms were controlled by central entities, such as social media companies and search engines. Marketing efforts were directed toward optimizing content for these platforms' algorithms to reach a wider audience.
- *One-way communication.* Marketing messages were primarily broadcast to audiences without much interaction. Brands relied on advertisements, banners, and sponsored content to convey their messages.
- *Limited user participation.* User engagement was limited to actions like sharing, liking, and commenting. Brands have a strong control over the narrative. Users can gather in a community, but it's not the norm. Users or customers can

also leave reviews without having the power to change the product.

- *Data ownership*. Web2 platforms own and control users' data. This data is used to target them with personalized ads.
- *User creation with limited to no ownership*. Users can create things, but they don't fully own them, nor do they control the monetization of their content.

People can publish stuff and talk to each other, but they don't fully own their work, their data, or their monetization.

On the other hand, companies can gather and use data and powerful tools to track, engage, and manipulate users to their benefit.

When you market in Web2, you have to imagine that a random person clicks on an ad or answers a phone call, and in front of this person, there is a whole team with specialized software, millions of data points, tested scripts, and optimized funnels that can take advantage of this person.

If the product is good and beneficial for the customer, we assume it's ethical. If it's not, it's unethical.

Companies and platforms are much stronger than users and customers. If you think about who is collecting the economic value, look at this illustration from a16z crypto:

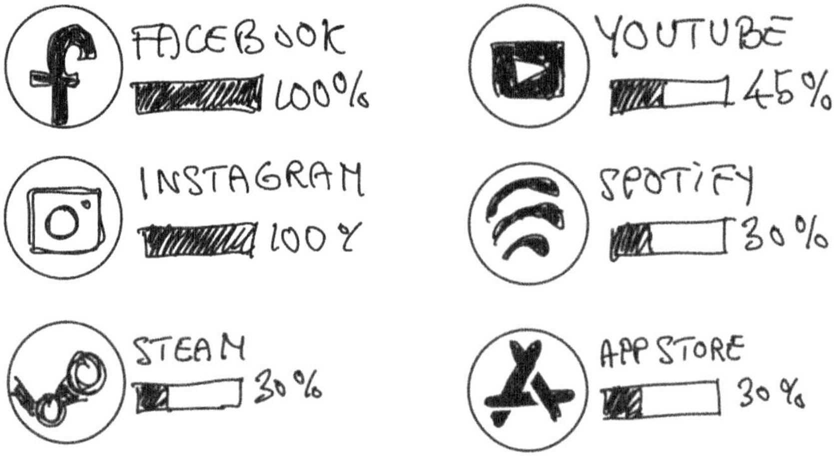

Source: a16z

Web3 Marketing

As we explained before, Web3 represents the evolution of the Internet into a more decentralized, user-centric, and interactive environment. To put it simply, **the whole idea is that people own stuff on the internet.**

Marketing in the Web3 era is about collaboration, user ownership, and tokenization.

Here are some key points about Web3 marketing:

- *Decentralization*: Web3 technologies, such as blockchain and decentralized applications (dApps), shift control away from central entities. This allows for more direct interactions between users and eliminates the need for intermediaries.
- *Two-way communication.* Web3 marketing encourages two-way communication. Projects can engage meaning-

ful conversations with their audience, addressing concerns and building stronger relationships. The audience is also gathering in communities where they engage with each other, with the project, and its founders, and impact the outcome. Talking to Mark Zuckerberg—impossible. Talking to Vitalik Buterin on an X.com (formerly Twitter) space—possible.

- *Token and smart contract.* Web3 introduces tokens and NFTs that can be used for various purposes—including rewarding users for engagement, referrals, completing actions, decision-making, and contributing to the development. Even if a token is usually not a share of the company or a right to its profits, tokens create a sense of ownership in the project. If the project does well, the token usually grows in value, which benefits holders.

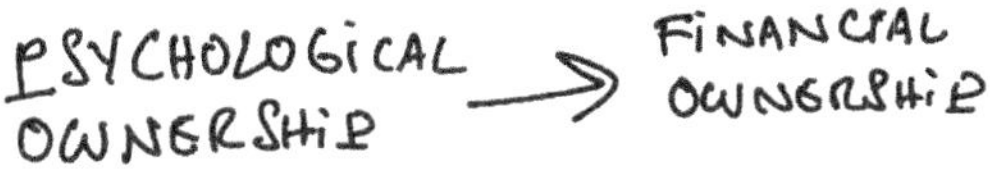

Source: alea.eth

- *User participation and governance.* Web3 enables users to participate in the creation of content and products. Projects can involve users in decision-making processes. It's common to ask the holders to vote on a decision. Tokens and NFTs are very often used as governance tokens as they hold voting power.
- *User data ownership.* Remember that Web3 means that you own stuff? The same goes for your data. Users have more control over their data and can choose to share it with projects in exchange for value (yet these features are still in their infancy).

Unlike Web2, in Web3, **platforms don't siphon all the economic value**. Uniswap is taking 0.3 percent and Ethereum 0.06 percent. OpenSea, with 2.5 percent, is already getting criticized for being too greedy, opening the door for competitors with less or zero fees (like Blur.io).

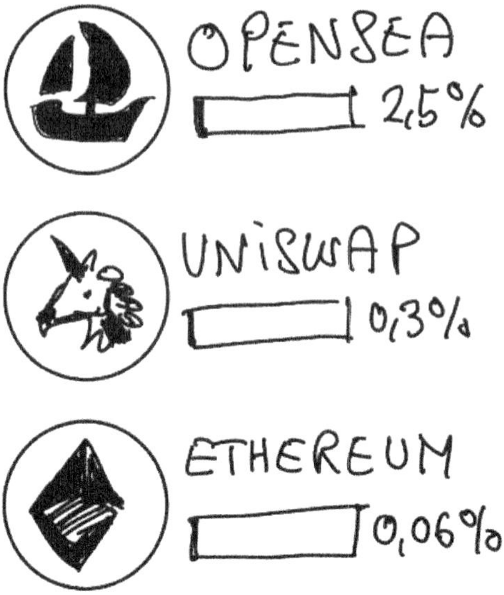

The consequence of this new reality is that **marketing in Web3 is about giving away a lot of power and initiative to communities of holders**. The word *community* is very important.

Marketing to Individuals vs. Marketing to the Crowd

In Web2, you market to an individual who is part of an audience or a segment of a demographic. Usually, users or customers don't gather to influence the project or interact with founders.

They are isolated from each other. They don't have ownership in the project (equity) or the project's destiny (governance).

In Web2, founders and marketers have all the leverage. The company always has the upper hand.

In Web3, as a founder or marketer, your degree of control is very limited. **You don't speak to isolated individuals but to organized or unorganized (usually the second) crowds.**

You need to manage the crowd's movement and sometimes (often, actually) its irrationality. The crowd oscillates between FOMO and FUD. Its mood can swing in a matter of hours.

For instance, it's not uncommon for the crowd to gather and try to oust founders or launch a manhunt against them if the project doesn't perform well.

In Web3, the community usually has the upper hand.

Key Takeaways

- Web2 is a one-way dialogue between the platform and the user. In Web3, it's two ways.
- In Web2, users own next to nothing. Web3 means that you own stuff.
- In Web2, you are marketing to an individual. In Web3, you're marketing to a crowd.
- In Web3, you aren't marketing to an individual but to a crowd.

SECTION 2

THE PROJECT

Building in Web3:

An Introduction to the Project

I test in prod.

—Andre Cronje

WIIFM

This chapter will teach you the different categories of projects that you can build in Web3. If you already have experience in Web3, you can go through it fast. If it's your first time in Web3, take the time to understand the following concepts.

Building a Web3 project is about *"trying some sh——t,"* as DeGods founder Frank would tweet. It's also about *"building first, fixing bugs later,"* as yearn.finance developer Andre Cronje would say.

Cronje's X.com (formerly Twitter) bio was, for a while, *"I test in prod."* This means to first release the product and then see if there are bugs while people are already using it. Which is the exact opposite of what's taught to developers.

In the context of Web3 with major hacks and rugs, this approach is bold, to say the least.

Building in Web3 has its own culture.

What makes Web3 product successful is usually a mix of the following:

- *Innovation* (aka *"You come up with something new."*)
- *Common sense* (aka *"Don't do stupid things."*)
- *Simplicity for the user* (aka *"I understand what's going on."*)
- *Transparency* (aka *"Founders won't take advantage of me."*)
- *Scarcity* (aka *"It's scarce so somehow valuable."*)
- *Utility* (aka *"It's not just a pump-and-dump but a useful thing."*)

Before going deeper into these notions in the coming chapters, let's understand the different natures of Web3 projects.

Web3 Projects Have Different Natures

Not sure what to build and how? The following list will answer all your questions.

PLATFORMS AND PROTOCOLS

Platforms and protocols are technologies that people can use or build over. They have different degrees of centralization. For instance, centralized exchanges (CEX) are often regarded as not being part of Web3 due to their opacity and their centralized nature.

Among the fairly decentralized platforms-and-protocols world, we can mention NFT platforms like LooksRare and Blur.io. In the decentralized world, DeFi protocols like Curve or Aave and decentralized exchanges like Uniswap are good examples.

Blockchains, layers 1 and 2, are also the platforms-and-protocols category.

GAME AND METAVERSE

Metaverse has been a vague buzzword to attract attention to Web3. In contrast, video games are seen as a real vector of onboarding to crypto.

Some initiatives are Web3 pure players (think about Sandbox or Decentraland), while others are Web2 players foraying into this new space.

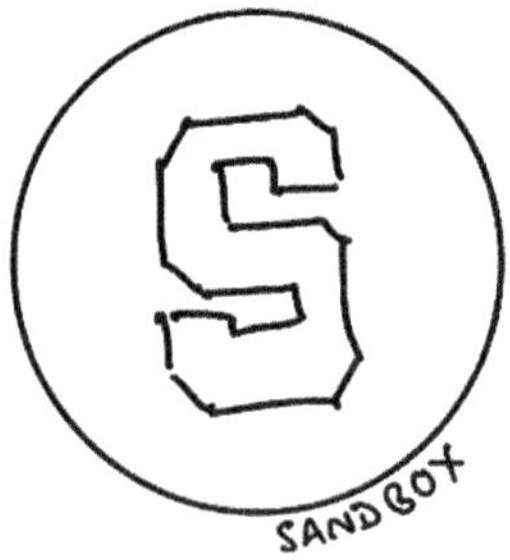

Think about the initiative of Meta (understand: Facebook) or traditional brands like Gucci entering the space.

> Definition: *layers 1 and 2*
> Ethereum (ETH) is like the main road (layer 1), where all the action takes place directly. Arbitrum is like a faster side road (layer 2) connected to Ethereum, making transactions quicker and cheaper.

TOKENS

Tokens can have many natures and functions. Some are utility tokens. You need to use them to perform a task or access something in a Web3 platform. That's the case with the LEO Token of the Bitfinex platform.

> Definition: *utility tokens*
> *Utility tokens* are like a special coupons you can use within a specific ecosystem. It's a digital token issued by a project or platform that grants access to certain products, services, or features within that ecosystem.

Others are purely governance tokens, giving the power of vote to holders. For example, Maker (MKR) is the governance token of

MakerDAO, a decentralized finance protocol that issues the Dai stablecoin.

> Definition: *governance tokens*
> *Governance tokens* are like a voting ticket in a digital democracy. They are cryptocurrency tokens that give their holder the right to participate in decision-making processes within a specific blockchain ecosystem or decentralized organization.

But most of them are experimental ideas without real utilities. You can call them memecoins or shitcoins. PepeCoin, for instance, is in this category. Shiba Inu, which kicked off in 2021 to reach $40 billion in market cap, started like this too.

NON-FUNGIBLE TOKENS (NFT)

Like for fungible (understand: *regular*) tokens, NFT can have a function within a platform (unlocking a feature, getting an improved version of the product, etc.). Still, most of them are funny experiments by aspiring crypto entrepreneurs.

Most profile pictures (PFP) NFT enter this category.

Some become blue chips and huge brands like the Bored Ape Yacht Club Collection, Azuki, or CryptoPunks, while most go up to only go down into oblivion.

In the future, we will see more and more NFTs with real utilities—for instance, real-world assets brought to the blockchain.

A MIX OF ALL THIS

Most projects are a combination of these elements.

A platform with a governance token (like Aave), an NFT with an extra token (like Bored Ape Yacht Club NFT and ApeCoin token), and a video game with both NFT and token (like *Axie Infinity*).

Web3 Builders Build on the Shoulders of Giants

In Web3, you never really build from scratch.

Even if you think about the infrastructure of Web3—that is to say, blockchain—most of them are built on top of others.

Let us explain.

Blockchains are created using a software development kit (SDK) that someone makes available. (For instance, the Cosmos SDK was used to create blockchains like Terra Luna.) Or they are created by forking another blockchain.

> Definition: *to fork*
> *To fork* means *"to copy and code."* Usually, when a project is forking another project, they add more features to suit a specific utility or strategy.

For instance, the Binance Smart Chain released in 2020 is a fork of Ethereum's technologies while adding new features to make transactions faster and cheaper.

Forking is also very common for projects built on top of blockchains. For instance, PancakeSwap and Trader Joe are forks of Uniswap's decentralized exchange DEX, respectively, on the Binance Smart Chain and Avalanche blockchains.

Ecosystem Awareness

Before building your Web3 project, you have to develop some ecosystem awareness.

DO YOU WANT TO WORK ON A SPECIFIC BLOCKCHAIN?

Understand who the key opinion leaders are, the biggest protocols developed on this blockchain, etc. Understand where the liquidity is and who has access to the crowd of holders.

DO YOU WANT TO WORK ON A SPECIFIC TECHNOLOGY?

Identify who the main competitors are, who are doing the same thing, and on which blockchain (and why). How many users do they have, and how many followers? Understand engagement and narrative.

RELAX (A LITTLE BIT) ABOUT COMPETITION

Last but not least, in the ecosystem, awareness means getting a little bit more relaxed about the notion of competition.

In Web2, the market and niches are saturated. In the business school language, it's called a red ocean. It's red from the blood of all the players fighting each other to the death.

Web3 is a very different story. **Everything has to be built. The space will grow 10x or even 100x in the coming years.** If you want to make it in Web3, your focus should not be market shares but your contribution to the growth of the market as a whole. **Cooperation over competition.**

What matters is not your slice of the cake but the size of the cake.

User Awareness

Very early in the process, the target user has to be clarified.

Are we talking about some memecoins for degens (with maybe further application in the future) or some foundational infrastructure of tomorrow's economy (DeFi protocols for instance)?

The more the user is a degen, the more short-term the project is. The time horizon is very short. Maybe a few days or a few weeks. Degen projects often don't last very long. In this case, the features have to be basic and fast to create (if there is any feature).

The vocabulary and roadmap should be simple.

> Definition: *roadmap*
> A *roadmap* is a development plan used by a crypto project or development team to plan and describe the development of their crypto project from start to finish.

The more the project is mature and designed for a mature audience, the more long-term it is. Communication may be more sporadic and focuses on technicalities.

You can take the time to develop things since the audience is expecting a more professional result and has a longer time horizon.

The Science of Common Sense

We're onboarding the next 1 billion users, bro.

—Some Web3 marketer

WIIFM

Web3 is an industry that struggles to explain what it does and why. Everyone talks in gibberish, and no one outside the industry understands what's going on. So adopting some common sense will give you a competitive advantage over the rest of the space.

Let's start with the basics. Because the basics are very often completely absent. We mean here: *common sense.*

With crypto volatility, crazy promises, overnight successes, major hacks, and scams at every corner, common sense is not only useful—it's a necessity to build anything in Web3.

We guess that in the coming years, the *"head of common sense"* will become a real job title in Web3.

When common sense is absent, confusion reigns. You arrive at the page of a Web3 product, and you simply don't get it. They talk about being a protocol while having all the communication codes of a memecoin. This doesn't make sense.

You're looking for information, and you simply can't find it. As a potential investor or community member, you're simply lost. So you move on to the next project, token, or product out there.

Web3 and Web2 are different fields, but in this chapter, we're going to borrow some key notions from Web2.

Secret No. 1—Copywriting Common Sense

Copywriting is the art of writing sales messages that turn visitors into customers and customers into hard-core fans.

Before creating a sales page or a website, copywriters have to ask and answer these questions:

- Why should I care?
- Why should I listen to you?
- Why should I listen to you now (and not tomorrow)?
- Who are you, and why should I trust you?
- Where is this stuff coming from?
- Why should I take action?
- Why should I take action now (and not tomorrow)?
- Is it risky? Is it legal?
- Do you have my back if something goes wrong?
- Where can I get help if I struggle with the product?

This is classic Web2 copywriting. But in Web3, this common sense is absent. Most Web3 pages simply do not answer these questions. They just throw on a page some weird notion that 0.001 percent of the world population can understand while thinking they contribute to mass adoption. (*"We're onboarding the next 1 billion users, bro."*)

You get something like, *"In a cross-sharded ZK-Rollup DeFi metaverse powered by quantum-resistant DAGs, users leverage NFT-backed memetic staking protocols to mint fungible delegated proof-of-authority tokens while participating in decentralized autonomous liquidity farming orchestrated by their AI-enhanced Shiba Inu consensus nodes."*

Secret No. 2—WIIFM

WIIFM in Web2 marketing stands for *"What's in it for me?"*

What are you offering to the visitors on your page? What is your product doing for them? Explain in (mostly) plain English and with limited jargon.

BLUR.IO CASE STUDY

Take, for instance, the platform Blur.io.

Blur.io identified one core problem of NFT trading: platform fees and royalties on one hand and user interface on the other.

Blur.io charges very low fees for its services, which makes it more affordable for users to buy, sell, and trade NFTs. This is in contrast to some other NFT marketplaces, which charge high fees that can make it difficult for users to profit from their trading strategies. Blur.io has a very user-friendly interface that makes it easy for users to buy, sell, and trade NFTs. The platform is also very intuitive, so users can easily find the features they need.

SOLANA CASE STUDY

Another team that nailed the WIIFM was Solana. Solana understood what people needed and were asking for.

To say it bluntly, 90 percent of people in crypto don't care about decentralization. **They care about good user experience, cheap**

gas fees, decent design, speed, and a chance to make some quick money.

Also, people don't care about going super deep into technical concepts. So why bother? Solana has played these cards very well.

It focused on the speed of transactions and very low gas fees, which are two of the most important factors for many users. Solana's blockchain claims that it can process over 50,000 transactions per second, and the average gas fee is only a few cents.

People love this. And developers go where users are. Despite having a very complex programming language for developers, Solana attracted many builders of NFT and decentralized applications (dApps).

> Definition: *dApps*
> *dApps* are the applications that make up the decentralized web. Most Web3 *dApps* look and feel just like regular websites and apps. The only difference is that you can access them by connecting your wallet and that they run on a decentralized network.

In addition to its focus on speed and low fees, Solana has also made several other strategic decisions that have helped it gain traction. For example, the company has introduced physical stores in several major cities.

These stores allow users to learn more about Solana and to purchase Solana-based products. Solana also launched a phone, the Saga, which is powered by the Solana blockchain and offers dApps instead of only regular apps.

Physical stores and phones are things people can touch and feel. It's a much more immersive experience than some unfinished and lagging metaverse experience. It's usually called **sensorial marketing**.

To touch, to feel, to smell (the store) creates a strong bond between the brand and its customers.

It's stronger and easier to grasp than a *"cross-sharded ZK-Rollup DeFi metaverse powered by quantum-resistant DAG . . ."*

Maybe it's not a surprise that StepN was launched on Solana.

StepN was a very successful *"move-to-earn app"* that was launched in December 2021. It quickly became one of the most popular NFT projects, with over 700,000 monthly active users at its peak.

The app allows users to earn tokens by walking, running, or jogging outdoors. The tokens can then be used to buy in-game items or exchanged for fiat currency.

Here are some of the factors that contributed to StepN's success:

- *Innovative concept.* StepN was one of the first move-to-earn apps, and it offered a unique way to earn rewards for physical activity.
- *Gamified approach.* StepN gamified fitness by incorporating elements of games like *Pokémon GO.* This made the app more fun and engaging for users.
- *Rising popularity of NFTs.* StepN took advantage of the rising popularity of NFTs by allowing users to purchase NFT sneakers. This gave users a sense of ownership and control over their assets.

The key lesson here is to **understand what people want, give it to them, and explain on your website how you're giving it to them.**

That's it.

Secret No. 3—New Vehicle, the New Opportunity

In Web2 marketing, a vehicle is a product or an offer that takes the customer from a situation of need or pain to a situation of salvation or happiness. It has been vastly popularized by ClickFunnels cofounder Russell Brunson.

In any given market, you have popular vehicles. These solutions are known and recognized.

They might work or not work (or not work as well as they claim), but they are the existing ones with the recognition and awareness.

Suppose you want to get market shares for your product or offer. In that case, you need to introduce a new vehicle (a new method of solving the pain) and a new, under-the-radar, and more innovative way to achieve the desire.

This new opportunity is called the *"new vehicle."*

Web3 offers a similar challenge. Ten thousand tokens are launched every year as thousands of NFT collections, hundreds of platforms, and protocols.

There are a lot of vehicles out there, and you need to stand out. **You have to think about crafting a *"new vehicle"* to become relevant.**

Having a *"one-sentence differentiation formula"* helps. Here are key sentences you could use.

IT'S THE FIRST ______.

Your product is the first one ever in its category. No one thought about it before. You're a complete pioneer. In the sphere of reflection tokens, SafeMoon is widely recognized as being the first one.

It's worth noticing that projects are often never really *"the first"* but the first that managed to gain attention and recognition. It has always been true in the history of innovations and inventions.

Bored Apes Yacht Club (2021) arrived long after CryptoPunks (2017), but in the minds of a lot of people, the Apes were here before the Punks.

IT'S LIKE ______ BUT ON BLOCKCHAIN ______.

This is one of the best new vehicles.

Take something that is widely successful on a specific blockchain and do the same on a blockchain that doesn't have it.

People will immediately assume it's relevant (usually it is) and that it's going to be successful (usually it becomes so). PancakeSwap was Uniswap on the Binance Smart Chain blockchain. Magic Eden was the OpenSea on the Solana blockchain.

IT'S LIKE _____ BUT ON A PLATFORM _____.

A platform here is not a blockchain.

Take, for instance, Unibot. *"It's like Uniswap but directly on the Telegram chat on your smartphone."* What you could do with Uniswap, now you can do it on the Telegram app. This is somehow an oversimplification, but people understand it and see instantly the value of it.

IT'S LIKE _______ BUT ON STEROIDS.

This is how a good friend introduced us to Shiba Inu a few months before the epic pump: *"This is like Doge but on steroids. If Doge pumps again, this will go even faster, even bigger to the moon."*

People who've missed an opportunity are looking for the next one in the category that'll do the same. This is why, in the wake of Doge and Shiba, *"dog coins"* like Akita Inu pumped super hard.

IT'S AGAINST _______ AND SO MUCH BETTER.

Often, you want to simply challenge the incumbent players, and being polarized and against is a driving force.

In Web3, people like to gather, complain against, and challenge established concepts.

For instance, PepeCoin positioned itself as being against all the current memecoins (starting with Doge) while claiming to be the only real genuine memecoin.

The following statement was published on their original website:

> *The dogs have had their day. It's time for Pepe to take reign. It's time for the most recognizable meme in the world to take his reign as king of the memes.*

IT'S LIKE IN FAVOR OF _______ AND IT'S COOL.

When people don't gather against something, they gather in favor of something.

It's a different type of energy. We can mention the Islamic Coin, which states:

> *Islamic Coin is a native currency dedicated to empowering an ethics-first Shariah-compliant financial ecosystem. Islamic Coin has a finite total supply, and 10% of each issuance is automatically dedicated for philanthropic purposes.*

They focus on their core value to gather crypto-educated believers around the project.

Secret No. 4—The Single Big Idea Strategy (Sharks, Spies, and Aliens)

Can I combine many WIIFM and vehicle ideas in the same project?

Said otherwise, *"If I add more features and new vehicle-style arguments, will it increase the awareness, desire, and demand around my product?"*

Short answer—in 99 percent of cases, *no.*

Complementary answer—thinking you're the 1 percent, the exception, usually is a mistake. We like you a lot, but let's assume you're not that special.

Think about it the following way:

You can have very good movies about aliens. You can have very good movies about spies. And you can have very good movies about shark attacks. But if you have in the same movie all three—sharks, aliens, and spies—it's usually going to be a very bad movie.

It's the same for your Web3 vehicle. **Keep it simple.**

Secret No. 5—Speed Wins, Ship Light

Web3 is a fast-paced environment, and those who move slowly are often left behind.

The saying *"One week in Web3 is like a year in real life"* is a reminder that the industry is constantly evolving and those who want to succeed need to be able to adapt quickly.

This means understanding the macro trends that are shaping the industry, such as the bull and bear phases of the market, as well as the microtrends (such as which blockchains are popular and which DeFi protocols are gaining traction).

It also means being able to pivot quickly if necessary, as the market can change in an instant.

One way to move fast in Web3 is to *"ship light."*

This means starting with a Minimum Viable Product (MVP) that has just the essential features. This allows you to get your product to market quickly and start gathering feedback from users. Once you have validated your MVP, you can then add more features and functionality.

Side.xyz is a good example of a project that has moved fast. The scope of the project is vast, but the team chose to move fast and ship light. So instead of waiting to have a comprehensive product, they launched a simple *"link in bio"* feature first. While the developers are building complex products, the marketing team is spreading the *"link in bio"* features to a qualified audience of creators and Web3 projects.

Secret No. 6—The Purple Cow Differentiation

Seth Godin is a marketing guru who has written several marketing books. One of his bestsellers is the *Purple Cow*. In this book, Godin argues that to be successful, businesses need to be remarkable.

To be remarkable means that people are surprised by it. It means that it triggers a conversation and a love-it-or-hate-it reaction. Does it feel risky to you? In the attention economy, not being remarkable enough is the biggest risk.

Think about a purple cow. It is something novel, not usual. And people would see this cow in the middle of a herd of cows.

Godin's definition of a purple cow is something that is *"remarkable enough to make people stop and stare."* It is different from everything else out there. It is something that people will remember.

In the context of Web3, differentiation can be achieved in several ways. Here are a few examples:

BLOCKCHAIN CHOICES

When a competition project is very popular on a blockchain, launch or develop your competitor on a different blockchain.

This has the benefit of differentiation while serving a community that is not necessarily using the competitor's solution.

Olympus DAO is a DeFi protocol on the Ethereum blockchain that launched the trend of the crazy APY. When we say crazy, we mean 100,000 percent APY. It launched a trend in DeFi to a crazy yield that lasted about six months. Wonderland TIME was a direct fork and competitor of Olympus. To differentiate itself, it went on the Avalanche blockchain, where it became very popular.

PRICING (FOR NFTS)

Usually, the rule is to be the most expensive in your market or the cheapest. But **just doing the opposite of the norm in a given context is already a good move.**

In the context of the bull run of 2021, the NFT collection from entrepreneurs Elio Trades and Alex Becker, NeoTokyo, differentiated itself by offering a free mint, which was unique in an environment where most projects were asking for hundreds or even thousands of dollars for mints.

CULTURE

Web3 is already a culture in itself. Within Web3, NFT and DeFi have their own cultures. Not to mention specific blockchains or sub-communities with their own identity and values.

Nevertheless, focusing on a strong culture is a way of differentiation.

For instance, GoblinTown.wtf NFT had an absolute degen culture where all community communication within the Telegram group involved people making weird goblin sounds and noises.

USER EXPERIENCE

In Web3, it's a common practice to have a horrible user experience (UX) or even user interface (UI).

Maybe developers take great pride in doing things normies cannot use. Or maybe it's a form of autism—who knows.

But what's sure is that providing a better user experience is a huge leverage of differentiation in the space. We mentioned the Solana example earlier.

Beefy Finance is another example. It's a platform that aggregates and displays yield strategies and liquidity providing—things that are usually complicated to understand and even more complicated to use.

Instead of making things super complicated (like literally everyone else back then), they designed a system where in one to two clicks, you could deploy the same strategy as combining yourself with several dApps, platforms, wallet actions, and dozens of steps.

There are many more differentiation options. Stay curious and playful.

Secret No. 7—Know Your Customer

In traditional marketing, we always ask ourselves:

- Who is the customer?
- What are his beliefs?
- What is his family status?
- Where does he live?
- What is his job and financial situation?

In our case, we should ask the following questions:

- Is it his first time in crypto?
- What has been his crypto journey? Which centralized exchange, which coins did he first buy, and when?
- Has he experienced a bear market?
- Has he been rugged?
- Which other coins or NFTs does he own?
- Whom does he trust? Or distrust? And why?
- Which country and purchasing power?
- What's his favorite blockchain and wallet?

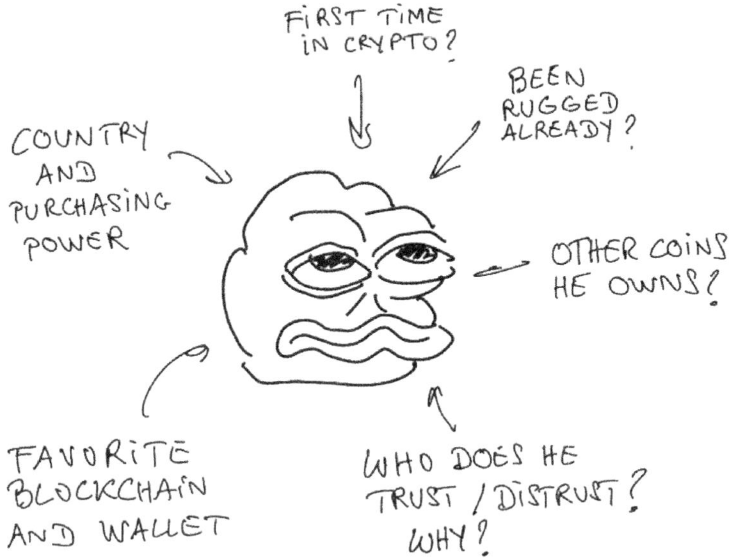

Secret No. 8—Exit the Technobabble and Know Your Customer

The more we will see crypto and Web3 adoption, the less we will see people being genuinely interested in super technical details.

People like to joke about *"I'm here for the tech."*

It means: *"I came for the free money. I have no idea what I'm doing. But now my bag is down 90 percent. I have no idea if and when it'll recover, so instead of getting angry I pretend that I'm here for the tech. But please tell us when we will go up again. I want free money. A lot."*

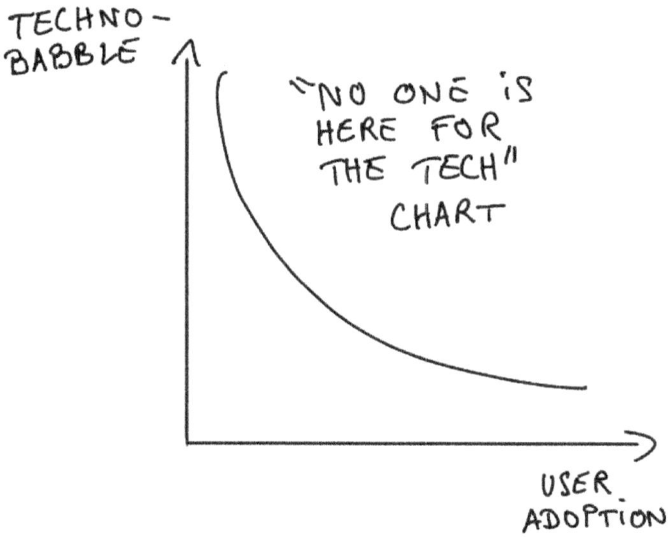

In reality, **almost no one is here for the tech. So don't bother them with crazy technobabble.** The more we see user adoption, the less people want to hear about technical stuff. Exactly like Web2.

Look at Web2.

Are people interested in SMTP (simple mail transfer protocol) or IMAP (internet message access protocol)? No. Users are interested in the experience of using Gmail or Outlook. Some might have privacy concerns and move to solutions like Proton Mail.

What about marketers and builders? Most of them care about email marketing strategies and opening rates.

Don't get us wrong—technical innovation is wonderful. It's just that 99 percent of people don't need and don't want to know the details.

It's even worse, technobabble is making people feel confused or even stupid—two things you want to avoid as a builder or as a marketer.

Generally speaking, in the past years, NFT did a decent job at making things relatively easy.

"Hey, it's a JPEG on the blockchain. There is scarcity. Set up your wallet in five minutes and buy our stuff."

Granted. Many were scams. And most of them fail to deliver anything. But **mainstream influencers shilling NFT brought more people to Web3 than geeks talking about Zk Rollups.**

"TALK TO ME LIKE I'M A CHILD OR A DOG" SEAL OF APPROVAL

Now that we know that most people are not *"here for the tech,"* you have to talk about something else than the tech.

It could be your mission, your movement, or the benefit of your product. Of course, mention also the risk involved.

Think about the now-infamous Terra Luna. They could have mentioned the *"byzantine fault tolerance (BTF) tender mint consensus algorithm built on Cosmos SDK."* Instead, they said, *"A decentralized internet needs decentralized money."*

A beautiful mission that anyone can understand.

What people got (WIIFM): You can make 19,49 percent a year on your *"dollar"* without any effort.

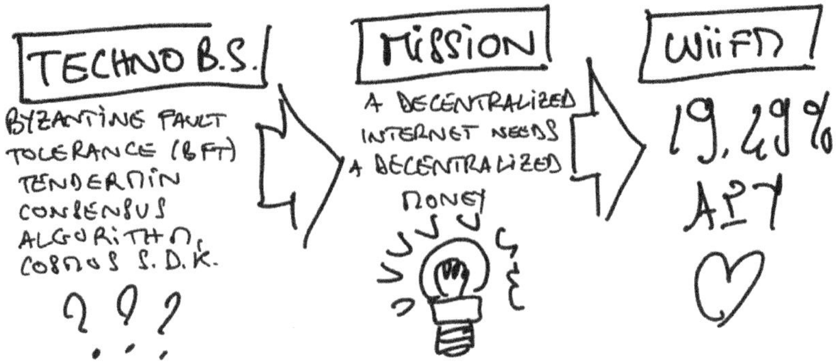

Of course, in this example, the fact of offering literary *"free money"* (while it lasted) also contributed to their temporary success.

Secret No. 9—The Web2.5 Approach

Cycle after cycle, it's getting easier to onboard people into crypto and Web3.

But you need to have a dynamic approach to it. **If you are 10 or 20 percent better at onboarding people into your community and product, you will mechanically win market shares.**

There are two forms of onboarding: culture and community on one side, tech and product on the other. In section 4, we will discuss the notion of community onboarding in-depth.

- **HERE ARE SOME WAYS TO IMPROVE THE TECHNICAL ONBOARDING**—*User-friendly wallet integration:* Offer seamless integration with popular Web3 wallets like MetaMask, Trust Wallet, or Coinbase Wallet. Provide easy-to-follow instructions for users to connect their wallets to your platform.
- *User-friendly one-click wallet creation.* You can use a solution like Magic Link to create an email-based wallet. Like

this, people don't have to hear about seed phrases and other technicalities. They use something they already know: an email log-in.

- *Onboarding incentives.* Offer small rewards, such as tokens or NFTs, to users who complete the onboarding process. This can encourage participation and engagement from the outset.
- *Add fiat on-ramp solutions.* Fiat on-ramp solutions are payment processors that accept and take the risk of crypto. People can pay with a card to buy your NFT or token. This way, they don't need to fund a decentralized wallet from a centralized exchange and then use a decentralized exchange or NFT platform to get your token.

Web2.5 and the Sorare Case Study

Generally speaking, the best way to onboard new users into a Web3 project is to have a Web2.5 model.

Let us explain.

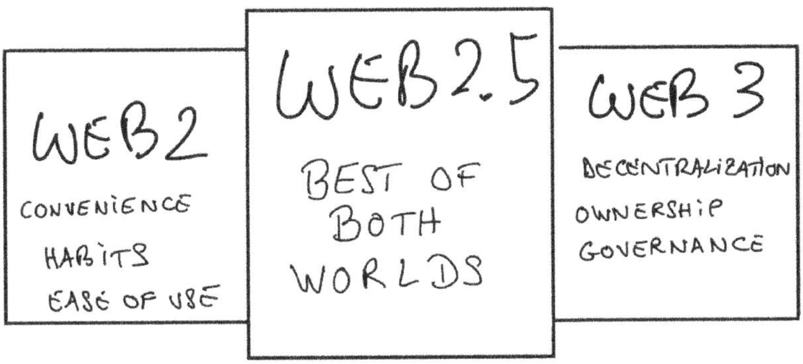

The Web2.5 Approach offers the benefits of the blockchain without the technical barriers and burdens. You combine the best of both worlds.

Take, for instance, Sorare.

Sorare is a fantasy football game built on the Ethereum blockchain. It allows users to collect, trade, and manage digital player cards. The cards are non-fungible tokens (NFTs), which means that they are unique and cannot be replaced.

Sorare is a Web2.5 product because it combines elements of both Web2 and Web3 technologies. On the one hand, it is a centralized platform that is controlled by Sorare. On the other hand, it uses blockchain technology to store and manage the ownership of the NFTs.

Here are some of the reasons why Sorare can be considered a Web2.5 product:

- *It is a centralized platform.* Sorare is a company that owns and operates the Sorare platform. This means that Sorare has control over the platform, including the rules of the game, the pricing of the cards, and the user experience.
- *It uses traditional web technologies.* Sorare is built on top of the Ethereum blockchain, but it also uses traditional web technologies such as HTML, CSS, and JavaScript. This means that Sorare can be accessed and used by users who do not have any knowledge of blockchain technology.
- *It has a user-friendly interface.* Sorare has a user-friendly interface that makes it easy for users to collect, trade, and manage their player cards. You don't have to worry about gas fees, connecting wallets, and confirming signatures. It's smooth. It's good. It's extremely easy to use.

You can use the product without having to perform any blockchain-related tasks.

Key Takeaways

- Ninety percent of people in crypto don't care about decentralization. They care about good user experience, cheap gas fees, decent design, speed, and a chance to make some quick money.
- Your product must be a vehicle that transports the user from the current to the future desired situation.
- Speed wins. Ship light and simple.
- One week in Web3 is like a year in real life.
- To stand out, be different. You can do this through the choice of blockchain, pricing, culture, and user experience.
- Exit the technobabble—meaning, talk to your audience like they're a child or a golden retriever.
- If you are 10–20 percent better at onboarding people with a Web2.5 approach, you will mechanically win market shares.

The Science of Transparency

The currency of leadership is transparency.

—Howard Schultz

WIIFM

There is a transparency nature in the blockchain where founders and the team often maintain a heavy layer of opacity over their actions and goals. This lack of transparency is prone to fuel distrust and accusations against the team in case things don't work out the desired way. So don't mess with transparency, and don't do shady stuff.

Let's start with Plato and some deep wisdom!

Plato tells us the story of "*The Ring of Gyges*," and it feels like Tolkien's *Lord of the Rings* got a little bit of help from our friend here.

So here is the deal:

Gyges is a shepherd who discovers a magical ring that grants him the power of invisibility. Super cool.

So what does he do?

He does what anyone would do.

With this newfound power, Gyges can act without fear of consequences. He can now engage in actions without being seen or held accountable.

He uses the ring to become invisible and eventually seizes the opportunity to kill the king, take the throne, and establish his rule.

Plato uses this story to explore the concept of morality and how individuals might behave when they believe they can act without being observed or facing any consequences.

The story raises questions about whether people are inherently moral or whether they would act unjustly if they could avoid detection. *"The Ring of Gyges"* thought experiment serves as a foundation for discussions on ethics and human behavior in philosophical discourse.

Basically, when people think others cannot see and track them, they start doing weird stuff.

Blockchain, Anonymity and Transparency

The beauty of blockchain is that we achieve at the same time a great level of transparency and anonymity.

Usually, these two notions are opposite. You have either one or the other. The more you have transparency, the less you get anonymity. And vice versa.

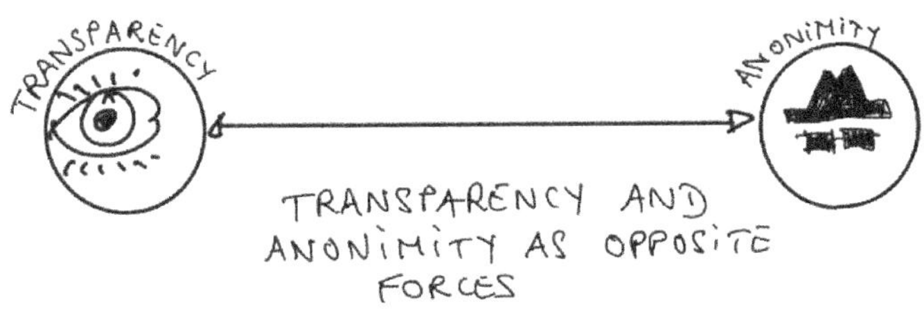

On the blockchain, you have both notions. As every wallet and transaction is visible to anyone, you achieve great transparency.

Bitcoin operates on a *blockchain*—a decentralized and immutable digital ledger that records transactions. This ledger is open and transparent, accessible to all participants within the network. Every Bitcoin transaction is documented, offering a comprehensive historical record, akin to a publicly viewable register.

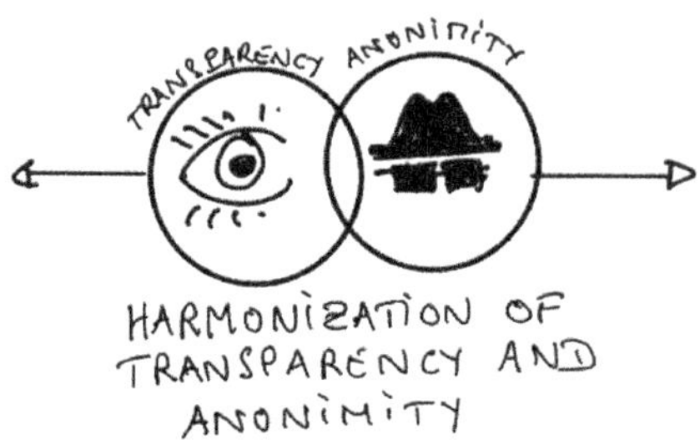

On the other hand, you cannot know (or not that easily) who owns the wallet, so people benefit from a fair amount of anonymity.

Of course, anonymity is not perfect, and some specific blockchains are working on increasing this privacy element (think about Secret Network, for instance, or other *"privacy chains"*).

Okay, enough with the theory! Where do we stand as Web3 builders and marketers?

Transparency Assumptions and Behaviors

Things can be fairly anonymous in Web3, hence the unethical behaviors of some people.

But here is how to think about it: **Just assume that sooner or later, everything will be public and transparent.**

Let's imagine a few scenarios:

The concept of *"know your customer"* (KYC) could take on deeper dimensions, potentially leading to more extensive personal data collection. Centralized exchanges might have to extend their scope by keeping tabs on decentralized user wallets. This would raise questions about the **balance between decentralization and surveillance.**

Some exchanges could also leak your personal information and wallet information. It happened to Celsius Network during its bankruptcy procedure, where the balance and transactions of all its customers were disclosed. A leak from a former employee is also possible. It happens all the time with banks and even sometimes with law firms. Think about the origin of the Panama Papers.

DON'T DO STUPID STUFF

Another scenario is the rise of artificial intelligence (AI) and analytics, introducing a growing invasive capacity and paving the way for more sophisticated ways to connect data. OpenAI's founder, Sam Altman, is trying to do exactly that with Worldcoin.

So let's assume that you won't stay hidden forever. **Don't do anything stupid, unethical, or illegal because sooner or later, you'll get caught**. Forensic science will catch up.

The *"Very Basic"* Science of Transparency

Transparency—or at least a certain level of transparency—is something you owe to your holders and community.

This transparency should not be about the personal information of team members. You can doxx yourself, but you don't have to (more on this in section 3). The rise of attacks, threats, and even kidnapping makes it not very safe to disclose personal information.

> Definition: *doxx*
> *To doxx* means "*to reveal your personal information (face, name . . .) to the public.*" *Doxxing* can also be the act of disclosing private or personal information of an individual without their consent.

So transparency is about different things that are much more important to holders and the project's success.

Here is what you need in order to be transparent:

VISION AND BELIEF

Express your project's goals and beliefs openly, without making crazy long-term commitments. Show and display your genuine enthusiasm for the project. Show how passionate you are and how much you believe in it.

Be transparent about where you want to go. Be transparent about your vision of this industry's future and how your project fits in. Basically, say, "*This is the future, and this is how we will make it happen and/or be part of it.*"

PROJECT AND FEATURES

Communicate your project's features, detailing both achievable and challenging aspects. Don't overpromise.

Don't create an impossible roadmap. This is misleading. It's the opposite of transparency. Instead, acknowledge that more features might be easy to create while others might be more challenging. Remind everyone about the experimental nature of the project.

Be transparent about the fact that features, priorities, and choices might change over time. In the context of Web3, where the regulation or market condition can change drastically, in the interest of the project, it's good to keep the options open.

Basically, say, *"We want to build this and this. Some stuff is easy, and we're confident. Other stuff is more complicated. And things might change."*

TEAM AND SKILLS

Explain who is in your team (use pseudonyms) and what their background or experience is. Same as for the features, don't make crazy claims. Don't invent skills they don't have.

The holders and the community should be able to have reasonable expectations while being hyped up by the vision of the project.

So don't pretend you're rocket scientists if you're not.

TOKENOMICS AND ALLOCATION

Provide transparent insights into tokenomics, token distribution, and dilution. People want to know who owns what.

If the founders or the legal entity behind the projects owns a lot of tokens, then disclose it and explain why. **Don't try to hide it.**

Explain the following: *"The team owns this and this. We keep X percent of tokens in reserve in this wallet that you can check. We will use it for this and this."*

FUNDING AND PROFIT MECHANISM

Disclose how your team generates revenue and how funds will be used. It's okay to make money—it's not forbidden! But it should be said.

It has to be transparent. And if things have to change, update the community. Explain why.

If you explain, people understand. If you hide, sooner or later they'll discover it, and the crowd will go after you.

So if you want to mint an NFT and buy a Lambo with the money, just say it. Assume the degen crazy identity of your project so people know what they're getting into. And by the way, people resonate very well with radical honesty and crazy personal goals.

RISK TRANSPARENCY

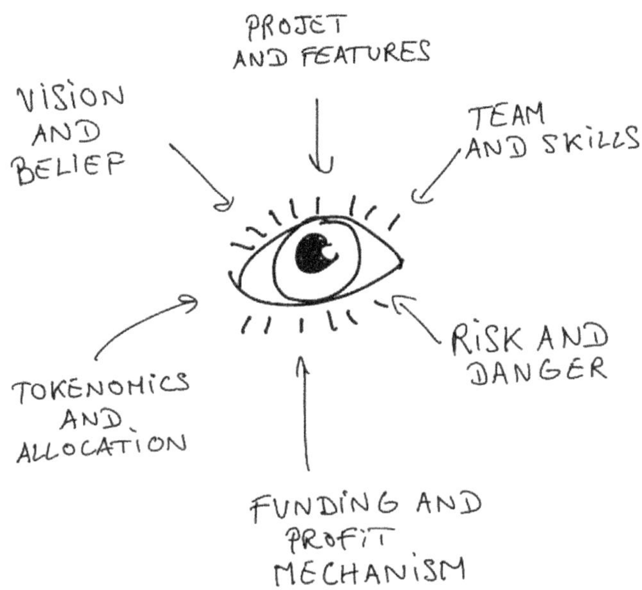

All right, this is the common sense part.

Just list everything that can go wrong. Everything that comes to your mind, write it down. Mention that the list is not exhaustive and that other problems might occur.

Be super clear about it. Ninety-nine percent of people know these risks very well, and they think they don't need a reminder. But do it nevertheless.

Basically, say, *"This can go belly up for all these reasons," and you list them.*

By following these rules, founders and projects demonstrate transparency and also basic respect for users' intelligence.

Most problems among humans are problems of communication. The more you hide, the worse it gets. Sanctuarize your identity and your family life, but be the most transparent builders about everything else.

People will appreciate it.

Trust and goodwill compound.

Since we're here—none of this is legal advice. We suggest you reach out and consult law professionals before doing anything in Web3. All the suggestions in this chapter are based on practical reasoning and ethical considerations.

And when in doubt, remember the Web3 Murphy's Law.

The Web3 Murphy's Law

You're likely familiar with Murphy's Law, which asserts that *"whatever can go wrong, will go wrong."*

In the context of Web3, there's a Web3 Murphy's Law that adds an interesting twist:

It suggests that the issues predicted by Murphy's Law will show up sooner than anticipated and with greater intensity.

It's going to be f——cked up. Always. And massively.

Whatever your intentions and goodwill, you will face FUD, people will threaten you, and maybe some hacker might manage to hack wallets or even the project. Haters will gather and call you any name. Maybe some members or even the majority of the community will turn their back on you.

And many more weird crazy things.

Your ability to manage this depends a lot on your transparency foundations.

Were the risks transparent? Yes!

Were the skills of the team transparent? Yes!

Were we transparent about how we make money? Yes!

Were we honest about our vision and mission? Yes!

Among other things.

By answering a big *yes* to all these questions, you can face FUD, accusations, and threats with serenity. Because you know you did your best and you were transparent about everything.

Mistakes and lack of skills will be forgiven if the transparency foundations are healthy.

Key Takeaways

- Assume that sooner or later, everything will be public and transparent and that forensics are catching up. Don't trust that the blockchain will be anonymous forever.
- Transparency is not showing your face but being open about the future of the project, profit mechanisms, and risks.
- Always remember Murphy's Law: *"Anything that can wrong will go wrong,"* and in Web3, that comes sooner than anticipated and with greater intensity.
- Most problems among humans are problems of communication.

The Science of Scarcity

Wow, that super-rare 3D Monkey with laser eyes for $800,000 is a steal.

—Somebody on X

WIIFM

The whole idea behind the Bitcoin and the Web3 narrative is scarcity. The real provable, unfalsifiable scarcity. When you design and upgrade your Web3 project, you need to always maintain a form of transparency. This chapter will teach you how using famous examples such as Yuga Labs, Azuki, RTFKT, and Ethereum.

At the dawn of economic theory and human desire, there was scarcity. It goes the same for Bitcoin and crypto in general.

Why are diamonds more valuable than water?

This paradox, first proposed by economist Adam Smith, questions the apparent contradiction between the high value of diamonds and the low value of water, despite water being essential for life.

Short answer—diamonds are scarce.*

Scarcity creates *value.*

Scarcity creates *desire.*

Scarcity creates *demand.*

It even seems that **the engine of modern economies is artificial scarcity.** Not everyone can enter Harvard or buy a new Rolex watch. People wait three years before they're able to buy some watch brands beloved by *"NFT bros,"* like Richard Mille.

The Value Matrix and the Role of Scarcity

A while ago, we tried to identify basically where the profits are. Where to go to maximize economic return on your effort. We started to build a matrix.

On the horizontal sections, we have two extremes: extreme relationship and extreme technology. We believe that the economic value is concentrated in these two extremes.

* It's actually not that true, but Adam Smith couldn't have known that in the late eighteenth century.

Anything in between can still make some money, but less and less over time. Small e-commerce stores, marketing agencies, etc. Their golden age has terminated. It might end up like agriculture. *True*, everyone needs some food, but there is no food for the people producing the food. Think about it.

So you can either be in an extreme relationship or an extreme technology.

Now let's check the vertical sections. **Your business can either use abundance or scarcity to drive value creation.**

This gives us the following matrix:

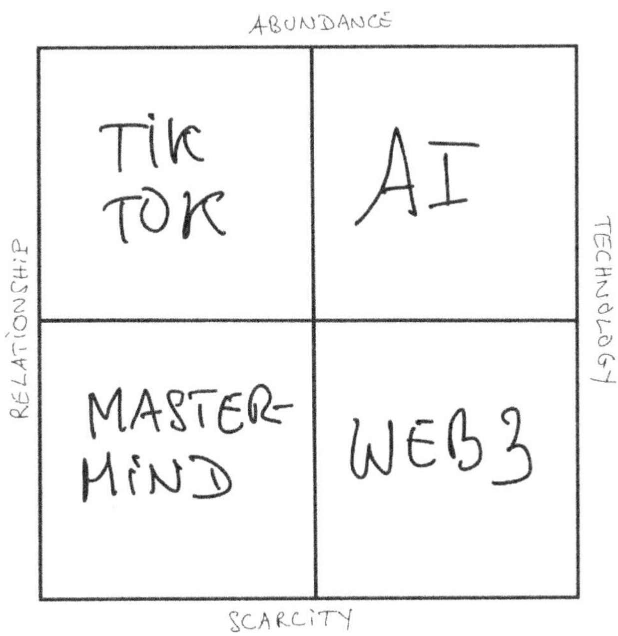

Basically, on the technological side, AI means abundance and Web3 means scarcity. Think about the 21,000,000 Bitcoins, the *"only"* 10,000 BAYC NFT, etc.

On the relationship side, TikTok would be the caricature of abundance while a closed mastermind of ultraqualified people would represent the scarcity.

You can adapt this matrix now to Web3 as a whole. You'll get something like this:

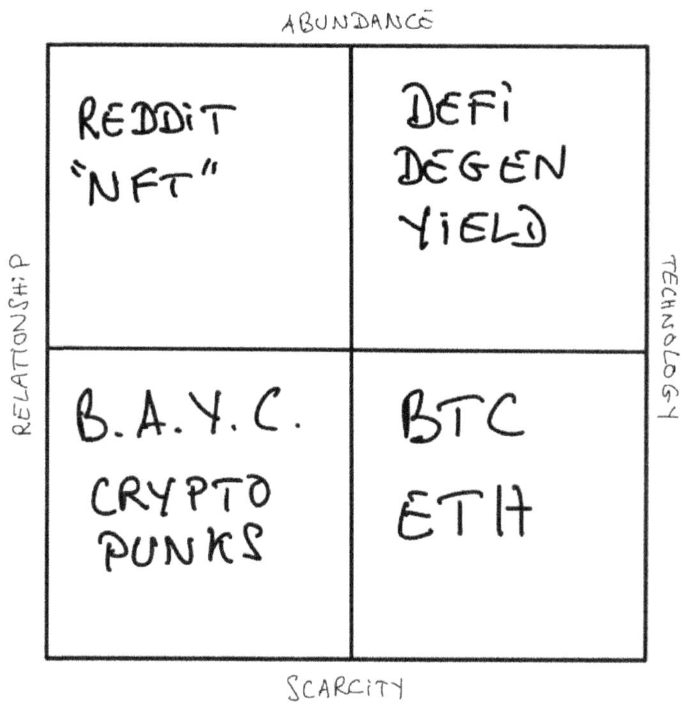

Abundance and technology give you these super-technical smart contracts with crazy tokenomics (that no one understands until they collapse, then it's obvious for everyone) that give you hundreds of thousands of percentages in APY.

Abundance and relationship give you these very basic Reddit NFTs that you can use as a profile picture on the platform.

Scarcity and relationship give you the Bored Ape. It's a lot about relationships, being part of the club, attending private events, joining token-gated spaces, etc.

Scarcity and technology give you Bitcoin and its 21,000,000 cap or the deflationary proof-of-stake Ethereum.

> Definition: *proof of stake*
> *Proof of stake* is like a lottery where your chances of winning increase with the number of tokens you hold. The more tokens you have, the more likely you are to validate new transactions and earn rewards. It's a way to encourage people to be responsible and be honest *"transaction checkers"* in the blockchain network.

Designing and Maintaining Scarcity

The name of the game in building the Web3 project is to design, maintain, and play around different forms of scarcity.

These are different forms of scarcity that need to be taken into consideration:

- *Scarcity of focus from users.* People are looking at many tokens, and they are bombarded with new ideas and theories every single day. You have to be ultrarelevant to capture this focus.
- *Scarcity of information about the project.* People are struggling to get the relevant information, they get confused, and they leave and move on to the next moonshot.
- *Scarcity of time used by the project.* Having a deadline to mint, maintaining pressure before a launch, and telling

people, *"This is just the start, don't wait too long before joining."*

- *Scarcity of quantity.* A limitation in the amount of tokens or NFT is something expected nowadays. The inflation of supply has been identified by many as a source of decreasing prices. Burning tokens is often seen as a good sign by communities (even if it doesn't affect price in the short term). You can also limit the amount of wallets authorized to mint or buy the presale.

Scarcity and Timing: The Azuki Case Study

Note—this case study is inspired by Lamboland X.com thread. Follow him at @LambolandNFT.

The Azuki collection was launched in January 2022 with 10,000 unique items. The collection quickly became one of the key *"blue chip"* NFT collections, and even during the bear market of 2022, where most collection floor prices dropped by 90 percent, Azuki maintained itself.

Definition: *floor price*
Floor price is the lowest price of an NFT within a collection that's available to buy. It can be a good metric for the health of a project.

A strong community with wealthy whales was swiping the floor, maintaining a healthy supply-demand equilibrium.

Until something crazy happened.

Summer of 2023, Azuki released their Elementals collection over their historic collection. They raised $38 million, but the floor price of the core collection dropped by 60 percent amid heavy FUD.

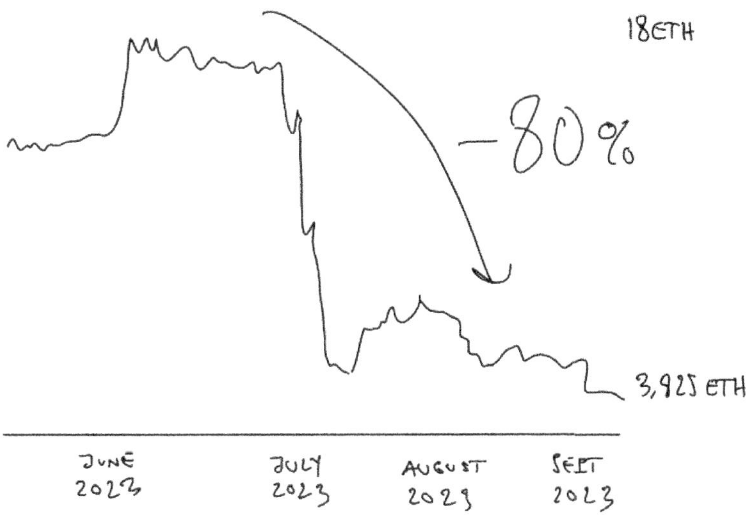

The new mint was widely regarded as a cash grab by the community.

Definition: *cash grab*
A *cash grab* is a low-quality, low-effort project designed only to make money and offer little value to the buyer. This term is often used in relation to poor-quality NFT drops.

Not only did it dilute the main collection, but the new art was also very similar to the original collection.

The balance between supply and demand was disrupted by this mint. There is now less demand for Azuki since people can now buy the same art (Elementals) for a fraction of the price.

And to make things worse, Elementals is a 20,000 NFT collection. This is a huge supply increase considering there are barely 20,000 people truly active in Web3 at the time. Pudgy Penguin CEO reacted by calling it a *"death sentence."*

This was the destruction of the supply-demand equilibrium.

It resulted in many people losing trust in the Azuki team, causing even less demand for Azuki assets. Many of these new NFTs were airdropped to the current holders.

Definition: *airdrop*
Airdrops are coins or tokens that are *"dropped"* into users' wallets without any action on the users' part. Similar to food being *airdropped* from helicopters, free money (or sometimes a scamcoin . . . beware!) is dropped in your wallet!

*"And many of the Azuki holders who got their free Elemental sold it right away. Since they treated it like a dividend. But since the Azuki and Elementals prices are pegged against each other, the more Elementals dropped, so did Azuk*i," comments Lamboland.

It's about supply, it's about demand, and it's about timing. Maybe in the context of a bull market, the price impact would have been very different.

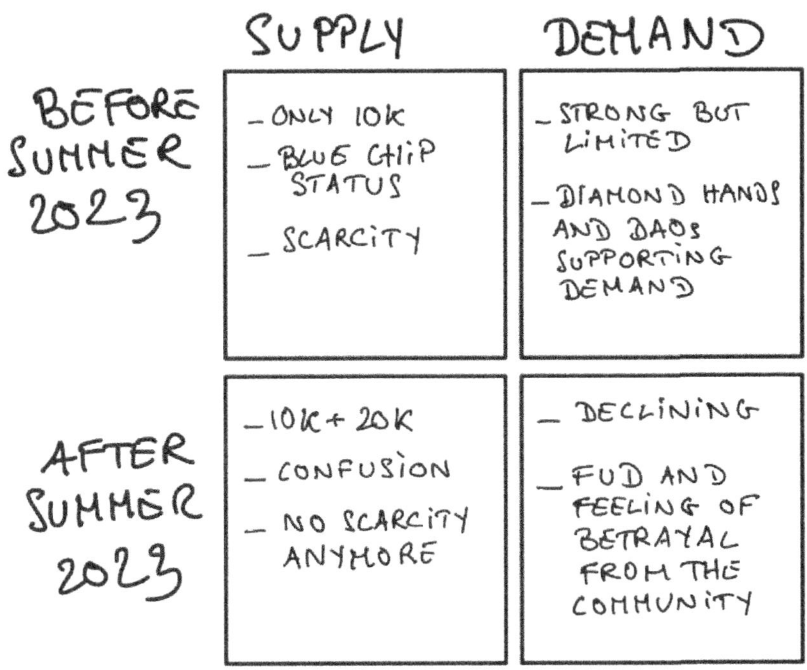

Scarcity and Strong Branding: The Yuga Labs Case Study

Yuga Labs started with a very strong Bored Ape Yacht Club (BAYC) Collection that quickly became the gold standard for NFT: 10,000 little JPEGs on the blockchain that humans were using as profile pictures.

BAYC has a very strong social and community dimension. Owning and displaying a bored ape as a profile picture means something.

The supply from the Yuga brand was first increased in June 2021. They introduced a dog NFT collection, the Bored Ape Kennel Club, but it didn't affect the supply-demand balance.

A very important milestone was the introduction of the Mutant Ape Yacht Club (MAYC) collection in April 2021. It happened the following way: 10,000 NFTs were airdropped to current holders, and 10,000 went to a public sale.

The public sale brought more demand and new holders to the community. So you had a higher supply combined with a higher demand.

It was in the context of a bull market.

So things went more than fine.

Yuga made $100 million from the MAYC mint. And most of that money came from people outside of their community. So it was a win-win-win situation.

At this stage, the supply-demand equilibrium was really well maintained.

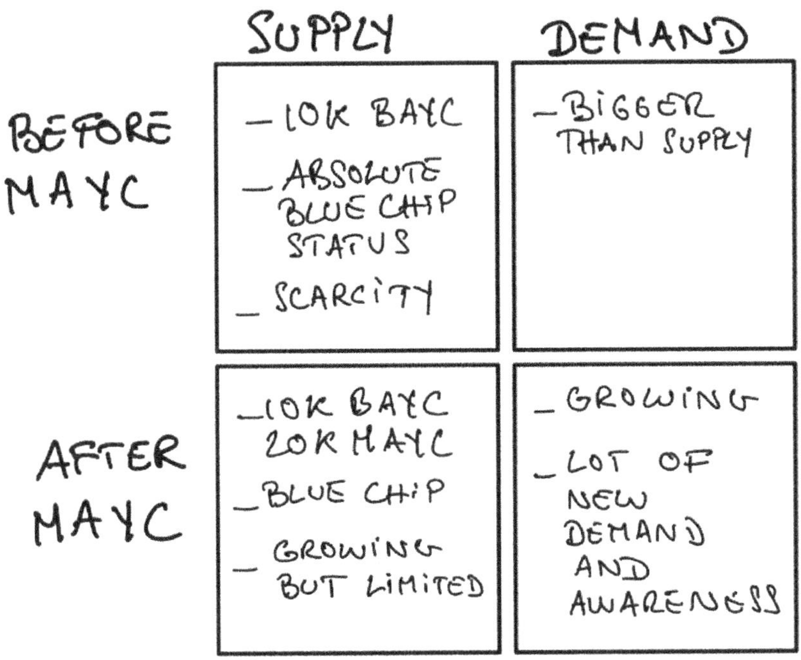

But then in March 2022, they launched the ApeCoin token. ApeCoin was a way for people who could not afford the Yuga NFT to have some exposure to the brand. Yet it diluted the demand for their highly priced NFT.

Before the ApeCoin, having financial exposure to the brand would cost you a fortune. Now you can have exposure for $20 in ApeCoin token.

But that's not all of it.

In May 2022, they introduced Otherside, a collection of 55,000 NFTs!

Financially, it was another big success. As Decrypt wrote, *"Yuga Labs Sees $561 Million in Otherside Ethereum NFT Sales Within 24 Hours."*

But at this time, the bull market was almost over and the brand was heavily diluted. Moreover, **there was a lack of clarity for the community and especially the potential new holders.**

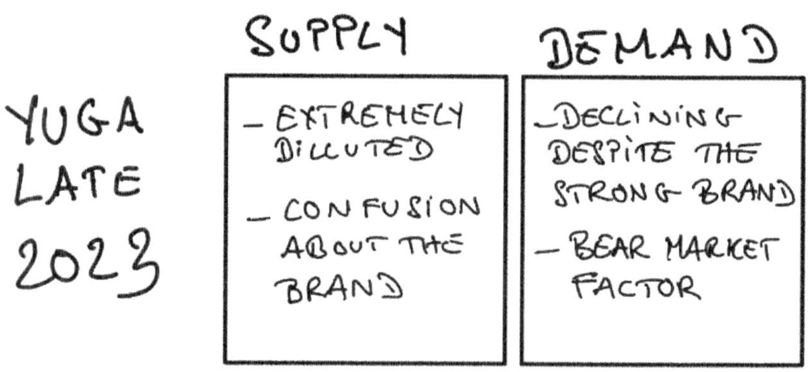

What should you buy? A mutant ape or an Ape? What is this "Otherside" thing? I see that the ApeCoin token is going down, is it going to affect the price of my Ape?

To make things even more complicated, Yuga introduced a series of NFTs on Bitcoin. They launched in March 2023 the TwelveFold collection on ordinals. While the supply wasn't big (only 288 NFTs), it added to the confusion leading people to question the brand's strategy.

> Definition: *ordinals*
> *Ordinal NFTs* are a new form of blockchain-based assets. They allow investors to create and purchase NFTs inscribed directly into the Bitcoin blockchain. *Ordinals* enjoyed much attention in the spring of 2023 but quickly faded away due to high network costs.

Scarcity and Confusion: The RTFKT Case Study

In old-school Web2 marketing, we consider confusion, skepticism, and boredom to be the three capital sins!

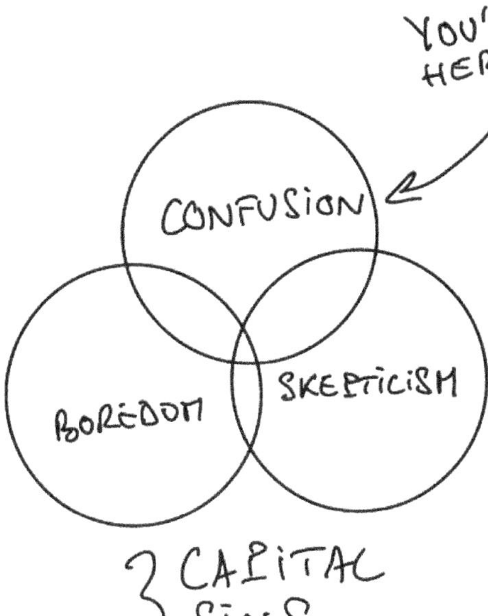

Confusion is the issue here.

RTFKT has a similar story to Yuga. They started early in the NFT craze and became big by partnering with big brands. They introduced multiple collections and gave tons of free NFTs to holders of previous collections.

However, it came at a cost . . .

No. One. Gets. It.

Everyone in NFT knows the brand. Everyone knows that they got acquired by Nike for an absurd amount of money. But no one understands the ecosystem.

What should you buy?

Where to start?

Are all these collections from RTFKT, or are some fake?

This is preventing people from joining the project and contributing to the demand. **Liquidity is also spread across too many collections.** As a consequence, the floor price dropped significantly over time.

We must respect RTFKT's success, but we're here to make better decisions.

THE RTFKT MYSTERY

If you want to increase the supply, you *also* need to increase the demand. And you need to offer a clear vision, a roadmap for people to follow, a simple onboarding, and an ecosystem they can understand.

NFT and Web3 are complicated and risky enough. You don't want to add complexity on top of that.

Scarcity and Narrative: Ethereum Case Study

Ethereum had an inflation issue. The network was creating more and more tokens by miners doing what miners do (they mine) without having a limited supply.

It worked for a while and was also criticized as being too energy-consuming.

So Ethereum moved to a proof-of-stake model. Basically, instead of having miners running complex hardware machines to secure the network, you have people staking ETH tokens to secure the network.

Definition: *staking*
Staking is when an investor holds, or *"locks up,"* their crypto assets for a certain period of time in order to validate and support the blockchain network. *(This is a huge simplification.)*

As a consequence of the pivot to a proof of stake, at each transaction, some ETH tokens get burned. **So not only is the supply not capped, but the supply of ETH is also going down.**

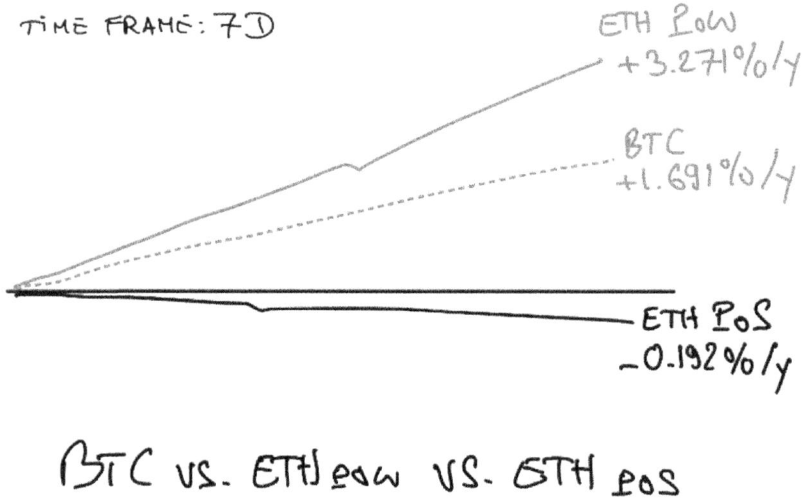

If you look at the simulation from the website Ultrasound.money, you see something like this:

Bitcoin has a strong inflation, thanks to miners doing their job.

Ethereum proof of work also had a strong inflation (bigger than the one of Bitcoin actually). Ethereum proof of stake is experiencing a minor deflation. The supply is going down.

This change also affected demand. With a proof-of-stake model, you can stake tokens and earn rewards (understand: passive income paid in ETH). So now, as an investor, you can really challenge the idea of holding Bitcoin, since Bitcoin is not generating any yield or passive income. Ethereum also got their narrative boost as they reduced their energy consumption by 99 percent. Demand is also growing.

To summarize, you get something like this:

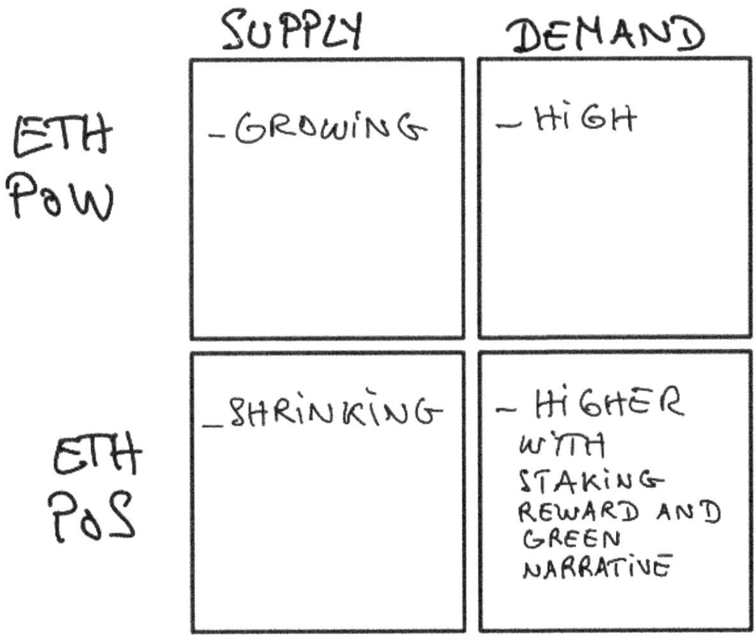

Key Takeaways

- Web3 narratives are mostly driven by scarcity. People respond to this.
- Good projects manage a fragile supply-demand equilibrium.
- Any increase in supply can be seen as a cash grab and can create confusion around the brand.
- Make sure to reward past holders when launching something new (check the *"The Science of Loyalty"* chapter for more information).
- Always work on the onboarding of new users to stimulate more demand for your tokens or NFTs.

The Science of Tokenomics

Tokenomics is the Science of Anticipation and Forecasting.

—Nathan Benchimol
CEO, Nomiks.io

WIIFM

Fail the tokenomics, and your project is doomed. Period. Tokenomics governs how the token economy works and is by nature hard (if not impossible) to change later on. In this chapter, we will cover the classic blockchain trilemma that any Web3 builder should know before moving on to a more practical trilemma that we call the Web3 trilemma. Don't worry if some of these concepts are strange to you—we will get to it step by step.

But first thing first . . .

What Is Tokenomics?

The term *tokenomics* is a mix of *"token"* and *"economics."* It refers to the economic principles and mechanisms that underpin a cryptocurrency or blockchain-based token system.

> Definition: *tokenomics*
> *Tokenomics*—derived from the words *token* and *economics*—is the study of the supply, demand, distribution, and valuation of cryptocurrencies.

Sounds complicated?

That's because it is!

But to put it more simply, it's about how you create tokens, how you distribute them, how the tokens work, what people can do with them, and everything around tokens.

Key elements of tokenomics typically include many words that describe easy-to-understand realities:

- *Token utility*—what can you do with the token? Access stuff, buy things, vote, etc.?
- *Token supply*—how many tokens are out there right now and in the future? Can you create more tokens in the future, or is it blocked? If the supply increases, we call it inflationary. If the supply is reduced (for instance, by burning tokens), it's deflationary.
- *Token distribution*—when will the tokens be distributed, and to whom? Do you have a presale or an ICO? Are you going to airdrop the community? Who gets what, and why?
- *Token governance*—who decides what and how? Can token holders vote? How does it work?
- *Token staking and rewards*—can I stake my tokens and get something in exchange? If yes, what?
- *Token burn*—will some tokens get burned (understand: *destroyed*) to reduce the supply and increase the scarcity?
- *Token interoperability*—will the token and protocol work with other blockchains and protocols?
- *Economic incentives*—are there mechanisms designed to encourage certain behaviors? For instance, contributing to the marketing or looking for bugs in the code and being rewarded for this?

All these notions are complex. If you're new to the industry, you'll get used to it as you see them everywhere. Most of this information is written in the contract or on the whitepaper.

> Definition: *whitepaper*
> The *whitepaper* serves as the foundational document that drives trust in a Web3 project. The *whitepaper* explains the visions, goals, technological choices, and governance model in a transparent manner.

The Three Actors: Predators, Players, and Holders

In token economy design, consider three key actors, as outlined by Nathan Benchimol from Nomiks.io:

- **Predators**. These individuals are primarily profit-driven. They are willing to sell, or *"dump,"* tokens if it's financially advantageous. Their focus is on monetary gains rather than the project itself.
- **Players**. Players actively engage with the token economy and the project. They are interested in the product's features and the project's long-term success. Their actions and involvement contribute significantly to the project's sustainability.
- **Passive holders**. Passive holders purchase tokens but typically don't actively strategize for profit-taking or delve deep into understanding the tokenomics and product intricacies. They are more focused on holding their tokens.

While all three actors play a role, players are crucial for the project's long-term success because they interact with and support the project's development. Predators—often represented by entities like VCs, launchpads, and business angels—may prioritize short-term gains, but their influence on the project's tokenomics can be substantial due to their financial backing.

Balancing the interests of these actors is essential in crafting a robust token economy.

The Long-Term Implication of Tokenomics

Well-designed tokenomics won't miraculously transform a bad project into a good one. However, poor tokenomics can indeed undermine the success of even the most promising projects.

Axie Infinity serves as a significant milestone in the Web3 space, demonstrating remarkable success with its *"play-to-earn"* model. Yet the presence of predators who rapidly extract value and dump tokens can disrupt the ecosystem. This can negatively impact players who are earnestly contributing and earning tokens, ultimately undermining their efforts.

Tokenomics should be viewed as the *"science of anticipation and forecasting,"* as Nathan Benchimol suggests. This perspective is critical because, unlike the traditional economy where interest rates, tax policies, and rules can be adjusted, **in the Web3 economy, once tokenomics are encoded in a smart contract, changes are complex and often impossible.**

Therefore, designing tokenomics requires forward-thinking—considering future market conditions, user behaviors, trends, and technologies. It's about understanding users, predicting market cycles, and predicting how the economy will respond to these changes.

The Blockchain Trilemma

If you've been long enough in this game, you know the famous *"blockchain trilemma."*

A *trilemma* is a situation in which three conflicting choices or requirements exist, making it challenging to achieve them simultaneously.

Why does it matter?

Because most of the thinking around tokenomics and Web3 building is around three core notions: scalability, security, and decentralization.

An educated audience will check your project through these lenses.

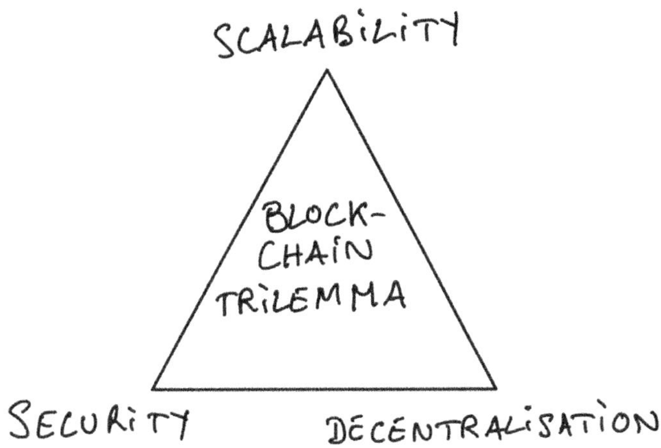

To keep it short, it is a concept highlighting the trade-offs among three essential characteristics of a blockchain or a cryptocurrency system:

- **Scalability**. Can you grow the number of users and transactions without crashing?
- **Security**. Can people easily attack the network? Are there vulnerabilities?
- **Decentralization**. How many people can participate in the decision-making and validation processes?

Because it's a trilemma, you can only have two elements, and you need to compromise on the third one. That's the idea.

Let's check three examples:

- Bitcoin: Bitcoin boasts unparalleled decentralization and robust security through PoW, but it faces scalability challenges with slower transaction processing and high fees due to its block size limitations.
- Ethereum (PoW): Ethereum as a proof-of-work model manages to have a high degree of decentralization and security but at the cost of scalability. The transition to a proof-of-stake model is aimed at fixing the scalability issues but might compromise decentralization.
- Solana: Solana employs DPoS for decentralization, but it faces centralization concerns due to limited validators. It offers speed and high throughput but may be less secure than Ethereum. Scalability is its standout feature, though at the expense of decentralization and security.

	DECENTRALIZATION	SECURITY	SCALABILITY
ETH POW	STRONG	STRONG	LIMITED
SOL	LIMITED	FAIRLY STRONG	STRONG
BTC	STRONG	STRONG	LIMITED

When you run a project and think about tokenomics, you have another trilemma.

Let's call it the Web3 trilemma.

The Web3 Trilemma

It looks like this:

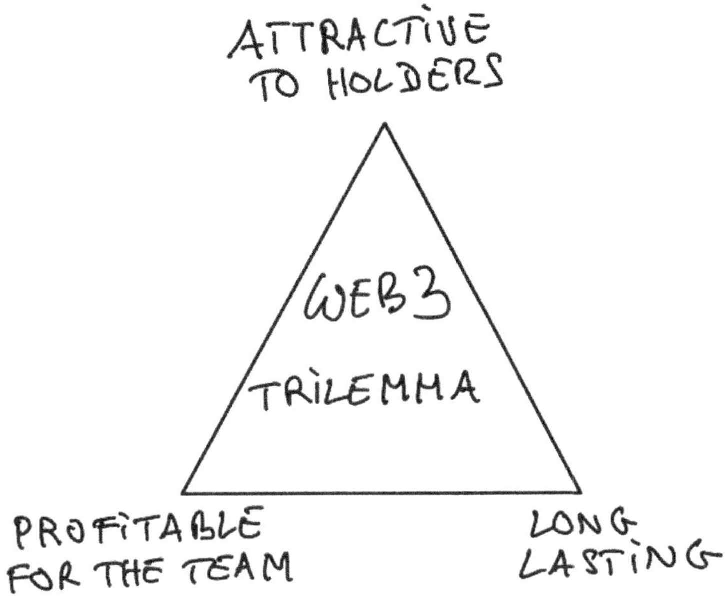

The following are the three corners of the triangles:

ATTRACTIVE TO HOLDERS

Holders in the Web3 space are primarily driven by the desire to profit. This can manifest through reselling tokens or NFTs at a higher price or earning staking rewards. The greater the potential for earnings, the more attractive the project is to these holders.

It's important to note that this **profit-driven mindset represents a significant portion of Web3 communities**. Many holders are primarily concerned with the token's price rather than considering the project's overall market capitalization (market cap, calculated by multiplying the number of tokens by the price of a single token).

Basically, they seek *"free money"* with expectations of substantial returns, often aiming for 100x or more, all while receiving passive income.

These expectations can sometimes be unrealistic, and it's crucial for project teams to balance these desires with the project's long-term sustainability and goals.

PROFITABLE FOR THE TEAM

Team members should be fairly compensated. While the mission is often a driving force, financial responsibilities are real. Team members, dealing with considerable stress, deserve compensation for their hard work and dedication. **People don't work for free.** They have rent to pay too.

Therefore, it's crucial to consider the percentage of tokens allocated to the team. Additionally, assessing whether selling a portion of these tokens could impact the token's price requires attention to supply-and-demand dynamics.

Finally, implementing vesting periods is a common practice to secure a long-term commitment from team members.

> Definition*: vesting*
> *Vesting* is a mechanism that allows Web3 companies to distribute tokens to their employees and other service providers over time, subject to certain conditions or milestones. This ensures that the team stays committed to the long-term future of the project, and it increases the trust of the investors.

LONG-LASTING

The project has a chance to live long. You want it to survive ups and downs. The shorter the life span of a project, the higher the suspicion of malevolent intentions. The longer it lasts, the more it makes money usually and the more it can innovate.

Good projects should recover from 90 percent of crashes, from FUDs, and from bear markets. They should also adapt to new environments, new technologies, and new paradigms.

Examples of Tokenomics

10,000 PROFILE PICTURES NFT

You create 10,000 unique NFTs with cute or less cute animal faces. You sell them in an epic mint. Usually, 100 percent of the money is going to the team. Unless they specify otherwise before the mint, it's up to them to decide what to do with the money.

- *Attractive to holders?* In the context of a bull market and euphoria, yes, it is. Depends on the mint price and innovation factors in the project, but yes, in the right context, it is attractive.
- *Profitable for the team?* Yes, they collect a lot of money they can use however they want. It happens fast, and it's a lot.
- *Long-lasting?* Usually, no. First, buyers buy to resell at a higher price. Most projects fail to build a strong brand, stay relevant, and develop new revenue streams to continue the development. The lack of utilities also often hurts the longevity of the project.

REFLECTION TOKEN

A reflection token is a token that collects a fee (called a *"tax"*) on each buying-and-selling transaction. This tax is then distributed between the liquidity pool, the team, and the holders. Percentages can vary a lot.

- *Attractive for holders?* Yes. The tax limits the action of bots (holders hate bots), the rewards are beneficial for them, while the growth of the liquidity pool gives them exit possibilities.

- *Profitable for the team?* If they receive a percentage of the tax and/or if they own tokens, then yes, it is.
- *Long-lasting?* Usually, no. These tokens go up in value, but very fast, holders will sell their bags to move on to the next opportunity. So these tokens tend to pump-and-dump despite the best efforts of the team.

LAYER 1 PROOF-OF-STAKE BLOCKCHAIN

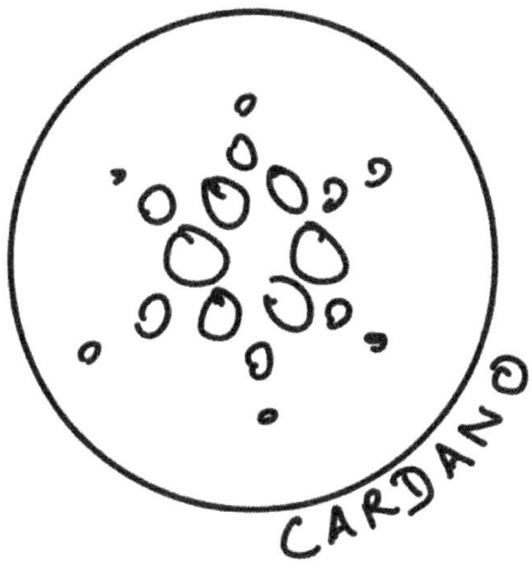

A proof-of-stake (PoS) blockchain is a consensus mechanism where validators are chosen to create new blocks and secure the network based on the number of coins they hold and are willing to *"stake"* as collateral.

Okay, basically, it's a blockchain where people can stake tokens to get a reward. Got it?

- *Attractive for holders?* Moderately. The market cap is usually high, meaning it won't go up 10x or 50x that easily. Staking and staking rewards are nice but have usually low (5–10 percent APY). For long-term holders, it might be interesting. If you can enter during the bear market, then it's attractive.

- *Profitable for the team?* The sheer size of such a project makes it interesting for the team. They can allocate 5 or 10 percent of the token supply to the team and future team members.
- *Long-lasting?* Somehow. The low token inflation and the ability to fund the team, in the long run, are making these tokenomics long-lasting. But blockchains fight for relevance. The success will depend on the capacity of the team to attract more builders and liquidity to the blockchain.

10,000,000% APY YIELD DEGEN TOKEN

During the 2021 bull run, a new concept emerged: the *"10,000,000% yield degen token."* The concept is simple: You buy the token, you stake it, and you get an absurd amount of yield. The yield is paid in the token of the project.

Of course, you assume it will crash anytime soon, but every day the project stays alive (and more people join), you make *"money."* One of the examples was Olympus DAO.

- *Attractive for holders?* In the context, yes. Of course, people expected it to crash, but each day that passed without crashing was a day where holders received absurd amounts of *"free"* tokens through the staking mechanism.

- *Profitable for the team?* Yes, if they get a supply of tokens and/or they can collect a fee on transactions, staking, etc.
- *Long-lasting?* No. Some managed to survive many months, but it ended badly.

NOUNS.WTF

Nouns.wtf (also called Nouns DAO) is one of our favorite projects out there.

It's an NFT collection on the Ethereum blockchain, initially launched in August 2021. Each day, one and only one NFT is auctioned. The highest bidder is minting the NFT.

All the money goes to a treasury managed by the holders through a DAO. Founders don't get the mint money, but for every nine minted NFTs, they get one for free that they can sell. Interesting concept.

- *Attractive for holders?* Yes and no. The scarcity of the NFT is enhancing the desire to own one of them. But the super-high price makes it hard for people to afford it. Holders and audiences have to be qualified (and rich) crypto enthusiasts. Depending on the blockchain, gas fees might be an issue (you have to pay gas fees to participate in the auction).

- *Profitable for the team?* Yes, but only in the long term. They don't get the money coming from the mint. They just get one NFT every nine days. To make money, they need the project to survive and be long-lasting.
- *Long-lasting?* Yes, by design. Holders control a treasury worth tens of millions of dollars, which gives the NFT a form of floor value (you divide the treasury by the number of NFTs, and you have a symbolic value). The team is incentivized to build in the long run, and the community is qualified and committed

To summarize our examples:

	ATTRACTIVE FOR HOLDERS	PROFITABLE FOR THE TEAM	LONG LASTING
10K PFP	IN RIGHT CONTEXT: YES	YES	USUALLY NO
REFLECTION TOKEN	YES	YES	NO
LAYER 1 POS	MODERATELY	YES	YES
10000000000% APY YIELD	YES	YES	NO
NOUNS DAO	MODERATELY	ONLY IN THE LONG RUN	YES

When in Doubt, Go Back to the Basics

The big idea here is the following: something somehow has to support your token. People only buying hoping to turn a profit is *not* a long-term strategy. It's a pump-and-dump scheme by design and by default.

So you need to have, within your project or strategies, a mechanism to support the price of your token. People need to hold it or use it for some reason other than profit.

As Peter Thiel once said in the backstage of SF Disrupt 2014:

> *The history of innovation has been one where most people who invent things get nothing at all. The Wright brothers came up with the airplanes but didn't get rich. Edison edged out Tesla. (. . .)*
>
> *To make money you need to do two things. Number one, you have to create something of value to the world. And number two you have to capture a fraction of the value you create.*
>
> *And often, people have completely failed at doing the second.*

He is not talking about Web3 and tokenomics, but it makes sense here too.

Think about the Cosmos platform and its native token Atom. The Cosmos SDK and platform enable other teams to create blockchains and platforms. You can count Terra Luna, Secret Network (a privacy-focused blockchain), and Akash Network (decentralized cloud computing) among the projects that were built on Cosmos.

However, the Cosmos SDK and platform do not directly capture any of the value created by these blockchains. This is because the Cosmos SDK is an open-source project, and anyone is free to use it to build their blockchain.

As a result, the value of the Cosmos ecosystem is spread out among the many different blockchains that are built on top of it. They invented things, and they had a token associated with these things, but people using these things didn't have to buy, hold, or use the token in question. Maybe it'll change in the future.

You need mechanisms to support the demand for your token.

As of the writing of this book, the Blur token of the Blur.io NFT platform is suffering the same fate. Blur tokens were massively airdropped to the community, but the project failed to introduce a mechanism to support the demand for the tokens. The airdropped people just sold the tokens, and the price went down 97 percent.

You need to think about long-term strategies to develop demand and use cases around your token. We will see many of them in the chapter *"The Science of Utility."*

Last thing . . .

Don't Burn Your Boats Too Fast

The story goes that when Cortés and his men arrived in Mexico in 1519, they faced a formidable task: to conquer the powerful Aztec Empire led by Montezuma II.

Quite a challenge.

Cortés knew that his troops might be tempted to retreat or abandon their mission in the face of overwhelming odds. To eliminate this option and to ensure his men were fully committed to the mission, Cortés ordered the burning of his ships, effectively stranding his expedition on the Mexican coast.

This action conveyed a clear message to his soldiers: there was no turning back, and they had no choice but to conquer or die.

The expression *"burn the boats"* has since become a metaphor for committing fully to a goal or endeavor, leaving no room for retreat or fallback.

It shows determination, resolve, and a desire to face challenges head-on, knowing that there is no way to return to the comfort of the past.

In Web2 entrepreneurship, this expression is very popular. But in Web3 and especially when it comes to tokenomics, it has a different meaning and risks associated.

Understand this:

The tokenomics of a project is going to be discussed at length by community members and the project's enemies.

You'll hear things like:

"The team has too many tokens, what if they dump it?"

"Ninety percent of tokens haven't been minted yet. It's too inflationary."

"The vesting schedule for VC is not long enough."

"The liquidity pool is not big enough to absorb big dumps and pumps."

Things never work perfectly according to the plan. Maybe you didn't sell all the tokens during the ICO, and now you have 50 percent of the supply of tokens minted and waiting on the project's wallet.

People are afraid the project might sell everything and rug the community. So people will ask for you to burn them. Maybe you should, but you should *not* rush.

> Definition: *to burn*
> *Burning* is like removing some coins from circulation and tossing them into a digital black hole, where they can't be used again. It's a deliberate act to make the remaining coins rarer, which can sometimes increase their value (if you burn a lot).

We'll explain soon why.

Other scenarios—you haven't renounced the contract. It means that you can still edit the tokenomics and make some changes. Some of them could be very dangerous for the community. For instance, you could maybe blacklist the community from selling or transferring the token, which would be the same as stealing from them. So everyone will hurry you to renounce the contract.

Should you do it?

Maybe, but not in the rush and under the pressure of a crowd.

Definition: *blacklisting*
Blacklisting is like banning someone from a club. When a wallet is *blacklisted*, it's marked as unwelcome, and transactions from or to that wallet are blocked or restricted. It's a way to enforce rules and keep bad actors or unwanted activity out of your project.

In both examples, people are somehow right. They ask you literally to burn the boats to show your commitment to the mission. But it's not coming without consequences

Once burned, you cannot recover the tokens. Maybe down the road, some VC might have been interested in an OTC deal to buy these tokens at a discount and with a long vesting time to protect the community.

Definition: *OTC deals*
OTC deals are like a private table at a fancy restaurant. Instead of buying tokens on the public market, VCs prefer private deals with projects. It's like having a tailored menu and personal chef, allowing them to negotiate specific terms and prices without ordering from the menu.

Once you renounce the contract, you can't make any changes to it. It's for good. So you have to think carefully about it.

Most of the time, people have legitimate reasons to ask you to renounce, burn, or perform an action that cannot be undone. They'll tell you that without this, the project won't work or won't take off, that no one serious will join it, etc.

This is a lie.

These same people have no issue investing in other projects with the same problems but enjoy stronger hype. So don't get fooled. Don't just act on the feedback of random people. Respect their opinion, but don't act blindly on them.

Ask your advisers, start a private conversation with key community members about it, and then discuss it with the community as a whole. It's okay to burn the boats, but don't rush it.

Key Takeaways

- Look at your Web3 project through the following triangle. Is it long-lasting? Is it profitable for the team? Is it attractive for the holders? The closer your answers are to a *"yes,"* the higher your chances of making it.
- Tokenomics can change over time. Don't rush to burn your boats too fast. Web3 can change very fast. Keep your options open.
- When in doubt, keep it simple. Add value to the world, and capture some of that value.

The Science of Utility

We raised $10 million, now let's give the holders some $10 merch.

—*Web3 NFT founders*

WIIFM

Utility is what makes the difference between gambling and the responsible adult world. Good Web3 projects, NFT, and tokens are . . . useful (crazy, right?). They are useful for something. If they have no use cases, then they usually follow pump-and-dump schemes. We chose to list many ideas of utility in this chapter, which makes it quite long. But the idea is for you to go through it fast and come back to it whenever you need utility ideas.

Everyone is talking about utility, and everyone has their own definition of utility.

Here is how we would define it:

***Utility* is the value your token or NFT provides to its holders, how it's used, and how they benefit from it.**

In theory, the *more* you have utilities, the *more* relevant your token or NFT is, and the more long-lasting your project is. That's at least the theory.

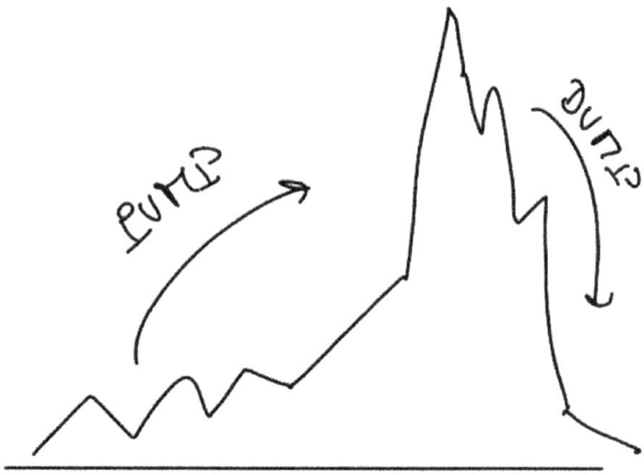

Utilities create demand and meaning around your product. Without utility, if the marketing is good, the token will pump-and-dump. And when something crashes, everyone gets angry very fast.

But if the token is useful, it'll pump-and-dump but higher and higher. Because whenever it dumps, some people will seize the opportunity to get it and use it. People won't buy the dip forever if a token is only about hype and fun.

The utility should help you escape the FOMO and FUD death cycles. Utility makes you relevant for months—and if possible, years—whatever the trend and the new hot stuff out there.

Let's put together a list of utilities with examples.

Here is how you should use this chapter. The idea . . . is to get ideas.

At the beginning of your project, **don't promise a lot of utilities**. No one cares about promises. Plus, promises are liabilities.

But keep in mind all the possible options for your project. Get someone a document where you can list tokens and their utility ideas.

When the time is right, introduce utilities to maintain the momentum around your project while multiplying use cases (aka reason to hold and use the stuff you created).

Utility No. 1—The Token-Gated Membership

Token-gating refers to a mechanism in which a person has to demonstrate the ownership of a token to enter a space (usually a digital space). The blockchain is used to verify that the owner owns the token and has the right to access the space.

Many NFT collections have adopted this utility. From Gary Vee's VeeFriends (a collection of 10,255 little animals drawn by hand by Gary Vee in person), to the ZenAcademy education platform from Web3 educator Zeneca, or to the PROOF Collective collection from serial entrepreneur Kevin Rose.

What's important is what's behind the token gate!

You have three cores of token-gated membership experiences:

1. *Educational experience*—humans have access to exclusive content.
2. *Horizontal relationship experience*—humans connect with other humans.
3. *Vertical relationship experience*—humans connect with inspirational figures.

TOKEN-GATED EDUCATION

Offering premium exclusive content and educational material behind the token gate is an easy way to create utility and value for a token.

For instance, crypto entrepreneur Zeneca opted for a learning platform to teach about Web3 opportunities. As the website states, ZenAcademy's mission is:

> *To cultivate a community of excellent humans. To empower them with the tools, opportunities, and networks to excel in Web3 and beyond. There's a place for everyone at the academy. Whether you're just starting, whether you're an artist, a dev, project founder, or a self-professed degen.*

The ZenAcademy student's ID NFT is your entry pass to join the community.

HORIZONTAL RELATIONSHIP

Among the horizontal relationships, we can mention the PROOF Collective NFT community launched by serial entrepreneur Kevin Rose in 2021.

The 1,000 PROOF NFTs give access to a closed community of like-minded artists, creators, and entrepreneurs involved in digital art.

Many creators purchased the NFT to join the community and grow their network.

VERTICAL RELATIONSHIP

As an example of a vertical relationship, VeeFriends from Gary Vee offers holders the chance to have exclusive virtual meetings with Gary himself via FaceTime, together with the opportunity to ask him about his thriving brand through live *"AMA"* sessions.

That's one of the many utilities of the VeeFriends NFT.

Utility No. 2—Access Physical Event by Holding an NFT or Token

NFT and tokens could make the sales of tickets for events obsolete.

How?

With three leverages.

AUTHENTICITY AND OWNERSHIP

NFTs can help stop ticket theft by proving that the ticket is real and that the owner has the right to use it.

Each NFT ticket has a unique digital stamp that makes it almost impossible to fake. Also, because the blockchain is transparent, every transaction is recorded and can be seen, which adds another layer of security.

POWER OVER THE SECONDARY MARKET

NFTs can also give event organizers power over the secondary ticket market.

They can put rules into the NFTs, like putting a limit on how much they can be resold for or making sure that a certain amount of any selling goes back to the company that made them.

This can stop scalping and make sure that both artists and managers get a piece of the success on the secondary market.

They can be set up to give backstage passes, merchandise, or savings in the future. This extra feature can make fans more interested and give them unique experiences that can't be had with regular seats.

EXAMPLES

They can also collect these digital tickets and keep track of their attendance at events to build their social profiles.

As a Web3 pure player, Bored Ape Yacht Club (BAYC) chose to expand outside the digital space to offer a physical, in-person experience with the ApeFest.

The utility of the NFT is to attend a physical event with other holders. ApeFest is where the community gathers once a year.

Other creators from outside the Web3 launched their NFTs with physical events as a key utility. For instance, Kings of Leon released in 2021 an album as an NFT, which included special perks like front-row seats to their concerts.

Utility No. 3—Unlocking Features on a Digital Product, in a Game or a Metaverse

The traditional business model of software and applications is to have a paid premium version or paid features.

On Side.xyz, for instance, we are using an NFT, the Side Card, to unlock features in our product.

With Side.xyz, Web3 projects and creators can create their Web3 profile page. However, the NFT will open many advanced features that will be released over time to keep the community hyped.

Another example is Stakedao.org, a famous DeFi investment platform. They launched their collection of 666 NFTs to unlock the best-performing yield strategies.

When it comes to games and metaverse, NFTs and tokens can be used as a currency to buy things or as access to discounts and special features.

For instance, Sandbox allows users to create and own digital assets—such as land, avatars, and wearables. Holders of SAND tokens can earn discounts on in-game purchases, access to exclusive events, and other benefits.

Utility No. 4—Offer Metaverse Experiences (For Boomers)

Okay, boomer, a metaverse experience is not just a digital experience. Or maybe it is. No one knows. Some say that using Zoom is already the metaverse.

Why do we even talk about it?

Because some huge Web2 companies decided to gamble their reputation on a buzzword. Facebook even changed its name to Meta and spent $36 billion* (as of 2022, so probably much more by now) on building little avatars with no legs.

Let's try to give some credit to this metaverse concept:

Metaverse is *not* a token-gated space to watch educational videos as a digital experience (see utility number 1).

Metaverse is an experience involving not only blockchain but a virtual and artificial reality to create a new experience.

The idea is not only to participate but to own things.

As Yat Siu, CEO of the gaming company Animoca, would say, *"The open, true metaverse has to be one in which you have ownership. Without ownership, it's meaningless."*

Facebook Meta is not the only one here.

Italian luxury brand Gucci partnered with key Web3 players like Sandbox and Yuga Labs (owner of the Bored Ape and CryptoPunks collections) to create a virtual fashion show experience for their customers, creating a limited-edition series of NFTs that unlocked a virtual runway show featuring the latest collection.

As *Forbes Magazine* quoted in 2022, *"Gucci Vault Opens In The Sandbox, Bringing Luxury Fashion Into The Metaverse."*

To go back to more down-to-earth utilities, platforms like Sandbox and Decentraland let crypto projects create and own digital space in their metaverse.

* In comparison, creating the iPhone cost Apple $3.7 billion according to Business Insider.

It's regarded as one utility. And it's quite cool. Your project could buy some land in these *"metaverses"* and do things there.

To say the least, we're only at the very beginning.

Utility No. 5—Buy or Give Access to Physical Stuff

By buying stuff, we mean here to get physical products you can touch, feel, and own.

Several scenarios are the following:

1. Humans can access the store and buy our stuff only if they have the token.
2. Humans get free stuff by buying our NFT.
3. Humans get an NFT when they buy physical stuff.

YOU CAN ACCESS THE STORE AND BUY OUR STUFF ONLY IF YOU HAVE THE TOKEN

RTFKT nailed this.

In 2021, RTFKT partnered with renowned artist Takashi Murakami to release the CloneX. It's a collection of 20,000 3D avatar-style profile pictures. Each NFT sold for 2 ETH, and the collection was sold out in a matter of minutes.

Following the acquisition of RTFKT by Nike, the brand dropped several NFT collections in addition to CloneX. Some are purely digital, while others are linked to physical products—for instance, a special edition of sneakers.

Physical sneakers contain scannable NFC tags that link to the NFT from which the clothing was claimed, creating lasting verification between physical and digital items.

You can have a similar experience, using the popular e-commerce solution Shopify. There are Shopify apps to create a token-gated store. Only people holding an NFT or a token can access the store and buy what you have to offer.

This is a very easy and great opportunity. People can only buy merchandise with the logo of your brand if they own the token or NFT.

It creates a super strong sense of exclusivity and belonging.

Another case study is the Doodles x Crocs Collection. Buyers were able to acquire a Crocs Box digital collectible with every purchase of the Doodles x Crocs Classic Clog Bundle. Once you opened the box, you received two Doodles Wearables. You used those to upgrade the visual identity of their NFT. And later that year, you could swap the bundle for a real-life Crocs pair.

Holders were able to access the new collection at a discounted price of $99 ($120 for nonholders) and one day earlier than the public.

YOU GET FREE STUFF BY BUYING OUR NFT

Beeple is famous for selling at an auction a JPEG picture for $69 million. Everyone, even in the mainstream media, talked about it back in March 2021.

For his collection *Beeple: Every Day*, he offered every holder a physical version (aka a physical token) of the artwork. Exactly 721 owners of the NFTs received the physical versions of their NFTs for free.

People liked it.

Services like Solid NFT enable creators and NFT holders to turn their digital NFT into physical art.

This is a nice plus for your community.

YOU GIVE A FREE NFT TO THE PERSON BUYING YOUR PHYSICAL STUFF

This utility strategy is very different because the first utility comes *before* you own the NFT.

Instead of launching an NFT and figuring out how to add utility, you could start with the utility.

When Luca Netz was named CEO of the NFT project Pudgy Penguins, he faced the problem of getting more traction for the project while developing new income streams.

Launching in the NFT bear market of 2023 a new NFT collection to bring more income would have been a catastrophe. So in 2023, they launched and successfully sold over 20,000 NFT-themed toys (making $500,000 in sales in only 48 hours).

Each toy was associated with a QR code that gives them access to Pudgy World—which is tied to a blockchain wallet, Soulbound NFT, and Tradeable NFT, accessible through email address sign-up.

It was explained the following way by the project:

> *Each toy comes with an official, scannable redemption code NFT adoption certificate that enables digital penguin customization. That way, you can obtain rare and epic traits and have a one-of-a-kind forever Pudgy Penguin registered to your name on the NFT blockchain. You can even trade the traits in the Pudgy Penguin marketplace!*

This is, for sure, a contrarian approach to utility that proved to be very successful.

Utility No. 6—Loyalty Program through Tokens and NFT

Loyalty programs with carton cards and stamps are from a different century. Literally. It's not even Web2. It feels more like, *"Hey, we just invented the printing press, and we're going to stamp some piece of paper."*

Tokens and NFTs could become a form of loyalty points while offering Web3 benefits and utilities.

When it comes to customer loyalty, Starbucks Coffee nailed it. And they are about to take it to the next level, thanks to Web3.

In 2022, Starbucks unveiled its Starbucks Odyssey loyalty program, the first enterprise-scale rewards program built on top of blockchain infrastructure.

The company statement says the following:

> *The new Starbucks Odyssey experience will offer members the ability to earn and buy digital collectible stamps (NFTs) that will unlock access to new, immersive coffee experiences.*

Starbucks is a business rooted in customer loyalty. You go to your local Starbucks coffee place, and usually, they remember your name and your favorite drink. The loyalty program even enabled the brand to become a bank where customers can deposit money for future coffee drinks.

The Odyssey program is an innovative opportunity for Starbucks loyalty members and partners (employees) in the United States to earn and purchase unique digital collectible assets through its loyalty program.

These digital assets will unlock access to new benefits and immersive coffee experiences. Starbucks is among the first companies to successfully incorporate NFTs into its loyalty program at scale, and it aims to foster a digital community that enables new ways for the company to engage with its members and partners.

Nike is working on a loyalty program called NikeConnect, which uses blockchain technology. Customers who participate in the program will earn NikeConnect tokens, which can be used to unlock exclusive content, experiences, and discounts.

Walmart is exploring the use of blockchain technology to create a loyalty program called Walmart Spark. Customers who participate in the program will earn Spark tokens, which can be redeemed for exclusive merchandise, experiences, and discounts.

Utility No. 7—Support a Cause, Raise Attention, and Contribute Financially

Supporting a cause has been widely used in the Web3 world as a marketing and attention-grabbing tool. But it doesn't mean it's not sincere or beneficial for causes.

Take for instance the NFT collection World of Women (WoW).

Their website is super clear on their mission:

> *We believe in giving back from Day 1. With the WoW community, we're taking action to increase diversity in the NFT space, educate and onboard the next generation of creators and builders, and create equal opportunities for everyone. The time is now.*

The projects have financially supported and brought the spotlight to initiatives like the following:

- *She's the first.* An organization that funds and supports local solutions to educate and empower girls across twenty-six countries.
- *Too Young to Wed.* An initiative fighting across-the-world child marriages and empowering women to decide when and with whom to marry.
- *Code to Inspire.* A program to support girls and women in Afghanistan by teaching them coding and graphic design.

Supporting a cause gives you good karma points while making you relevant to a targeted audience.

Utility No. 8—Governance and DAO

Most tokens called themselves *"utility"* and *"governance"* tokens (maybe to avoid regulatory crackdown).

Governance is a key utility of almost every project on the blockchain. Blockchain was about decentralization from day one. In this context, each token is a voting right to participate in the decision-making of the project.

Sometimes the voting implies staking the token, but not always. Take for instance the decentralized finance protocol Aave.

You can vote with your AAVE tokens or with stkAAVE (Staked AAVE) tokens. Staking your AAVE tokens will give you additional voting power, but it is not required. If you do not want to stake your tokens, you can still vote with your regular AAVE tokens.

In the NFT space, Doodles is an NFT project that provides utility to its community by allowing token holders to vote on future releases and events. Nouns.wtf (which we will cover in-depth in the *"Typologies of Launches for NFTs"* chapter) also lets any NFT holder offer a proposal and vote on proposals of other holders.

Utility No. 9—More Money . . . Rewards, Royalties, Dividends, Airdrops, Staking Revenues

"I'm here for the tech" is a common joke in Web3. The majority of stakeholders are here for the money.

And the money part is the best marketing for Web3 as a space. And it's not that bad. People indeed come for the money but stay for the community, the mission, and the technology.

So let's speak of *"more money"* as a utility.

Big disclaimer (before we start):

None of this is legal advice. Promising revenues, profits, or passive incomes might change your token's or NFT's nature. It might turn your project into a regulated financial product. Right now, the regulation is lacking clarity (depending on countries). But we strongly recommend you consult a lawyer regarding this "more money" utility and if or how you can use it in your marketing material.

Now that that's been said, there are more money utilities for your token.

AIRDROP

Some savvy creators airdrop tokens into their holders' wallets—in a bid to keep collections fresh and alive and keep holders engaged with the brand.

Probably the most well-known example of this done well is ApeCoin, the token that powers the Yuga Labs ecosystem. Regular ApeCoin drops to holders fuel purchases and trades and keep holders excited about the collection. At least for a while.

REVENUE SHARING

NFTs and tokens are often part of a business. The business or protocol has revenue streams and maybe profit. It's possible to incorporate revenue sharing into the utility and allow the holders or stakers to receive part of these revenues.

Take, for instance, Justin Bieber. In 2023, he tokenized his song *"Company."* Two thousand NFTs were offered to mint for a price tag of 0.017 ETH. Each NFT earns 0.0005 percent royalties when the song is streamed.

Offering profits and revenues to holders works, but it can also attract the wrong kind of holders. You don't want to have people only there for the money. Usually, whenever the money stops coming and slows down, they turn their back and leave the project as quickly as they arrived.

WHITELISTING

Having a whitelist means you (or more specifically, your wallet) are allowed to enter a project before the rest of the community. It could be for an NFT mint or a token's presale or an ICO.

Whitelisting usually means that you can arrive before the others and at a better price. In other words, whitelisting is an early access that reduces the dangers of any risky investment. If your project assures that addressed crypto wallets can mint one or more NFTs of an upcoming project, holders will feel they have the privilege and some unfair advantage over the rest of the world.

REFLECTION REWARDS

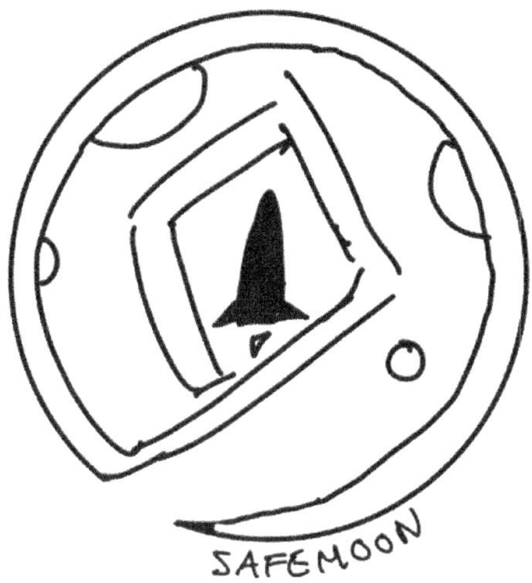

Reflection tokens like SafeMoon made this concept popular.

On each transaction on decentralized exchanges, a small fee was collected by the smart contract and then distributed to token holders. Buying and selling were taxed, and holders were rewarded. It was seen as a smart way to increase retention on the project.

SafeMoon managed to reach more than $5 billion in the market, mostly thanks to this reward mechanism.

STAKING

Staking is a broad term. In a more narrow definition, for proof-of-stake blockchain (like Cardano, Solana, or Ethereum), staking tokens contributes to the proper functioning of the blockchain, and stakers get paid for this.

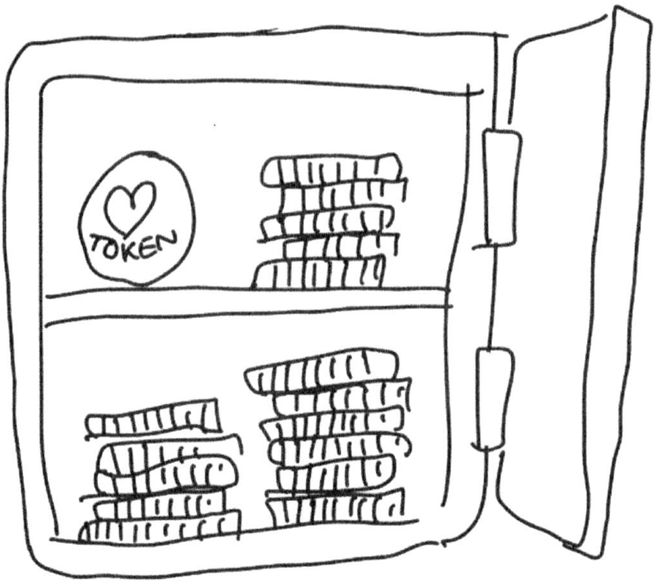

Staking has a vaguer meaning where it becomes more about *"locking"* tokens in a smart contract in return for utilities (e.g., governance) and revenues (e.g., staking reward).

Some projects even choose to have dual staking where holders can stake the NFT and the tokens at the same time.

For instance, users stake their ApeCoins and MAYC/BAYC NFTs in the ApeCoin DAO. The ApeCoin DAO uses the staked tokens to vote on proposals that affect the future of the ApeCoin ecosystem. In return for staking their tokens, users earn rewards in the form of more ApeCoins.

Sorare—this fantasy football game lets users stake their NFT player cards to earn rewards. Rewards can include ETH, rare player cards, or access to exclusive events.

Utility No. 10—NFT Licensing

Licensing refers to rights, including commercial rights, around your NFT (in this case, this utility is for NFT only).

CREATIVE COMMONS ZERO (CC0) LICENSE

Many collections have adopted the Creative Commons Zero (CC0). For instance, Nouns NFT. This means that the copyright for all NFTs is relinquished and dedicated to the public domain. This allows anyone to use, remix, or modify Nouns NFTs without legal restrictions.

The CC0 license is a powerful tool that can help promote creativity and innovation.

This licensing model has been praised by many in the NFT community. It is seen as a way to break down the barriers between creators and users and encourage the free flow of ideas.

Here are some of the benefits of using the CC0 license for Nouns NFTs:

- It allows anyone to use, remix, or modify Nouns NFTs without any legal restrictions.
- It promotes creativity and innovation by encouraging people to use Nouns NFTs in new and interesting ways.
- It helps to build a strong community around Nouns NFTs by giving everyone a stake in the project.

In the case of this licensing model, owning the NFT does not give you much regarding licensing rights and commercial use as anyone can use it (even if you're the real owner).

Thanks to this CC0, the Lil Nouns NFT collection was launched as a subcollection of Nouns DAO.

FULL-OWNERSHIP LICENSE

This type of licensing gives the holder of the NFT the most control over the underlying digital asset. They can use it for personal or commercial purposes, and they can even sell it to someone else.

The full-ownership licensing model is becoming increasingly popular as NFTs become more mainstream. This is because it gives holders more control over their assets and allows them to monetize them in a variety of ways.

Here are some of the benefits of using the full ownership licensing model for NFTs:

- It gives the holder the most control over the underlying digital asset.
- It allows the holder to monetize their asset in a variety of ways.
- It can help to build a strong community around the NFT project.

The Bored Ape Yacht Club (BAYC) uses a full ownership licensing model for its NFTs. This means that the holder of a BAYC NFT owns the copyright to the underlying digital asset and has the right to use it for personal or commercial purposes.

The Made by Ape platform lists and provides licenses to projects wanting to build on top of their NFT or their brand. We can mention the Mutant Grape Wine Club or the Bored Treat dog food.

Utility No. 11—NFT Breeding

Breeding is a general term that can be used to describe any process of creating new NFTs from existing ones. It is often used interchangeably with the terms *merge*, *mating*, and *hatching*.

NFT MERGE

Merging is a process where two or more NFTs are combined to create a new, more powerful NFT. For example, in the *Axie Infinity* game, players can merge their Axies (NFT creatures) to create new Axies with better stats.

NFT MATING

Mating is a process where two NFTs are paired together to create a new NFT offspring. For example, in the *CryptoKitties* collection, users can mate their CryptoKitties (NFT cats) to create new CryptoKitties kittens.

NFT HATCHING

Hatching is a process where a new NFT is created from an existing NFT. For example, in the *Gods Unchained* game, players can hatch new cards from eggs that they have earned in the game.

The most successful breeding experience was the creation of the Mutant Ape from Yuga Labs.

Mutant Apes were created in the Yuga ecosystem through a process called Mutant Serum. The Mutant Serum is an NFT that once combined with a Bored Ape Yacht Club (BAYC) NFT creates a new Mutant Ape NFT.

The Mutant Serum was released in two phases. The first phase, which took place in August 2021, saw 10,000 Mutant Serum NFTs airdropped to BAYC holders. The second phase, which took place in September 2021, saw 10,000 Mutant Serum NFTs sold in a public auction.

When a Mutant Serum NFT is combined with a BAYC NFT, the resulting Mutant Ape NFT will have a random set of traits. These traits can include different facial expressions, clothing, and accessories.

Utility No. 12—Discount and Special Deals IRL

IRL means *"in real life."*

Here are two examples:

CRYPTO.COM CARD

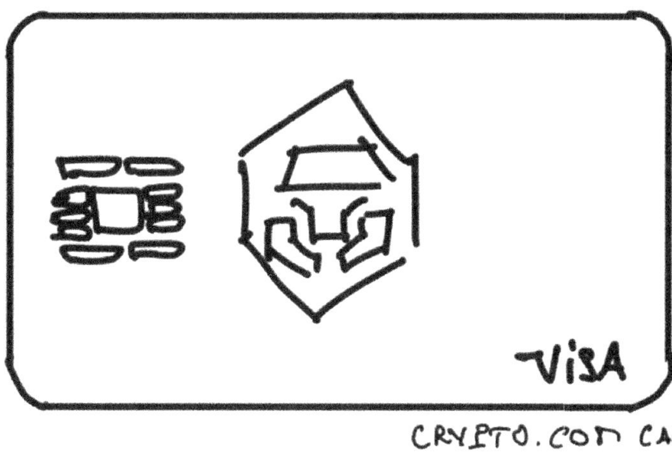

CRYPTO.COM CARD

The Crypto.com card is a debit card that offers users a variety of benefits, including cashback in CRO tokens, airport lounge access, and discounts on travel and other purchases.

The cashback rewards are based on the tier of the card that you hold. The Obsidian card, the highest tier, offers up to 8 percent cashback in CRO tokens. The Ruby Steel card, the lowest tier, offers up to 2 percent cashback in CRO tokens.

TRAVALA NFT

Travala is an online hotel- and flight-ticket-booking platform where you can pay in crypto. They have 2.2 million hotels and rooms listed and accept over 90 cryptocurrencies as payment methods.

Travala launched an NFT that provides holders with a variety of benefits, including discounted travel. Holders of the Travala NFT can earn discounts on travel bookings through the Travala platform. The discounts are based on the rarity of the Travala NFT.

Utility No. 13—Real-World Assets

As Coindesk.com writes, *"Traditional finance giants are excited about the idea of putting ownership of assets like precious metals, art, homes, and more on the blockchain."* And this started before the traditional finance giants got interested or ever heard about tokenization.

But let's first explain this notion.

Real-world assets (RWAs) are tangible or intangible assets that exist in the physical world and have intrinsic value. **The notion of real-world assets in blockchain refers to the process of tokenizing these assets on a blockchain.**

Tokenization consists of converting an asset into a digital token that can be traded on a blockchain network. By tokenizing RWAs, they can be made more liquid and accessible to a wider range of investors. Also, you can fractionalize assets.

For instance, Andry Warhol's artworks have been tokenized on the Ethereum blockchain in 2023. A company called Freeport offered fractionalized shares of Andy Warhol paintings, creating 1,000 tokens that represent shares of the work that anyone can buy. As of this writing, for just under $200, anyone could own 1/1000th of Warhol's *Rebel Without a Cause.*

In the future, NFT and tokens will be used to own totally or partially real-world assets like houses, paintings, cars, gold, etc. It might be one of the biggest utilities for NFTs and tokens.

The advantages of keeping the ownership of the real-world items on-chain are many:

- It lowers costs by removing middlemen like lawyers, brokers, banks, etc.
- It allows fast, efficient 24-7 trading of items that traditionally only could be done during *"working hours."*
- It lowers the barrier to entry and creates more liquidity.
- Its transparent process increases trust and accountability for traders.

The Bank of America called RWA tokenization a *"key driver of digital-asset adoption."* According to one of their reports, the tokenized gold market has captured over $1 billion in investment. Right now, the future looks bright for tokenization with global business advisory firm Boston Consulting Group forecasting that the market for tokenized assets could mushroom to $16 trillion by 2030. Not bad.

Utility Strategy

To sum up, we know there is a link between the utility of a token or an NFT and its price actions (and the longevity of the project). It's not a perfect causality, more like a correlation. But there is something there.

The more useful a token is, the better it is for holders.

At the end of the day, you can break down utilities into three categories: benefits, usability, and profitability.

- *Benefits.* The benefits of an asset are the tangible and intangible advantages that it provides to its owner. For example, a utility NFT might provide its owner with discounts on travel, access to exclusive events, or the ability to use it as a profile picture.
- *Usability.* The usability of an asset is how easy it is to use and interact with. For example, a utility NFT that is difficult to use or understand will have less utility than an NFT that is easy to use and understand.
- *Profitability.* The profitability of an asset is the potential for it to generate income for its owner. For example, a utility NFT that can be used to earn rewards or that can be sold for a profit will have more utility than an NFT that cannot be used to earn rewards or that cannot be sold for a profit.

Key Takeaways

- Utility is the value your token or NFT provides to holders, how they use it, and how they benefit from it.
- Think about utility in three main categories: benefits, usability, profitability.
- Benefits—discounts, loyalty programs, new features, memberships, physical events.
- Usability—how easy can I use it?
- Profitability—NFT licensing, airdrops, revenue sharing, royalties, dividends, staking revenues.
- Excessive development harms the relevance of the subject.

The Science of Decentralization

Which Lambo should the founder buy?

—A *"DAO"*

WIIFM

The more a project is decentralized, the harder it is to manage but also the more antifragile and lasting it is. But decentralization is not something you decide by decree or implement overnight. This chapter will teach you how to achieve it through a series of pragmatic steps.

This chapter is an adaptation (or even a rip-off) of Marc Zeller's great article "The Decentralization Journey" *on the AaveChan blog. Credit for good stuff goes to him. Any errors and omissions are ours.*

Blockchain is about decentralization. The idea is to avoid having a centralized entity (like a central bank in traditional finance) controlling everything and being able to make discretionary decisions.

Through decentralization and governance, Web3 aims to develop better infrastructures to create, store, and transfer value than the ones we already have.

But things are not that simple. **Decentralization is not a binary thing. It's a process with four main stages.** It starts with something super centralized and hopes to reach a decentralized *"stateless state"* at the end of the process.

It looks like this in Marc Zeller's model:

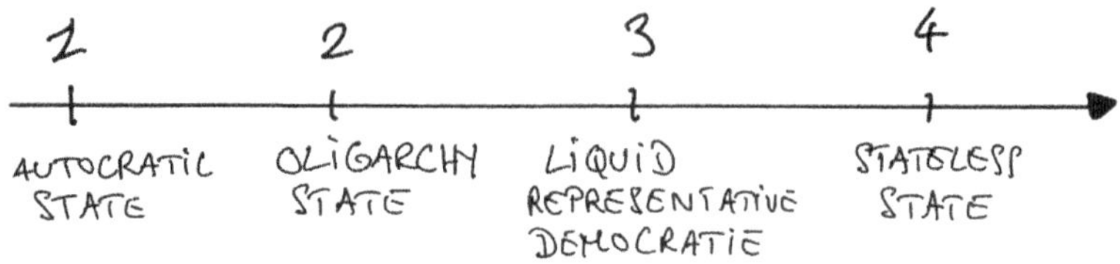

Stage No. 1—Autocratic State (Team-Run Projects)

Most dApps start their journey in the autocratic stage. During this stage, **founders and developers have near-complete control over the project**. There are little to no checks and balances.

This centralization of power and decision-making is necessary to move fast and create things. At this stage, you have no idea if there is demand or interest for your project. You might not even have a community. It's just you and your buddies.

The focus is to build your Minimum Viable Products (MVPs) and strive for Product-Market Fit (PMF). Autocracy gets stuff done.

If you introduce a token, it's more like a *"fan club ticket"* than a genuine governance instrument. **Holders have limited influence over decision-making and primarily serve as supporters of the project.**

If there is any governance, it is typically minimal and what is often mocked as *"decentralization theater."*

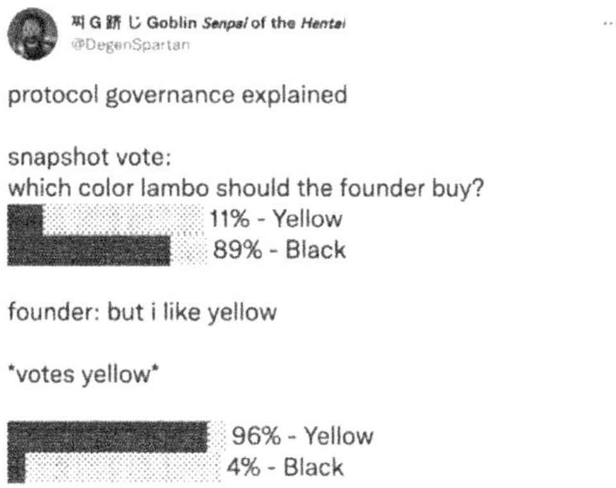

Strategically, **you can let the community vote on obvious decisions** they'd all agree on. Voting is not necessary, but it entertains the *"decentralization theater"* while educating the community about the importance of voting and contributing to projects (versus being silent spectators or loud gamblers).

You have a product, a token, and demand for your stuff.

You can now move on to stage 2.

Stage No. 2—Oligarchy State (VC-Run Davos)

Your stuff works, and business angels or venture capital firms are now investing in your token. As a consequence, **the circulating supply is concentrated among a few early investors**.

It's an oligarchy state. Rich people decide about stuff. You have to see this phase as a necessary transition between autocracy and further decentralization.

Dealing with investors and VCs teaches you to manage people, control the narrative, and integrate different opinions into your decision-making process.

Regular token holders can vote, but they don't have a lot of voting power in comparison with the team, early investors, and venture capital firms. It might cause some frustration, and many will call your project *"too centralized."*

You're laying the groundwork for moving into the mature DAO stage.

How do we move on to stage 3?

As Zeller notes:

> *The answer is simple but hard to implement:*
>
> - *Find PMF & achieve DAO revenue*
> - *Implement a DAO culture & welcome delegate platforms*
> - *Implement robust DAO frameworks*
> - *Fight voter apathy*
> - *Use DAO revenue to dilute teamwork with DAO service provider work*

You start to have a real economic model and revenues while the community of holders is taking more and more part in the decision. You need to grow the community to dilute the oligarchs.

Early investors are taking profit and exiting while you distribute more to the community (airdrop, staking revenue, etc.). You want to create independent delegators that people (including oligarchs) are delegating to.

> Definition: *delegators*
> *Delegators* are individuals who hold tokens in the DAO and are given the authority to vote and make decisions on behalf of others who have delegated their voting power to them.

Then you move on to stage 3.

Stage No. 3—The Liquid Representative Democracy

DAO is maturing, the project is growing, and we are moving into a liquid representative democracy. **This stage can only be achieved if the token supply is distributed enough to dilute the influence of the oligarchs from stage 2**.

The big change here is that the oligarchs are not in charge. We're in a democracy now. People vote and have an impact on decisions.

In the mature DAO stage, there is a healthy revenue stream, and service providers are paid by the project for their work. Governance is transparent and predictable, with well-defined frameworks in place.

Token holders with active roles receive distributions from excess protocol revenue via staking or other protocol roles.

According to Zeller, almost no project has reached the mature DAO stage yet. Yet he credits some leading DeFi projects, such as MakerDAO and Aave, for being on the verge of transitioning from late stage 2 to stage 3.

Stage No. 4—The Stateless State

The last stage is the stateless state stage. It represents the holy grail of decentralization.

It is incredibly challenging to achieve and is best suited for fully mature projects or those laser-focused on specific *"DeFi LEGO bricks."* Similar to a stateless society, the idea of reaching this stage without perfect code and execution is naive.

Currently, Zeller only recognizes LUSD, Ethereum, and Bitcoin as the only significant actors in the stateless state stage.

One might argue that direct democracy, similar to the one practiced in ancient Greece, would be the ultimate goal for DAOs and an alternative *"stage 4."*

However, it's important to consider the limitations of such a system. In ancient Athens, only around 40,000 free males (out of an estimated population of 250,000) participated in the direct democratic process, while slaves and women were responsible for the majority of labor.

This raises the question of whether individuals who work full-time jobs would have the time or inclination to participate directly in DAO governance.

Transition through Dilution

As projects move through the stages of decentralization, **it is essential to recognize that the transition from one stage to another should not be a forceful, sudden overthrow, or *"putsch."***

Instead, the process should be incremental, marked by a progressive dilution of power and control.

The development team's authority in the autocratic stage should be progressively diluted by the influence of early investors and other stakeholders in the oligarchy stage. Then the power of the oligarchs should be further diluted by the chosen representatives in the mature DAO stage. This gradual dilution allows for a smooth transition and helps avoid drastic disruptions that might destabilize the project.

A well-executed dilution process encourages collaboration and fosters a sense of shared responsibility among stakeholders. It also ensures that each stage benefits from the insights and contributions of a diverse group of participants, driving the project toward true decentralization and ultimately benefiting the entire community.

By adopting this approach, projects can navigate the decentralization spectrum more effectively, striking the right balance between efficiency, governance, and shared decision-making. This careful and considered transition between stages will not only improve the likelihood of achieving a truly decentralized future but also inspire confidence in the broader DeFi ecosystem.

Key Takeaways

- Centralization and decentralization are not binary but are processes that take time.
- Decentralization and democracy are not useful in the first stages of a project (they might even be detrimental).
- Transitions between phases happen with dilution. Early investors exit or delegate while the community gets airdrops and staking rewards.
- This process lets the community learn about their responsibilities and take a deeper part in the project decisions and development.
- Perfect decentralization and mature DAO are hard, if not impossible, to reach for most projects.

The Science of Simplicity

Don't overthink, it's like Dogecoin but on steroids.

—*A friend*

WIIFM

Only simple things can scale. Complicated stuff makes people feel smart but always causes problems down the road. In this chapter, you will learn to build simple things. Once that is done, you can start adding more complexity to the project.

The $18 Million *"I Feel Smart but I'm Stupid"* Story

Let me (Tugan) tell you a story. When we first launched Side.xyz (back in the day, it was called Unity—we changed the name in between and merged with a different team), we had a community of Web2 entrepreneurs. It was the last months of the 2021 bull market, and the euphoria was at its apex.

We wanted to make things different and make our community feel special. So we came up with a great and very intellectually stimulating plan:

1. Members of the community will be able to mint an Ethereum-based NFT for free.

2. This NFT will give them access to the token presale at a discounted price (and more utility down the road).
3. The purchasing power during the presale would depend on the NFT card you have. If you want to buy more tokens during the presale, you need to buy more cards on the secondary markets.
4. To buy the presale, you need to connect your wallet to our website and stake your NFT.
5. The presale will be open for a limited period, then we will have the token ICO.
6. ICO will have several rounds at different prices. The earlier you come, the better.

On paper everything is great:

- We're making a present to our community (NFT is for free).
- People can enter the project at a better price.
- We can raise funds for Side.xyz and build great stuff.

How did it work in practice?

Back in December 2021, minting the NFT would cost $200 to $300 in Ethereum gas fees. So the free NFT turned out to cost a fortune for small holders. Most people couldn't simply afford to mint.

As a consequence, we had to cancel the mint and move to the Polygon blockchain (which was offering much cheaper gas fees). We offered to people who minted to refund the gas fees (with Side tokens) and to airdrop them with a new NFT on Polygon.

But now that we were on Polygon (a blockchain less mainstream than Ethereum), the community had to set up the blockchain Polygon on their wallet and get some Matic tokens.

It was not super complicated, but each step was hurting our conversion. People just gave up. Most of them didn't have Matic tokens. We whitelisted everyone and airdropped some free Matic tokens so they could mint the NFT for free.

Now people have the NFT on the Polygon blockchain, but our token is on the Ethereum blockchain. It was fine, but confusing.

In the meantime, people were losing patience, and we were reaching day after day a new ATH, letting more and more smart people believe the crash was around the corner.

Nevertheless, some whales wanted to invest hundreds of thousands into our token. Instead of taking their money, we told them to get more NFT on the secondary market to have more purchasing power for the presale. It cost them money that they didn't invest in our project.

After this, we had to do the presale. Of course, the website was complicated and crashed multiple times before we could manage a presale.

Bonus point—after this presale, you had an NFT that had zero value and needed to find utility for. Congrats, you created a liability for your project.

The community got confused. Potential holders became impatient and moved on to other opportunities. Time was playing against us. People willing to invest were struggling to invest.

Had we simply given people an Ethereum address to send funds to, we would have raised $20 million instead of $2 million.

An $18 million mistake.

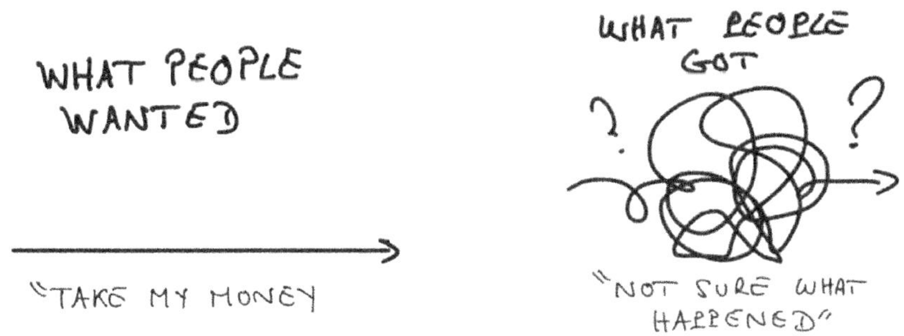

Here is the lesson:

Complicated stuff doesn't work. Always focus on simplicity. It's only when something simple works that you can add things. Don't get fooled by stimulating ideas.

A Case Study of Shiba Inu—The 150,000,000% Simplicity Secret Sauce

Shiba Inu was launched in 2020 as a reaction to the popularity of Dogecoin (launched in 2013) within the crypto community. The token has zero utility. It was simply a memecoin in the *"dog coin"* category.

As CoinTelegraph writes, *"After gaining a lot in value in 2021, it officially became Dogecoin's rival, leading Floki Inu, Akita Inu, and Dogelon Mars."*

(Yes, there is a market for dog coins.)

Shiba Inu started as a simple thing—*not* with a complex roadmap, esoteric tokenomics, promises of technological developments, multiple tokens, NFT, and other components.

The success of Shiba relied on the *"zeitgeist market fit"* but also on its simplicity. It was easy for people to grasp. When I (Tugan) was first introduced to it a few months before the pump, people just told me, *"Don't overthink, it's like Dogecoin but on steroids. It is useless, but if Doge pumps again, this stuff will go to the moon."* (And it did.)

It felt like a leveraged Dogecoin.

Got it simple.

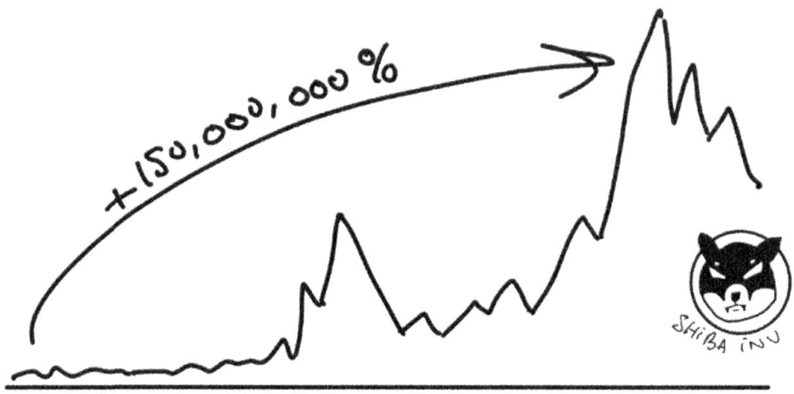

As CoinTelegraph reports:

> *In the range of one year, from August 2020—when the cryptocurrency was created—until October 2021, the SHIB coin raised from a low of $0.000000000056 to an all-time high of $0.00008616, rising an incredible 150 million percent.*

From the simplicity of Shiba Inus's message emerged a community of fans that would support and defend the token. The tokens were part of their identity and gave them a lot of fun.

The competition to grow bigger than Dogecoin was also a strong narrative and driver for the community. Ultimately, Shiba managed to briefly flip Dogecoin on October 29, 2021.

Over time, Shiba Inu added some complexity to develop an ecosystem:

- *SHIB (ERC-20 token)*—the original Shiba Inu token, launched in August 2020. It is a decentralized cryptocurrency that is not backed by any government or financial institution.
- *LEASH (ERC-20 token)*—a deflationary token that was launched in June 2021. It is designed to appreciate over time.
- *BONE (Erc-20 token)*—the governance token of the Shiba Inu ecosystem. It was launched in July 2021. Users can stake BONE to earn rewards and participate in voting on proposals for the ecosystem.
- *Shibaswap (decentralized exchange)*—a decentralized exchange (DEX) that was launched in July 2021. It allows users to trade SHIB, LEASH, BONE, and other ERC-20 tokens.
- *Shiboshis (NFT collection)*—a collection of 10,000 NFTs that was launched in October 2021. The Shiboshis are a collection of digital art representations of Shiba Inu dogs.
- *Doggy DAO (decentralized autonomous organization)*—a decentralized autonomous organization (DAO) that was launched in November 2021. The Doggy DAO is a community-governed organization that allows users to vote on proposals for the Shiba Inu ecosystem.
- *The Shiba Inu Blog*—the first blog launched on February 28, 2022, was titled *"2022 The Year of Learning."* It was written by Shytoshi Kusama, the lead developer of the Shiba Inu ecosystem.
- Shiba Eternity—a free-to-play mobile card game that was launched on October 6, 2022. It was developed by PlaySide Studios in partnership with Shiba Inu Games. The game is

inspired by Japanese martial arts and features a collection of 100 unique Shiboshi NFTs.

- *Shibarium (layer 2 blockchain):* A layer 2 blockchain that is being developed by the Shiba Inu team. Shibarium is designed to improve the scalability and efficiency of the Shiba Inu ecosystem.
- *Shib: The Metaverse (metaverse project)*—a metaverse project that is being developed by the Shiba Inu team. Shib: The Metaverse will allow users to create, own, and customize their virtual worlds.

> Definition*: ERC-20*
> *ERC-20* is a token standard used on Ethereum- and EVM-compatible networks that allows developers to build token applications that are interoperable with other products and services.

These are just some of the products that are currently part of the Shiba Inu ecosystem. The team is constantly working on new products and features, so this list is likely to grow in the future.

One of the reasons why Shiba Inu is still alive as a community in the bear market following the 2022 crash is the development of this ecosystem.

First, you start with simplicity.

You don't overpromise. Then you add complexity. But only step by step. You enhance the existing product, add ideas, and iterate. In the meantime, you build the community and create a strong culture around the project.

The Science of Simplicity

Follow these rules to keep things simple.

SIMPLE RULE NO. 1—HAVE JUST ONE MISSION

The mission could be to have fun, fight an enemy (like Shiba did with Doge at its start), etc. The mission could be anything from supporting charity to the development of a new technology. But it has to be one and only *one*. Don't get people confused. Don't pick too many fights. Avoid dispersion.

SIMPLE RULE NO. 2—FOCUS ON ONE BLOCKCHAIN

Avoid having your ecosystem spread on different chains. It makes it difficult for your community to follow up and gather your different assets.

It's also forcing your community to learn how to use more tools and own more tokens to pay gas fees. When the DeGods ecosystem left the Solana blockchain, they migrated to Ethereum for some collection and Polygon for another one (y00ts). The community was spread on two platforms. Ultimately, the team left Polygon and renounced the $3 million grant Polygon offered them to join them.

SIMPLE RULE NO. 3—HAVE A SIMPLE ROADMAP

Don't overpromise things. Don't announce dozens of crazy features. First, because it doesn't work (people are not stupid). Second, because it can be leveraged against you.

If you list things just to try to be appealing but you have no intention of developing them, it could be seen as manipulation and as a fraud.

SIMPLE RULE NO. 4—MAINTAIN A CONSISTENT BRANDING

All your social networks should have the same visual identity and the same tone. If you add more tokens, NFTs, and platforms to your project, they should keep the same visual identity, wording, and culture. Think about all the dog-related features in the Shiba ecosystem.

SIMPLE RULE NO. 5—GATHER ALL YOUR INFORMATION IN A SINGLE AND SIMPLE PAGE

Your community should be able to get all the key information in a manner of seconds without having to scroll through multiple pages or multiple subproducts of your project. Gather everything in one place. Use a Side.xyz project page to enhance clarity and trust.

SIMPLE RULE NO. 6—SIMPLIFY THE TOKENOMICS, OR MAKE SURE IT MAKES SENSE

Ideally, try to maintain a simple tokenomics. It's not always easy as projects have to evolve. But try to make things as easy and transparent as possible. If you introduce new tokens and NFTs, in a way, they should support and give utility to the existing token.

SIMPLE RULE NO. 7—ONE IDEA AT A TIME

This is called product and communication planning. Have a private roadmap of communication, features development, and announcements. Make sure to have just one narrative at a time. Make sure to launch features one after the other and not several products or tokens at the same time (unless it's very necessary, like a platform and its governance token at the same time).

Key Takeaways

- Always remember: subtract, before you add.
- Shiba Inu case study—no complex roadmap, esoteric tokenomics, and promises. *"This is like Doge, but on steroids."* Later they added more complexity, once the original vision was proven.
- To stand out, impress by simplicity and ease of use.

The Science of Loyalty

I'm a big cohorts guy.

—Frank DeGods

WIIFM

We all know how traitors end!

Loyalty is not really a science. You have it or you don't. But in a spirit of consistency with previous and next chapters, let's call this *"The Science of Loyalty."*

Loyalty is at the core of human societies. Decisions on wars, alliances, and social cohesions have been, for centuries, rooted in the notion of loyalty. The French revolutionaries beheaded their king the minute they felt he was becoming disloyal to the people when he tried to flee aboard.

You have basically two forms of loyalty. **Reciprocal and nonreciprocal loyalties.** *Reciprocal loyalty* means that it's going in *both* directions. The two people are loyal to each other. On the other hand, *nonreciprocal loyalty* means that a person is loyal to the other one but the opposite is not always true.

Let's do a deep dive.

Loyalty, Power, Human Interactions . . . and Guillotines

Loyalty is often a form of political system and social organization. It's about the distribution of power, roles, and responsibility. **It's about making the present and the future clearer and more understandable for participants.** They know what to expect and from whom.

Think about the European Middle Ages (I know, ages away from your next NFT mint). The loyalty system was the bedrock of society. Without it, society would have simply collapsed into anarchy.

Peasants had to pledge loyalty to their lords (they were almost their property in some way). Lords had to pledge loyalty to higher-ranking lords, and these higher-ranking lords had to pledge to the kind. Generally speaking, everyone has to pledge loyalty to the kind.

In return, the king is loyal to the *realm* as a whole, and lords have a form of responsibility to their vassals and peasants. The king had to protect and take care of them. It wasn't great for everyone, but it was a functioning social order.

That's, of course, an oversimplification, but this idea of reciprocal loyalty while having a very strict hierarchy is paramount.

To take a last example, before going back to Web3, one of the reasons King Louis XVI of France was guillotined on January 21, 1793, was his failed attempt to escape abroad. The countries he wanted to escape to were in a war against the French revolutionary power.

Escaping meant joining the enemies of the Revolution. It felt like disloyalty against the people and the realm. This treason triggered his execution.

Keep in mind that for most people, the king was still an important figure and that a constitutional monarchy was one of the options on the table. So executing him wasn't something casual.

What we're trying to say is, **loyalty matters a lot to humans.**

(Your NFT and token holders are mostly humans.)

The Loyalty Paradox in Web3

If you haven't noticed by now, Web3 is full of paradoxes.

Here is a good one: **Holders and stakeholders of a project expect complete loyalty to the project from founders, while *not* being loyal in return!**

Loyalty from the team toward the projects and holders feels like a guarantee against exit scams and rugs. So it makes sense to expect this loyalty from the team.

If you raise an ICO and simply leave with the money, it's treason (not to mention the possible legal implications of it). The expectation of founders' loyalty is the healthy part of Web3 loyalty. People expect the team to not take advantage of them and somehow commit to the project.

It makes sense.

But here is the unhealthy part: The community, or the crowd of degens, will pretty much expect founders to be *"married"* to the project, to be 100 percent committed, to have zero personal life, to work 24-7, and to not do anything else besides the project. In some cases, they don't even want you to get paid for your work.

Not only is this not reasonable, but also it's hypocritical.

Let us tell you a story.

A good friend of ours launched an NFT collection during the 2021 NFT bull market. Let's call him Boris. The mint was successful, and the project was full of promises. Contrary to plenty of projects in the NFT space, the team did work very hard to deliver on what they promised.

Unfortunately, in the meantime, the hype changed and the floor price went down.

That's part of life.

But the team kept going.

One day one member of the community came to Boris and insulted him, telling him that the whole team was inefficient, that things should be done better, faster, etc.

He was really upset. To understand his situation better, Boris asked him which NFT he held from the collection (assuming he had many of them, given his state of mind). The guy answered, *"I don't have any. I sold them at the ATH three months ago."*

Boris was speechless.

It might sound crazy for you who's reading the book, but this is the reality of Web3.

Holders have little to no loyalty to the project (or to founders), but they expect founders to have 100 percent loyalty to the project (and indirectly to holders).

That's the loyalty paradox. *You have to be loyal to people who are not loyal in return.** Web3 loyalty is mostly a nonreciprocal loyalty where . . .

Money Doesn't Buy You Loyalty, Loyalty Does

To go deeper into the concept of loyalty, understand this: Money will not buy you loyalty.

Paying your team too much will buy you time and no loyalty. People will be there only for the money.

It's even worse if you get them used to being paid way over the price of the market. You put them in a form of pressure. They are afraid that it might stop. They'd be very angry at you if it stops, and they know they won't get the same money elsewhere, so the end of the project will mean downgrading their standard of living.

Expect them to go talk to the press and spread rumors about you once you're successful.

Paying people too much simply makes them delusional and stressed. We will discuss this in-depth in section 3 about the team.

The same goes for holders. Holders making money and seeing their bags pump will give you attention. They will cheer you up. They'll say you're the boss, the OG, the visionary.

As long as things go up and only up.

At any time, they'll simply sell their bags, leave, and forget about you.

And if they don't do it and the value of their bags goes down, you'd become their absolute scapegoat (see chapter *"Web3 Founder as God, Web3 Founder as Victim"* for more details).

When in doubt, think about the past key builders from the Ethereum community. They built their wealth and reputation on Ethereum's success before using this wealth and fame to create their competing product while trashing Ethereum.

Money doesn't buy loyalty.

Loyalty buys loyalty.

The DeGods Cohorts Loyalty Design

DeGods is an NFT ecosystem launched first on the Solana blockchain in October 2021 by Frank DeGods and his team. Frank comes from work on start-ups and understands the key performance indicators (KPIs) and analytics better than most founders in Web3. As he said himself in an interview with PROOF NFT founder Kevin Rose, *"I'm a big cohorts guy."*

By attracting and maintaining a very loyal following, Frank did the following:

Whenever the project was making a move or introducing an innovation, he would always make sure to reward the most loyal holders.

One way to do it is basically to airdrop all the holders with the new things, as Bored Ape did in August 2021 when they launched the Mutant Ape collection.

However, according to Frank, is it not precise enough to get loyalty. You need to create **segmentation and small cohorts within the**

community. You cannot just airdrop all 10,000 of our holders every single time you introduce them to something.

Plus, it doesn't feel very personal.

It feels like a way to just launch something else while avoiding getting the core community angry at you for not focusing on the main collection that they hold.

"You have to create subsections within your community to properly reward people for a long period of time," said Frank.

Loyalty has to go to people and assets. Let us explain.

- **Loyalty to people**. This is the obvious one. They purchase your token and NFT, and probably they still hold it. You need to reward people.
- **Loyalty to assets.** You already launched token A, and now you start token B. Token B has to give value, support, and utility to token A. If it doesn't, the demand will simply move from token A to token B, and the first one will go down while the second one goes up. Not ideal.

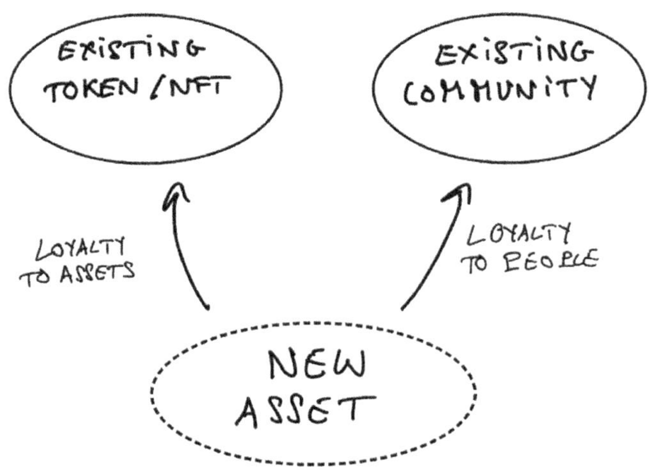

Loyalty Cohorts Engineering

Let's invent a scenario to think about how to design, engineer, and reward loyalty.

STAGE 1—YOU LAUNCH TOKEN A

You reward active members of the community with small airdrops of token A. The token will become the governance token of the project. Now people can vote and decide about things. Their voices matter.

STAGE 2—YOU LAUNCH TOKEN B ON TOP OF TOKEN A

You should give more utility to token A (loyalty to asset) while rewarding people who hold token A (loyalty to people).

So token B will be a reflection token that airdrops token As to holders. * Let us explain. Each time someone is trading token B on a DEX, you'll collect a tax, and this tax will be used to buy back token A and airdrop it to holders of token B. The more people trade token B, the more buyback there is to token A. That's an example of loyalty to asset token A.

Now you need to reward loyal holders of token A. You use the following cohorts of people who purchased token A and never sold any (aka diamond hands). You can simply airdrop some token Bs to this cohort. That's an example of loyalty to people in the cohort.

---

* This is called a "baby token." When a token has a tax on buying and selling and this tax is used to buy back and reward the holder with a different token, it's called a baby token.

STAGE 3—NOW YOU INTRODUCE AN NFT COLLECTION OF 1,000 PROFILE PICTURES

It's a way to create a sense of culture and social identity related to your project. Let's call it NFT C. Each day, 1 NFT C will be offered to mint with an auction. The highest bidder will be able to mint and become the proud owner of the JPEG.

But you have the following rules:

- Only people who hold 100 token As and 500 token Bs in their wallet can participate in the auction and mint. This is a very specific cohort.
- Fifty percent of the funds raised by the mint will go to a treasury managed by the DAO (whose governance token is token A). The community decides what to do with this money (spend on marketing, give to a charity, airdrop it to holders, etc.).
- Fifty percent of the funds raised by the mint will be used to automatically buy back token Bs and burn them.

STAGE 4—YOU INTRODUCE A DUAL-STAKING CONTRACT OF TOKEN B AND NFT C

People can stake a pair of tokens B and NFT C. They cannot stake the NFT or the token B individually. It has to be the pair.

Stakers will receive a reward in token A, hence increasing their voting power in the governance.

Furthermore, the longer you stake, the higher your rewards paid in token A. Each day, your APY is growing by 0.1 percent (until a ceiling).

This is just an example.

The key to rewarding laser-focused loyalty and engineering positive behavior is to be able to rank and classify holders in cohorts and groups so you can be precise in your actions.

In this example, we had the following cohorts:

- Cohorts of active community members (mostly off-chain data)
- Cohort of token A diamond hands (on-chain data)
- Cohorts of people holding 100 token As and 500 token Bs
- Cohorts of people holding at least 1 token B and at least 1 NFT C

WHOM TO REWARD

- Active community members
- Members who stay around a FUD and defend the project
- Members who refer the project to other
- Members who refer the project to others *and* who hold the token / NFT
- Holders of the token / NFT
- Diamond hand holders (never sold any tokens)
- Quantitative holders owning more than X tokens
- Dual owners of several tokens or NFTs from your ecosystem
- Stakers of your token / NFT
- Dual stakers of your tokens / NFT
- Long-term stakers
- Governance participants in the DAO
- Governance participants in the DAO *and* owning more than X tokens
- Governance participants in the DAO *and* who are diamond hands

HOW TO BE LOYAL TO A PREVIOUS TOKEN / NFT (BASICALLY TO SUPPORT ITS PRICE AND DEMAND)

- Sales from the new token will be used to buy back the previous token / NFT.
- Tax on the new token will be used to buy back the previous token / NFT.
- Ownership of the previous token / NFT is required to do anything with the new token.
- Dual ownership is required to perform a specific task or access benefits.
- Previous token / NFT gives you rewards (staking/airdrops) in the new token.
- Previous token / NFT can be burned to get the new one.

It's your job as a Web3 builder and marketer to design and combine cohorts, think about new utilities, and come up with creative ways to maintain the demand for all the assets while making the community feel special. One of the challenges here is **to do it while keeping things simple.** Newcomers to the community have to be able to understand the tokenomics, projects, utilities, etc. fast.

Key Takeaways

- Money doesn't buy loyalty, loyalty does.
- In Web3, communities expect you to be loyal to them, even if they are not loyal to you.
- Think about building loyalty cohorts. First, you have people. The longer they stay around, the more they get. Second, you have assets. The more the ecosystem grows, the more they increase in value.

The Science of Trust

Don't trust. Verify.

—Anyone using the blockchain

WIIFM

About 99.9 percent of Web3 projects fail. Some of them . . . on purpose (then it's a scam). Everyone working in this industry has been called *"a scammer"* at least once. Trust is a big issue here. This chapter will teach you how to build trust around your project.

Writing about trust in Web3 is interesting since the **blockchain was created to avoid asking the question of trust.** The blockchain's slogan is, after all, *"Don't trust, verify."* Nevertheless, blockchain and building in Web3 are a lot about humans having interactions. Which requires . . . trust.

Trust is paramount if you want to attract holders, develop a community, and build a project. People have to receive trust signals in the middle of the noise.

Here is an inexhaustive list of trust factors.

Trust Signal No. 1—Security and Audit

In 2022, cryptocurrency businesses experienced an alarming $3.8 billion in theft, marking a new record for a single year, as reported by Web3 analytics platform Chainalysis.

This figure surpasses the $3.3 billion stolen through crypto hacking in the previous year, highlighting the growing security challenges facing the crypto industry.

So security matters.

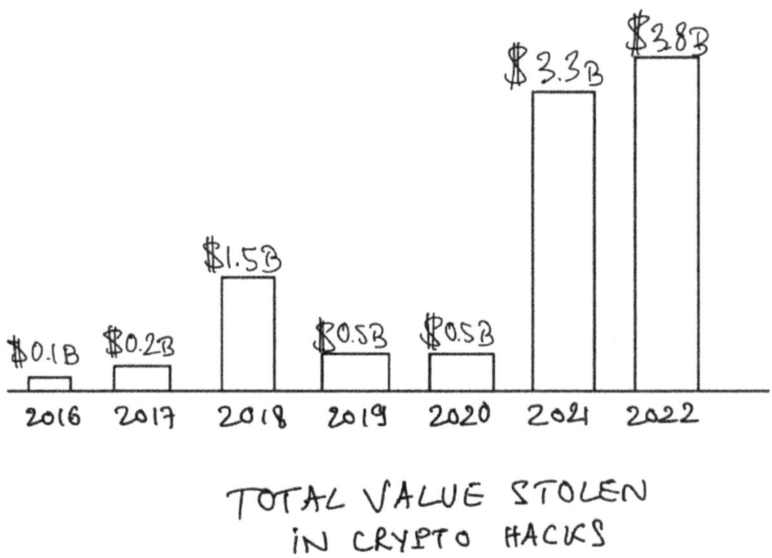

Security audits are a vital pillar of trust in Web3 projects. They serve as a safeguard against vulnerabilities that could compromise user assets and system integrity.

Showing project code and smart contracts to external security audit firms assures users and stakeholders that their tokens and wallets are protected.

Also, it demonstrates a strong commitment to transparency, responsible development, and adherence to best practices. As security breaches can have severe consequences, including financial losses and damage to trust, regular audits are not just about the present, but they also ensure the long-term viability of the project.

Trust Signal No. 2—Founders' Profile and Track Record

One of the first things people check on a project is, **what do we know about the founders?** While being doxxed can increase the trust factor by a magnitude, it's not necessary (especially knowing the risks associated).*

Holders will ask themselves, *"Okay, founders and developers are not doxxed. But what do we know about them?"*

It would be great if all the team members had their own social media accounts where we could read content, understand how they think, and check their commitment to the project.

How much you have been posting about the project and for how long are analyzed by the community.

As a founder, having a blue chip NFT as a profile picture across your social media (think about a Bored Ape, Crypto Punks, DeGods, or Azuki) will drastically increase the trust people have in the project's founder.

In case you wonder, *yes,* this is not rational, but humans aren't that rational after all.

If founders have done successful projects in the past, it's a positive signal.

---

* See the *"To Doxx or Not to Doxx"* chapter in section 3 about this issue.

Trust Signal No. 3—Whitepaper

The whitepaper serves as the foundational document that drives trust in a Web3 project. The whitepaper explains the visions, goals, technological choices, and governance model in a transparent manner.

Since the 2008 Bitcoin whitepaper from Satoshi Nakamoto, whitepapers have been part of the crypto and Web3 culture.

It's expected from all projects to have one. If you don't have one, you need to explain why! (It's fine too, as long as the explanation makes sense.) One of the first questions people ask is, *"Where is the whitepaper?"*

While focusing on whitepaper, **you have to keep in mind your target audience.** In the case of a memecoin, maybe the approach to the whitepaper could be more *"funny"* and *"detached."* See for instance the project Australian Safe Shepherd dog token (better known as *ASS token*) that introduced their whitepaper and roadmap the following way:

AUSTRALIAN SAFE SHEPHERD ($ASS) WHITEPAPER AND ROADMAP

Other technological projects put the focus on the math, technology, or even philosophical choices that motivate their works.

Speaking of math . . .

Trust Signal No. 4—Some Math and Science Behind the Tokenomics

The inclusion of math and equations in a project can evoke trust through the psychological mechanism known as *"perceived competence."*

People often attribute greater competence to individuals who employ scientific or technical language and methods. This perception of competence can, in turn, influence trust.

Humans tend to associate scientific rigor with authority and reliability. When a project adds mathematical models and equations, it shows a commitment to data-driven decision-making and taps into the perception that science and mathematics are trustworthy.

"Trust the science," as the saying goes.

Here again, there is some irrationality. Most crypto holders are not literate enough in math to truly understand the equations and math formulas.

But it feels like science. And *science* is synonymous with *authority.* Math enables engineers to design skyscrapers and planes, so the project should not collapse overnight if there is some math.

It's unfortunately not that simple, but you get the idea.

The idea is not to invent some fake science to manipulate people but to see what can be explained or contextualized by math and equations in your project.

Trust Signal No. 5—A Big, Ambitious, and Positive Vision for the Future

Having a big vision creates trust because it reflects a sense of purpose, ambition, confidence, and commitment.

People like to follow entrepreneurs or politicians with a strong, positive vision for the future. Think about Nelson Mandela's fight against apartheid, Obama's 2008 campaign, or Elon Musk's plan to colonize Mars.

It resonates with people. It's also a differentiation factor in a world where people shy away from having big ambitions. Moreover, **humans like to be part of something bigger than themselves.**

Also, leaders with a strong vision and mission don't give up easily. So you rather want to bet on them. You have the feeling that the project will face difficulties but manage to overcome obstacles.

A big vision captures the imagination and brings a sense of responsibility and accountability. Both reinforce the trust in the project.

For example, aiming to fix global supply chain issues using tokenization and blockchain sounds more trustworthy than launching a token called *HarryPotterObamaSonic10Inu.**

But once again, it also depends on the target demographic of the Web3 project. Dogecoin has a larger market cap than many big family-owned industrial conglomerates!

---

* Yes, it exists.

Trust Signal No. 6—Clean UI Website

The user interface (UI) of your website has to match the vision and mission of the project. A memecoin is not supposed to look like a website of the foundation of a layer 1 blockchain with hundreds of millions in financial backing and billions in total value locked.

Nevertheless, the more serious the project, the better and more professional your website has to look. **Always make sure that the first visual impression is the right one.** People always have a confirmation bias. If the first impression gives the signal of a *"shitcoin,"* people will simply find all the reason to believe your project is a shitcoin.

Visit websites of competing products in your niche to understand expectations and standards, and send them to your designer.

It's really a matter of consistency.

Trust Signal No. 7—Existing Vibrant Community

A vibrant community is a very strong form of social proof. It signals that many other people (mostly humans, but also some bots) do enjoy, use, and trust the product. They have an interest and are invested in it.

What's interesting is not only the number of followers or members in a group but the *intensity* and quality of the connections among the members. Do people have conversations with each other? How many messages are posted on Discord every minute? How many tweets are posted? Are some content creators part of the community?

If the project is already live, people might check the blockchain scan of the project to check the number of holders and compare it to the audience on different social networks. Both can be faked and manipulated, but it's still considered valuable data.

> Definition: *blockchain scan*
> A *blockchain scan* is a web interface that allows users to query the contents of the blockchain, like a search engine for the blockchain. Information on the blockchain can be searched, like transactions and addresses balances. (By the way, never fake your engagement, and never use bots. In the long run, it could play against you while being very ethically questionable.)

You might face a chicken-egg problem here.

People will come if there is an active community. But for an active community to be there, people have first to come. You solve the problem by **having the founders, developers, and the team available every day on the chat and welcome any visitors.** So from the trust perspective, either you have a community or you have very available founders.

Trust Signal No. 8—The Social Media Consistency

The social media presence of the team and project has to be consistent.

When were the social accounts created? If all founders and projects accounts were created two weeks ago, it's not making people believe that there is a lot of work done.

Builders like to mention how much experience they have and how long they've been working on the product, but if the X.com account was created only a few days ago, this claim doesn't sound very trustworthy!

So the earlier you build the social presence and start to post, the better. Let's say you have an idea or better a strong desire to build something, create a social account, and start posting *as soon as possible*.

Also, when people check a project, they're immediately going on X.com, Telegram, and Discord of the project. Usually, people visit the account of the project on different networks to check some inconsistencies.

If you have 30,000 followers on X.com but only 87 on Instagram, chances are the 30,000 followers are mostly fake followers or bots.

You need to have consistent numbers and avoid buying fake followers or attracting bots through airdrop campaigns and giveaways.

Trust Signal No. 9—Transparency about Token Allocation and Profit-Taking Mechanism

This point has been discussed in a previous chapter dedicated to transparency. But the token allocation, the profit-taking mechanism, where the money is, and what will be done with it are *key* in order to be trusted.

Confusion on these points is always a strong red flag. On the website or the whitepaper, you need to be able to easily find this information.

If, for instance, the project or the team holds a big percentage of the supply, it has to be explained. **Everything is fine as long as it's transparent and has rational explanations.**

Be transparent on all the sensitive topics.

Trust Signal No. 10 (Optional)—Backed by Investment Funds and Web3 Foundations

This trust signal is about your relationship with Blockchain Aristocrats, foundations, centralized exchanges, and investment firms. If you got grants from protocols or funding from centralized institutions, it's always good to mention it.

Even if the *"smart money"* doesn't have such a perfect track record (think about Three Arrows Capital, Terra Luna, and FTX), people generally trust them.

Not all this smart money is considered equal. Some VC and business angels have a stronger brand. Think about Mike Novogratz or a16z. They enjoy a much stronger reputation than the average VC.

Let's keep in mind that this trust signal is, of course, optional. You don't need it to succeed.

Trust Signal No. 11—Daring to Have a Contrarian Approach

This is a paradox. Founders have the feeling that to be accepted and trusted, they need to do be *"like the other ones."*

It might be true in many cases. But herdlike behavior is not always in your best interest. If your niche starts to be saturated, it might feel like you're just following the trends without having your own idcas while lacking courage.

Having a contrarian approach might therefore be a trust signal.

Instead of slightly iterating what your competition is building, charging, or promoting, have the guts to go down a completely new route. You will gain respect and trust from both outsiders and insiders.

A great example of this was the Moonbirds NFT collection minting for 2.5 ETH at a time when most projects minted for 0.1 ETH, or Neo Tokyo's NFT minting for free at a time of overcharged mints.

Trust Signal No. 12—Caring about Details

Great products are built by maniacs. Or at least this is the official propaganda of Silicon Valley. Steve Jobs and his *"reality distortion field"* is the perfect example.

If we have the feeling that we just don't care about details, if too many things are clumsy and incomplete, trust will slowly but surely be hurt.

Think about your project like a Jenga tower. Making a mistake is like removing one building block. Make one slight spelling error in your announcement, no problem. It happens. We're humans. But make them over and over again, and your tower will start to crumble.

Keep in mind that distrust and panic spread very fast in Web3. If you allow mistakes, and the culture within the team is not around excellence and work ethics, you will soon run into problems.

If, on the other hand, the community feels that there is a sense of deep caring about details, that things are clean, and that announcements are well written, trust will grow.

Key Takeaways

- Web3 is full of snake oil crooks, and in bear markets trust is just above zero. Gaining the trust of your users is your most important job.
- Trust compounds, and so does distrust.
- Throw all your biases aside, open an incognito window, put yourself in the shoes of your user avatar, and ask yourself, *"Do I trust this?"*
- Have the guts to swim against the stream.
- The devil is in the details.

The Science of Longevity

You win by staying alive long enough that you outlast everyone else.

—Alex Hormozi

WIIFM

There are two reasons to stay alive as long as possible. First, the longer the project lasts, the more you have chances to build and deliver something meaningful. Second, the longer you stay alive, the more you can make money (after all, Web3 is still a business). This chapter is the conclusion of all our previous chapters in this section of the book.

We can define *longevity* as the *"act of staying alive longer."* Easy one.

But why are we talking about longevity here? It's not a book about biohacking.

We're talking about longevity first because Web3 projects die very fast. And dying sucks.

Remember: **Web3 is faster entrepreneurship**. Things grow, make money, and die way faster than in the Web2 or in *"real life."* Web3 is a cemetery of tens if not hundreds of thousands of projects that have failed.

Compare Web3 projects with baby turtles (careful, it's going to be gory).

Baby turtles crawl out of their eggs on a beach in the Caribbean to try to reach the water while avoiding being caught and getting eaten alive by crabs and seagulls. The few that reach the ocean now have to deal with another set of predators (fish, sharks, etc.).

It's a baby turtle world, where 99 percent of projects die before achieving anything.

Many have to die so a few can become rich and famous. So staying alive is pretty much the name of the game!

Also, the longer you stay alive, the more you make money, and the higher the probability that you can innovate enough until you come up with something groundbreaking.

To put it bluntly:

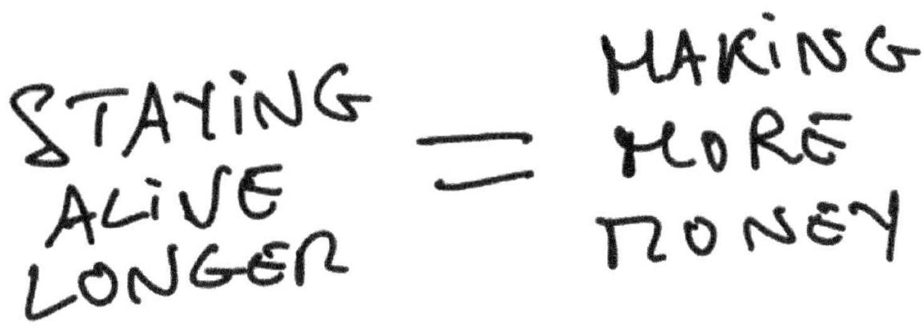

Then it's up to you to decide (with or without your community) how you allocate this money.

Longevity Wisdom No. 1—Survival > Success

As Web2 startup mentor and cofounder of Y Combinator Paul Graham wrote, *"The most important thing is to survive. Most startups die. If you can survive long enough, you'll eventually succeed."*

It's more important for a start-up to survive than to be successful immediately. Forget the headlines. Forget the *"cool"* factor. That's not the job. **The job is to survive where everyone else dies.**

Paul Graham's advice to focus on survival over immediate success is still relevant in the Web3 space. The Web3 ecosystem is still in its early stages, and there is a lot of uncertainty about which projects will ultimately succeed.

Look at the best-performing tokens of the 2017 ATH. Most of them were nowhere to be seen in 2021 ATH. New projects, technologies, and platforms took the spotlight and attracted most of the liquidity.

The best projects take time to become large successes.

Think about the CryptoPunks NFT collection. They were first introduced in 2017, and they had to go through a tough bear market.

No one cared in 2017.

No one cared in 2018.

No one cared in 2019.

A few insiders cared in 2020.

Everyone wanted one in 2021.

Everyone copied them in 2021, 2022, 2023 . . .

CryptoPunks drove the narrative of the 2020–2021 NFT bull market. Now you can see CryptoPunks in the private collections of billionaires, on the profile pictures of celebrities, and even in some museums.

One was even displayed in the Centre Pompidou Museum in Paris. As Decrypt wrote, *"Among the original artworks by Matisse and Picasso, visitors to Paris' famed Centre Pompidou can now find a unique new exhibit: a CryptoPunks NFT."*

SURVIVAL > SUCCESS

Survival is more important than success.

If you stay alive long enough, you increase your odds of success.

Longevity Wisdom No. 2—The Hype/Product Ratio

To survive is often a balance between the hype and the quality of your product.

$$H/P\ \text{RATIO} = \frac{\text{HYPE}}{\text{PRODUCT}}$$

Kevin Rose* called this a **hype/product ratio.** When his NFT collection Moonbirds was introduced, hype was huge, but the product was still in its infancy. As he said, *"Our hype is at 10. Our product is truly at a 1. It's up to us to close that gap."*

If the hype is way higher than the product, focus on the product. Ship light and ship fast. Show your holders and community that things are getting built. They cannot wait six or twelve months for a feature to be implemented. You need to feed them something fast.

---

* Kevin Rose is the founder of several NFT collections like PROOF NFT and Moonbirds.

On the contrary, if you have a high product but the hype is low, then it might be time to allocate some resources to marketing and community building. The coming chapters will teach you how.

Longevity Wisdom No. 3—The Business Model Issue

Good businesses are businesses that retain and rebill existing customers. Web2 is often about the monthly recurring revenue (MRR) or annual recurring revenue (ARR). The whole idea is to have a recurring business, with income streams coming every month or year to keep the boat afloat.

Most (if not all) NFT and token projects have this problem here.

They made a lot of money during the token's ICO or the NFT's mint. Sometimes tens of millions in a matter of minutes. And then they make almost nothing.

With NFTs, you can collect some royalties, but it's getting trickier and trickier to get them (trading platforms like Blur.io let you trade without royalties).

With a token, you can discreetly sell some tokens every month to get some cash. But that's not a business model.

Web3 projects that figure out a way to generate revenue every month are the ones that are the most likely to go through bear markets while being able to pay their teams.

Think about Nouns DAO, which is still printing money every single day. Maybe they nailed the business model issue for NFT. For a token, it's about creating utility and demand for the token within a service or a platform.

In conclusion, *"Web3 and crypto, in general, is very market-driven, so you have highs and downs. When we build, we always are considering the long game"* (Stani Kulechov, founder and CEO, Aave).

Grow Web3 Together with Us

Web3 is not about competition. It's not about the size of your slice. It's about growing the size of the cake.

It's about attracting more smart people, creating more innovation, and more cool stuff happening.

And that's great for everyone.

No matter if you're an investor, a marketer, a community member, or an airdrop hunter, you want to have more things going on.

And the easiest way that you can do this . . . is by helping us promote this book.

If this book helped you, or believe that it can help others, you can do us one big free favor.

Your review costs no money and less than sixty seconds to make, but it can change Web3 forever.

If you are reading on Kindle or an e-reader, scroll to the bottom of the book, then swipe up, and it will prompt a review for you.

If for some reason these changed, you can go to Amazon (or wherever you purchased this book from) and leave a review right on the book's page.

Thank you!

Tugan and Apollo

Key Takeaways

- It's not about when you can enter—it's about how long you can stay.
- To survive, you need to balance the hype and product quality. If there is no hype but there's a great product, focus on the hype. If there is no product but there's a lot of hype, focus on the product.
- The fundamental issue of Web3 is that it's not a cash flow business. Most projects raise millions but have no plan for recurring revenue. Projects that can generate cash flow during a bear market are the ones that will be around long enough to make it.

SECTION 3

THE TEAM

The Minimum Viable Guru: An Introduction to the Web3 Team

I'm not your guru.

—Tony Robbins

WIIFM

A Minimum Viable Guru (or MVG) is a semipublic figure that leads a Web3 project and gets the attention of the community. An MVG doesn't need to show his real identity (we will see in the next chapter why it's actually a horrible idea) but should use a few leverages to create a solid relationship with an audience. This chapter is purposefully quite long to really give you all the tools and hacks to create your MVG.

The Web3 space has a love-hate relationship with celebrity entrepreneurs and inspiring figures. The crypto history is paved with success stories that fail in an epic fashion.

Think about Do Kwon (Terra Luna), Sam Bankman-Friend (FTX), Alex Mashinsky (Celsius Network), Su Zhu and Kyle Davies (Three Arrows Capital), and many others.

You might argue that none of these entrepreneurs were truly about decentralization, but in people's minds, they're part of crypto.

Other figures are simply controversial and might fall at some point. Take Justin Sun (from the Tron blockchain and BitTorrent), who was almost described by The Verge as an international fugitive when they wrote:

> *Brash and outspoken, Tron founder Justin Sun has always been a controversial figure in crypto. More audacious than his reputation, Sun has an even riskier approach to U.S. and Chinese financial regulations — and is often trying to evade them.*

Haters of Chengpeng Zao (CZ) from Binance claim that he is hiding in the United Arab Emirates and cannot travel to the United States. And let's not mention all the controversies around Tether's founders (Brock Pierce, Reeve Collins, and Craig Sellars), their link to Bitfinex, the multiple lawsuits, and conspiracy theories.

The goal here is neither to tarnish the reputation of builders nor to give our opinion about them. It's about **understanding the dynamics of leadership, fame, and failure in Web3**.

Also, always keep in mind the 100 percent rug rule.

Definition: *100 percent rug rule*
Hundred percent of people in Web3 and crypto have been called *"crooks"* and *"gangsters."* In the same way, 100 percent of projects that might see their price go down at some point have been accused of being *"rugs"* and *"scams."*

Who is your MVG?

What Is an MVG?

MVG stands for Minimum Viable Guru. The notion is inspired by Eric Ries's book *The Lean Startup*. In the book, Ries introduced the concept of a Minimum Viable Product (MVP).

An MVP is the most basic version of a product that includes only the essential features needed to demonstrate its core functionality and value to early users.

The MVG follows the same logic. **It's about creating a semipublic figure that is public and interesting enough to inspire and drive traction to the project, without being too public, without being too transparent about personal information.** An MVG is also not a full-time influencer.

It's the minimum viable to inspire and drive a community around a project. Being an MVG is also an **antifragile asset**. Becoming a trusted voice in the space is a business in itself. It makes you interesting to connect or to work with.

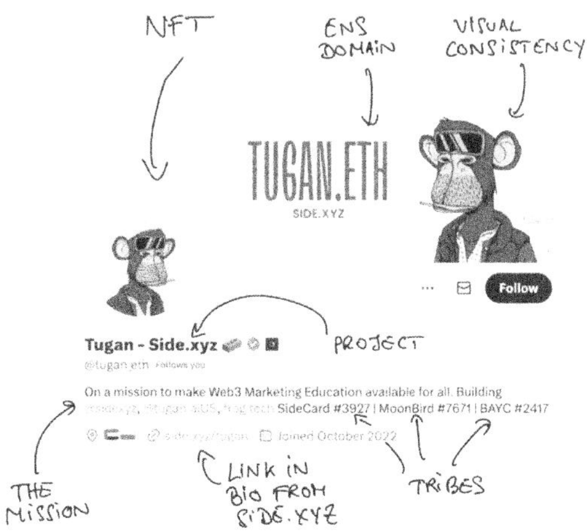

It's how you last and matter in Web3. Just imagine having a qualified audience and being able to onboard them into your next venture. You immediately have hundreds, if not thousands, of users and holders without having to spend any time or money on marketing.

So how do you become an MVG?

Who Is Your MVG?

You don't have to use your real first name. Mentioning your last name is something to avoid.

Your name or pseudonym has to be easy to pronounce. Ideally, you should try to get the Ethereum Name Service (ENS) around your name so you have a .eth at the end. For instance, Tugan.eth.

For your profile picture, you can take an NFT from a blue-chip collection or actually any collection. **It's better to have the NFT of a cheap collection you love than a picture of an expensive NFT you don't own**. Web3 is about ownership and transparency. Don't display something that's not yours. People will react very negatively to it.

With Side.xyz, you can create your page where people can know what you work on and which team you're part of—a page generally talking about what to learn about you.

It's very important that you decide about a visual identity (colors, profile pictures, font, etc.) and that you have the same across all social networks. You should be easily recognizable.

What Is Your MVG's Niche?

Let's assume that the world didn't wait for you.

Whatever your positioning and ideas, someone had the same and is already there. The barrier to entry to become a semipublic figure and create content on the internet is close to zero. As Gary Vee likes to say, *"Anyone can start to create content, but only a few manage to attract and keep attention."*

To be heard, you need to be specialized, to be *"niched."*

Here is how to understand the notion of niche.

Crypto and Web3 are the market. It's broad, it's big. Being specialized in *"crypto"* is too vague, too large, and too competitive. So you want to focus on something more narrow.

Introducing . . . *submarkets.* Think about NFT, Web3 gaming, or DeFi. These are submarkets of the Crypto Web3 market.

But it's still too broad! Then come the niches. A niche within DeFi could be something like *"liquid staking on ETH."*

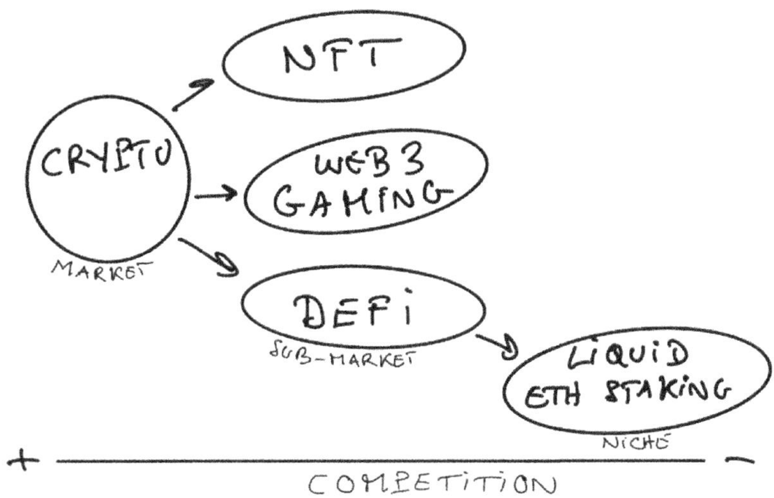

If you specialize in this niche, you have a chance to become relevant. After all, you're specialized because you're focused.

Someone who wants to learn about *"liquid staking on ETH"* wants to follow and place his trust in someone who has dedicated his focus to this.

Okay, let's say you want to expand. That's fine.

Start dominating your niche and creating your little monopoly there. Only after this is achieved can you start addressing another niche, and another one, and another one, until you own your submarket.

Facebook is the perfect Web2 example. Facebook didn't start with targeting the whole world. It first built a monopoly on the Harvard campus. Then it moved to the Ivy Leagues before spreading to all universities. You know the rest of the story.

It's okay to start small and niched. Then you expand. Not the opposite.

What Is Your MVG's Mission?

What do you stand for? Why do you do what you do?

People are more inclined to follow individuals who have a clear and compelling mission. A well-defined purpose resonates with their values, aspirations, and desire for meaning, creating a sense of purposeful direction and connection.

People are not stupid. Your mission has to be true to you. Sometimes the mission is about being *"a complete degen looking for the next 10,000x token."*

For others, like us, our mission is to create the best Web3 marketing and building education. We believe that most projects that fail don't fail on purpose (aka are rugs) but simply fail because people have no idea what to do and how to do it. This book is our answer to this mission.

What Is Your MVG's Hidden Motive (If You Have One)?

If you have a hidden reason or motive behind what you do, it might be worth mentioning it. It will boost trust.

For instance, you want to take revenge on life, show everyone that you're not a loser, and launch the biggest NFT collection the world has ever seen.

Many people in crypto will consider this a stimulating hidden motive. It makes you more trustworthy than saying, *"I'm here to make the world a better place."*

(Once again, people are *not* stupid.)

When Tugan was teaching marketing in the French-speaking market, he mentioned that the hidden goal was to identify talents that he could work with and create businesses together.

Side.xyz, Tugan.ai, and Frog.tech are all businesses that were launched with former *"students."*

Guess it worked out . . .

Who Are the *"Common"* Enemies of Your MVG?

Having a common enemy unites people. It creates a sense of unity and purpose.

It's *"us"* versus *"them."* In this context, collective identity and cooperation are necessary to overcome challenges posed by the enemy.

The enemy doesn't have to be well researched. Do Kwon, former CEO of Terra Luna and Anchor Protocol, mobilized his FU Army behind the enemy MakerDAO, the issuer of the stablecoin DAI and therefore direct competitor to his own stablecoin, UST.

Do Kwon
@stablekwon

By my hand $DAI will die.

5:54 AM · Mar 23, 2022

804 1,553 5,347 111

The Shiba Inu community gathered behind a shared desire to beat Dogecoin.

The MVG and his project *cannot* be *only* against something. They have to be bigger than this. But having enemies helps.

Which Tribe and Group Is the MVG Part Of?

Human Evolution 101—if you're alone in the wilderness, you die. That's it. You fail at the natural selection game.

Your MVG has to be part of groups. It could be a specific blockchain you work on (you're in the group of builders on Avalanche blockchain). It could be a specific industry (play-to-earn games). It could be about one or several projects (for instance, you're part of the Bored Ape community because you own one).

By asking the question of the group, we ask the following questions:

- Who is behind you?
- Who is your tribe?
- With whom are you connected?
- Whom do you know?

Audience reacts to this. Logically, being part of a high-status community (e.g., BAYC) will increase your status.

Does Your MVG Have an Autistic Routine?

Having an autistic routine means that you do a specific but uncommon action every day, week, or month in a super predictable way.

This action has to stand out.

Saying *"GM"* on X.com is weird and repetitive, but already too common for the industry.

Your autistic routine has to break the codes. It has to create a sense of extremism or novelty. It doesn't have to be about work or Web3.

Alex Becker wakes up every morning at 4:00 a.m., shares a motivational quote, and asks his community to *"pound it back."* He never misses a day and demonstrates his hard work ethic.

Feels quite autistic to us, while being easy to remember.

Create Rituals for Your Audience and Community

Rituals create a sense of predictability. Predictability makes people feel safer, especially in a rapidly changing world.

Religions used them to create bonds and gather the community. Rituals also offer ways to celebrate achievement, mark milestones, and honor shared values.

These rituals don't have to be complicated. On Side.xyz, community members say *"GB—Go Build"* in the chat every morning to signify that they are building something in Web3. The ritual also goes against the *"GM"* movement, which the community has identified as an enemy.

From the community's perspective: *"People that say GM are lazy and don't build things. I take on a new identity by saying 'GB' every morning."*

Besides that, the leadership team of Side holds a daily AMA at 10:00 CET time for fifteen minutes. It's every day, and it creates a new routine for people to join the chat, say *"GB"* and then listen to the founders for fifteen minutes.

DeGods holders meet up and drink Shoebeers (yes, that's a beer out of a shoe).

Having weekly or monthly *"Ask Me Anything"* (AMA) sessions could also be powerful.

What matters here is not the act of talking with the community but the consistency behind it that compounds over time.

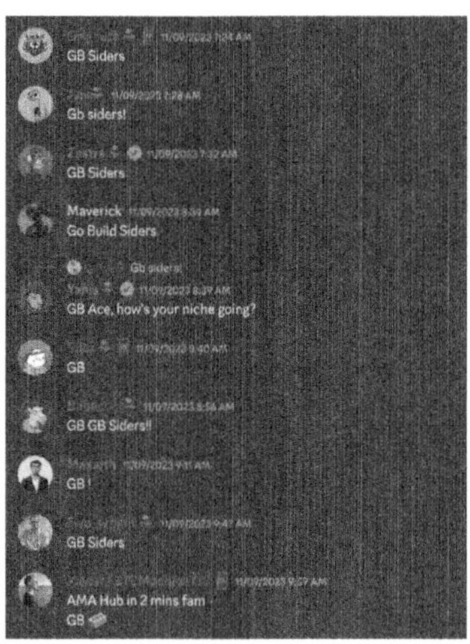

Is the MVG a Human?

Since the MVG doesn't necessarily show their real face, real name, and personal life, it might be hard to connect and have a deeper bond with them.

Maybe it's a bot. Maybe it's produced by some click farm somewhere.

To compensate for this lack of transparency, you can share things outside your work or main topics. It could be about food, movies, hobbies, traveling. Here is an example of the *"Life of Tugan."*

The goal is not for this stuff to be important but to make you feel like a human. It should not be more than 5–10 percent of the content you create. It's more like, *"Oh, by the way, I've watched this movie, and I liked it. It reminded me of . . ."*

Balance between Your Classics and the News

We live in an attention economy. Every MVG, every NFT collection, every token, and every protocol is fighting for attention. We're all fighting for *"market shares"* in people's minds. Market shares in people's minds mean market shares in the real economy!

As an MVG, your job is to become and stay relevant. There is one guy who nailed it, and it's Justin Sun from the Tron blockchain.

He is just hijacking every single piece of news to make people talk about him. Hate him or love him, but he always manages to be newsworthy.

A bankruptcy? He offers to bail out. A drama? He gives his grain of salt. A token pumping and dumping with an air of conspiracy? People will assume Justin Tron is not too far behind it.

Whatever topics in Web3, Justin Sun is around the corner and in the news. The Verge nicknamed him the *"Hype Man of the Century"* in a 2020 article.

But in the meantime, your MVG needs to have his *"classics"*—the topics and subjects he is focused on and where he becomes a trusted voice. If you only strive for attention, you don't build up trust.

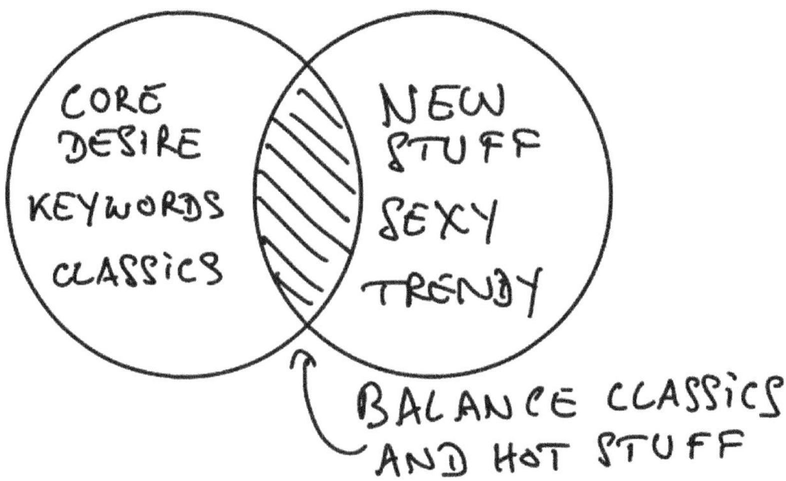

So you should balance content about your classics and some content about hot topics to be in the news.

How Should People Describe You in One Sentence?

People should be able to summarize your MVG with one single sentence and a picture. They should be able to give a vague (and sometimes rude or inappropriate) description of who you are.

They should be able to say, ***"That's the guy who ______,"*** and people would be, *"Oh yes, I know who you mean."*

For instance, Changpeng Zhao (or CZ): *"Oh that's the Chinese dude who owns Binance."*

CZ is a Canadian national, and simply calling him *"Chinese"* might even sound racist (it is in some cases), but that is the one-sentence summary. People instantly know who we're talking about.

People should be able to fill the sentence *"This is the guy who ______"* or *"This is the woman who _______."*

If people cannot do this, you're not memorable enough. So go back to work.

Where Is Your MVG on Russell Brunson's *"Prolific Index"*?

"Your audience must be fascinated with you and what you teach," wrote Russell Brunson in his book *Expert Secrets.*

It's a great book about turning knowledge and passion into a Web2 business. What's interesting for us is the notion of the ***"prolific index."*** *Prolific* means *"being able to produce a lot of inventive things."*

You have to understand that an MVG evolves in a constantly changing environment with new ideas, concepts, gurus, and technologies. This is especially true in Web3, where every month a new blockchain technology pops up while dozens of Web3 games and/or NFTs are launched every day. Not to mention dozens of tokens every hour.

Everyone is trying to yell louder than the other one, hoping it'll bring attention to their stuff. Talking louder and yelling are not helping. What helps is understanding Russell's prolific index.

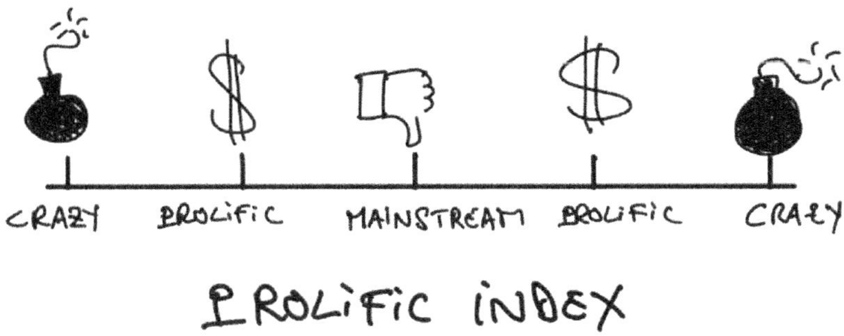

Basically, in the middle, you have the mainstream information and ideas. That's the thing you can hear everywhere. It's boring. There is nothing new or stimulating there. Most wannabe MVG start to create content in the exact middle. They are boring in an ocean of boring people.

On the extremes, you have crazy ideas. These are offensive, dangerous, and sometimes just stupidly illegal. You don't want to go there. Newbies are going there for the quick buck for the attention dopamine, but it doesn't end very well.

The opportunity is to locate yourself between the mainstream and the crazy. It's stimulating but not dangerous.

Here is an example:

- *Mainstream*: You need to dollar cost average (DCA) and wait five years to be rich in crypto.
- *Crazy*: You can become an overnight millionaire by gambling on the new shitcoin.
- *Prolific*: Don't gamble nor invest. Build and market the new shitcoin, and then turn it into a whole ecosystem over time like Shiba Inu did.

If you have been in crypto long enough, when you hear DCA, you sigh. You have heard it a thousand times in your crypto journey. It's boring. It might be true, but it's not stimulating.

The crazy thing is stimulating but simply dangerous. This is how people get rekt and end up hating crypto.

But being a builder is about offering a new way of life in the next frontier of entrepreneurship.

Always ask yourself, *"Are you in the mainstream zone? Are you writing or talking about something everyone is already talking about? Are you saying the same thing as them?"*

To differentiate your content and reach the prolific zone, you have three core strategies:

1. *Precision*: Go into super narrow details, data, anecdotes, and hidden stories that the others are not talking about. They talk about *"news A"*—find some conspiracy or crazy data point about it.
2. *Radicalization*: Go more hard core and deep into the mission and consequence of the info. Everybody says A is positive—explain why A is a revolution, that everything will be different from now.
3. *Contradiction*: Go against the current mainstream. Everybody thinks that A is great news—explain why it's a disaster.

You can also combine these strategies!

Top Steps for *"Not-So-Secret"* Growth

The best way to grow an audience and be interesting is to do something, then talk about this thing, and then talk even more about it (quantity) before getting better at talking about it.

(In case you wonder—yes, we stole this stuff from Alex Hormozi.)

STEP 1—DO SOME STUFF.

Basically, first, you do something. You build something, you join a project or a group. You contribute. Doing things makes you interesting and legit. If you don't have your own project for now, join an existing team and project. Become a contributor and content creator around it.

You want to create a positive feedback loop. The project's community will follow you while your followers will discover the project. It's a win-win situation.

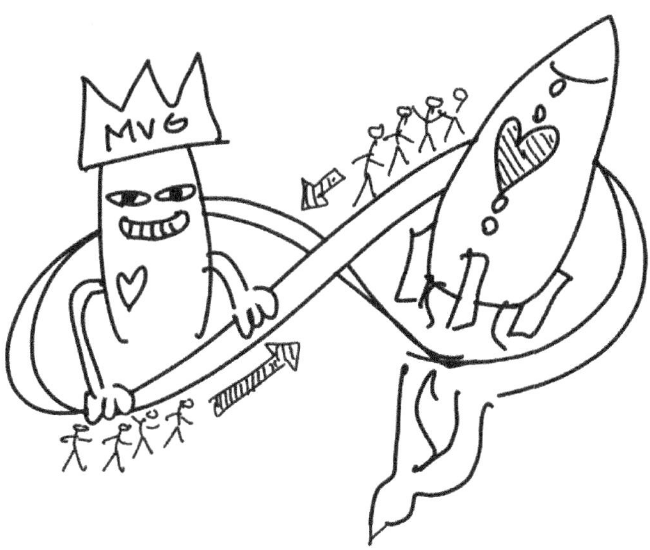

STEP 2—TALK ABOUT WHAT YOU'RE DOING.

Then you talk about it. You write about it. You create videos about it. You create content. It's okay if the content sucks. It doesn't have to be great. It has to be published. The more you give, the more you grow.

Projects have inherent traction, and people want to interact with the team or insiders. The more you talk about the project, the more you will feel like an insider, and people will be interested in what you have to say.

STEP 3—TALK MORE ABOUT WHAT YOU'RE DOING

Now you do much more content. You can go on several social platforms and formats. You play the quantity game. If you want to 10x the output, you have to 10x the input. Big secret, we know. But no one is doing it. People post four times a week and wonder why they don't grow.

STEP 4—TALK BETTER ABOUT WHAT YOU'RE DOING

Finally, you get better at doing it. Call it *"learning by doing."* The best way to become good at something is to practice a lot. Now you do a lot, and a lot, of good stuff.

Content creation is like money you don't have to invest. Every view, impression, click, or follower is something that, in theory, you have to pay for with ads. Here you get it for *"free"* by producing stuff. You could receive the equivalent of $1,000 or $10,000 per day without having to invest one cent.

So do things, talk about it, talk more, and finally, talk better! Hormozi used it to gain millions of followers and sell hundreds of copies of his books while growing his business, Acquisition.com.

As he said, *"Fame is the most efficient business model."*

It takes time. **Your real competitive advantage is patience.**

Before moving to the next chapter, let's check the things you should avoid.

Things That Are Hurting Your MVG

Here is a small list of things that might look like good ideas but are generally not good at all:

- Shilling, pushing, and selling too many different things too many times. Ideally, an MVG supports one or two projects at one time.
- Retweeting and sharing things that add zero value.
- Being inconsistent in your work, either having no consistency in your visual identity or having an unclear niche.
- Stealing other people's content. It's okay to look for inspiration, but do not steal.
- Retweeting and sharing contests and giveaways. It makes you sound desperate for money.
- Being too needy for attention, begging for likes, attention, and people.

- Getting into fights and disagreements with followers. A lion doesn't care what the sheep think.
- Being afraid to be controversial and having an opinion outside the mainstream.

The Leadership Paradox in Decentralized Web3

Let's start with the paradox.

Web3 is about decentralization. It's about avoiding that some small group of people or entities get too much power. But in the meantime, humans, in general, and especially in Web3, crave leadership. **They wait for a charismatic figure to step up, make decisions for them, and show them the way.**

In his 1576 essay *"Discourse on Voluntary Servitude,"* French author Étienne de La Boétie pointed out the fact that people do *not* want to take responsibility, make hard choices, and assume the consequences. They prefer to give this responsibility to someone else, even at the cost of their freedom.

It's interesting to note that usually tyrants in La Boetie's book do not take power by force. Power is given to them by people refusing to take responsibility.

The point is not for you to become a tyrant. Just to understand social dynamics.

Web3 feels the same. Investors, holders, and users all wait for someone to step up and lead them, to guide them to a brighter future. These figures have to manage teams of developers and builders to create awesome products. **This is a core paradox of Web3, where collective governance and decentralization of power should be at the core of the industry.**

Our take on this is that a strong figure is needed to launch and lead a project, but in the long run, power and decision-making should be progressively transferred back to the community.*

This leading figure is what we call an MVG.

---

* We saw this in the chapter "*The Science of Decentralization.*"

Key Takeaways

- People like to hand over hard choices to leaders, even if it comes at the cost of their own freedom.
- Everybody should and can be a guru.
- The barrier to entry for content creation is basically zero. To stand out, choose a hyperspecific niche.
- A short MVG checklist: compelling mission, common enemies, a tribe, an autistic routine, rituals for the audience. This will allow you to become *"He's that guy who . . ."*
- The best way to start growing is to **do**, **talk**, **talk more**, **talk better** (in that order).
- And finally, be very precise in the curation of your MVG and leave no room for spelling errors and short-minded promotions that hurt the trust of your audience.

To Doxx or Not to Doxx

Maybe Satoshi chose to stay anonymous for a good reason.

—Apollo

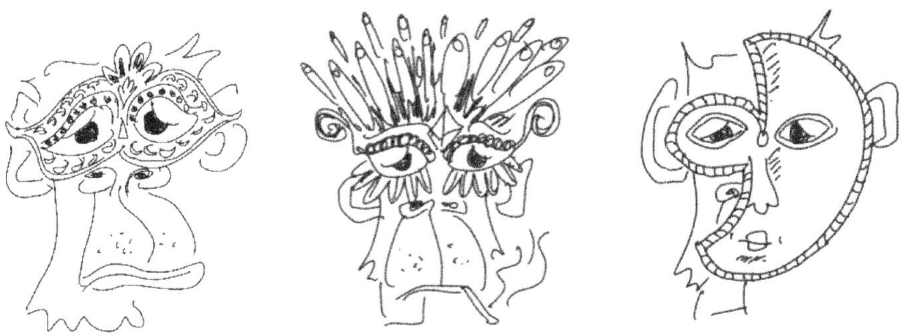

WIIFM

This chapter and the next one are the two chapters about healthy paranoia. The vibe in these chapters is very different from the rest of the book. As Intel cofounder Andy Grove wrote, *"Only the paranoids survive."* You'll learn why it's unfortunately actually not a metaphor.

Welcome to one of the core dilemmas in Web3.

First things first: ***doxxing*** **signifies disclosing elements of your identity or your identity as a whole (first name, last name, picture, nationality).** Sometimes you're not the one choosing to doxx. Some malevolent people (or jealous people in your social circle) simply doxx you.

By doxxing yourself, you increase trust in your project and companies. It means you are committed to the project, and holders love it.

But let's keep something in mind:

There is this famous saying in Web2: *"If no one insulted you each day before noon, you haven't done your work."* This is common for Web2 marketing.

In Web3, the vibe is a little rougher. The saying could become, ***"If no one has sent you death threats before noon, you haven't been building and marketing enough."***

Understand the Local Culture: *"Don't Doxx, It's Fine!"*

Web3 is a world where someone a with frog profile picture interacts casually with someone else who has a monkey profile picture. Both of them trust the investment recommendation to invest in a token called Cum Rocket Inu from an anonymous person using a cartoon camel as a profile picture. In the meantime, Elon Musk is pouring gasoline on the fire while the SEC is suing everyone they cross.

Some of the most trusted or entertaining figures in this space are not doxxed.

Think about Punk 6529, Minister of NFTs, or Zach XBT. No one cares about their faces (except maybe some people angry at them).

In Web2, not doxxing is seen as malicious.

In Web3, it's a different game.

And for good reason.

Don't Forget the *"Crypto Wizkid Cemetery"*

Crypto entrepreneurship is like trying to become an oligarch in the '90s in Russia. It looks wild and funny from the outside. But from the outside only.

There is a famous dark humor joke from this time: Each time a businessman or a banker would be found dead, or assassinated, the police would report the reason for the death as *"not good enough private security."*

Funny, but not funny.

Crypto and Web3 are unfortunately very similar.

Disclaimer: **The following pages are going to be morbid, but we think it's necessary to be very clear about the risks associated with Web3 entrepreneurship.**

Here is a list of the famous suspicious, and sometimes violent, deaths in crypto. The list of dead less famous or anonymous crypto entrepreneurs, investors, and influencers is way longer.

In 2014, Autumn Radtke, a twenty-eight-year-old entrepreneur and CEO of First Meta Pte. Ltd., a currency exchange, tragically passed away in Singapore, with her death ruled as a *"suicide."*

As we will soon discover, **most of the deaths of very rich and famous people in Web3 are caused by *"suicide," "accident," "sudden heart attack,"* etc.**

Moving on to 2018, Matthew Mellon, who turned $2 million into nearly $1 billion in XRP tokens, suffered a sudden heart attack while in a drug rehabilitation clinic in Cancún, Mexico. Remarkably, nobody could access his substantial cryptocurrency fortune except for him.

In 2020, a similar mysterious incident occurred with Gerald Cotten, the CEO of the defunct crypto exchange QuadrigaCX. During a visit to India, he passed away, leaving the keys to access cryptocurrencies worth hundreds of millions of dollars undisclosed. Speculations arose, including theories that he faked his death, leading to the creation of the Netflix documentary *Trust No One*.

In 2021, legendary Romanian Bitcoin investor Mircea Popescu, reportedly holding a fortune of over $2 billion, died. His wealth was estimated based on his holdings of 30,000 Bitcoins during the cryptocurrency's peak before his passing. Tragically, he is said to have drowned off the coast of Costa Rica, swept away by ocean currents.

An accident . . .

In late October 2022, Nikolai Mushegian, cofounder of MakerDAO, was found dead on a Puerto Rican beach shortly after tweeting about intelligence agencies pursuing him. His tweet claimed a plot to frame him with a planted laptop by his ex-girlfriend, who was allegedly a spy, and predicted he would face torture.

Continuing the unfortunate series of events . . .

In November 2022, the cryptocurrency world witnessed the demise of broker Javier Biosca, who was found dead in Estepona, Spain. At that time, Biosca was under investigation for his involvement in what would become known as the largest cryptocurrency fraud in Spain.

Just a day later, Tiantian Kullander, cofounder of Singapore's virtual currency trading platform Amber Group, passed away mysteriously in his sleep. Kullander, at just thirty years old, had cofounded a company with an estimated value of $3 billion.

Two days following this tragedy, Russian crypto billionaire Vyacheslav Taran met a tragic end in a helicopter crash. The crash occurred near Villefranche-sur-Mer, France, a popular tourist destination. The helicopter had taken off from Lausanne, Switzerland, and claimed the lives of fifty-three-year-old Taran and the thirty-five-year-old French pilot who accompanied him.

Another accident . . .

More unfortunate events unfolded the same year when Park Mo, the vice president of Vidente, the largest shareholder of the South Korean cryptocurrency exchange Bithumb, was found dead in front of his house during the early-morning hours.

In 2023, the crypto community was shocked by the gruesome discovery of the dismembered remains of forty-one-year-old crypto entrepreneur, Fernando Pérez Algaba.

His remains were found in a suitcase near a stream in Argentina by two children playing. Fernando Pérez Algaba had gained notoriety as a crypto influencer, often showcasing his extravagant lifestyle to his

916,000 Instagram followers, which included luxurious cars, jet skis, and lavish parties.

For this one, it was hard to pretend it was an accident, a suicide, or a sudden heart failure.

The following are some headlines about crypto influencers or traders being kidnapped, tortured, and murdered:

- *"Crypto Billionaires' Back-to-Back Deaths Spark Wild Theories among the Community"* (Cointelegraph)
- *"Death in Crypto: Three Notable Crypto CEOs Died Abruptly within a Short Period in 2022* (crypto.ro)
- *"Curse of the Crypto Whizz Kids: Missing Millions, Mysterious Deaths, and Wild Conspiracy Theories Surrounding the Untimely Demise of Digital Currency Tycoons—After Young Star Becomes Second to Die in Four Weeks"* (*Daily Mail*)
- *"Crypto CEOs' and Founders' 'Sudden Deaths'—What We Do Know, What We Don*'t*"* (*Newsweek*)
- *"Mystery of Crypto CEO Who Died—or Did He?—Taking $250 Million with Him* (*New York Post*)
- *"OneCoin Founder Ruja Ignatova Allegedly Killed and Tossed into the Sea in 2018"* (CoinGeek)
- *"Another Crypto Millionaire Christian Peev Found Dead"* (TechNext24.com)
- *"The Body of an American Crypto Trader Dismembered and Flushed Down the Drain"* (Protos.com)
- *"An American 'Crypto-Anarchist' Fled the Country. He Was Just Killed in Mexico's 'Murder Capital'"* (*Washington Post*)

And if you're more in the kidnapping vibe, here is a selection:

- *"Director of UK-Based Crypto Exchange Kidnapped in Kyiv"* (Cointelegraph)

- *"Kidnapped for Crypto: Criminals See Flashy Crypto Owners as Easy Targets, and It Has Led to a Disturbing String of Violent Robberies"* (Business Insider)
- *"Some Teenagers Are Making a Fortune Trading Bitcoin—One Even Got Kidnapped Because of His Success"* (*Fortune*)
- *"Singapore Crypto Consultant Kidnapped for $1 Million Ransom"* (Cointelegraph)
- *"Fallen 'Crypto King' Who Owes Millions to Investors Was Kidnapped and Tortured"* (Yahoo Finance)

You get the idea.

Doxxing is not something you should not take lightly.

Why Does This Happen?

The conspiracy theories point to a deep power struggle between centralized finance and a new world. If you start digging, you'll find weird and interesting *"coincidences."*

In a more basic approach, **there is a lot of money and crypto, and it's attracting organized crime.**

Understand this:

In Web2 or in the traditional economy, to steal an entrepreneur's wealth, you still need to go through the banking system and go through the antifraud and KYC systems. You cannot empty a bank account with millions on it that easily. The net worth of Web2 entrepreneurs is in shares of companies. To transfer them, you need the work of an attorney or notary.

You cannot just steal stuff that easily.

Web3 is different. The wealth is not in company shares but in fungible tokens on a wallet not always associated with a name. Tokens can be stolen, moved instantly around the world, and exchanged for different coins almost instantly. Solutions like Tornado Cash are enabling criminals to hide their tracks.

> Definition: *Tornado Cash*
> *Tornado Cash* is a decentralized privacy tool in the world of cryptocurrencies. It's like a mixer for digital money. When you put your digital coins (like Ethereum) into Tornado Cash, it shuffles them with coins from other people. When you withdraw, you get coins that are hard to trace back to your original ones. Yes, it's too good to be true. The founders are facing charges for laundering over $1 billion worth of tokens.

Keep in mind that some criminals are okay to risk their lives for $10,000, so imagine what they might do for hundreds or thousands—if not millions or billions—of dollars' worth of crypto.

That's the game you're in.

In the next chapter, we will discuss your security, whether you're doxxed or not.

Build Before Thinking about Doxxing

The basic idea is the following:

If you're not doxxed, you still have the choice to do it. You're free to choose and change your mind. You have options.

Once you're doxxed, you can't go back. You can't change your mind after. Your face is out there forever for criminals and predators to see.

Our recommendation would be to first stay nondoxxed and build.

Once you're successful and rich, then decide if it makes sense for you to be doxxed and to assume the risk (and the financial burden of private security in some cases).

Look at examples like Pacman, the founder of Blur.com. He stayed nondoxxed while building his billion-dollar company, and once he achieved the behemoth status, he chose to doxx himself.

Turns out Pacman (that was his pseudonym) is Tieshun Roquerre, a twenty-four-year-old MIT dropout. He previously launched the crypto domain start-up Namebase, which he raised $5 million for and then sold to Namecheap within three years.

Successful NFT entrepreneur Frank DeGods unveiled his face and real name only after launching successful NFT collections.

So if you want to doxx, here is our advice: **take your time, build first, and only then doxx.**

Real Doxxing Is Not What You Think

"It's not who I am underneath, but what I do that defines me."

These were Satoshi Nakamoto's last words.

Kidding. It's from *Batman.*

The idea is that your actions, what you stand for, what you build, your focus, and your passion are much more important than your name. Your project won't take off tomorrow just because you showed your cute little face.

Everyone in crypto is fine with founders not being doxxed. There are many more important things to disclose. We mentioned it earlier in the *"Science of Transparency"* and *"Science of Trust"* chapters.

Auditing your smart contract, releasing features fast, taking time to listen to the community, and empowering people will create much more trust than doxxing yourself.

The Minimum Viable Guru (MVG) that you built is enough to get the trust and recognition. **Don't let your ego or overconfidence lead you to risks.**

(Once again, we're not against being doxxed, but not everyone lives in a place like Dubai with maximum security.)

Key Takeaways

- You don't have to doxx. Web2—yes. Web3—no.
- Doxxing comes with high security risks that need to be calibrated and estimated.
- Once you doxx yourself, you cannot go back. Take your time and build in the shadows first.
- Real doxxing is not about showing your face. It is about showing your actions, beliefs, what you stand for, and what you can deliver.

How to Stay Alive

People who need bodyguards don't leave recommendations on Trustpilot.

—Someone's bodyguard

WIIFM

We continue with paranoia. This chapter is a form of *"science of common sense"* . . . to avoid problems. We got the opportunity to work with founders who faced very critical situations. It's something nothing prepares you for (unless you've worked in the army or police force). So we thought it makes sense to have this chapter in the book.

We never thought that a chapter like this would actually make it into the book. But after finishing the previous chapter, we got in touch with security professionals who work at LimaProtection.com to give you an overview of the best practices.

We never thought that this might be a chapter in the book, but after the previous chapter, it made sense for us to ask security professionals at **Lima Protection** to give you the best practices.

Full disclaimer: We know people who work there, and we have a relationship with this firm.

This is what we learned after a lengthy talk with them.

Common Sense about Security

Let's start with the common sense checklist. All this should be obvious, but we still see people making these mistakes. **Better be paranoid (and safe) than sorry.**

1. Don't share your face and real name if you don't have to (see previous chapter).
2. Don't show the face or say the names of family members, colleagues, or loved ones.
3. Don't link professional profiles to your profiles. Don't share your professional things on your profiles.
4. Don't say where you live. Avoid saying the country. Don't mention the city.
5. Don't organize crypto and Web3 events at your home.

6. Don't share on social media places where you like to go (restaurants, for instance).

7. Don't write reviews online about physical places you like to go (or make sure to do it with a different name and email address and never mix them).
8. Don't say where you're on holiday right now. No pictures, no mention. Post only after you leave the place. If it's a place where you'd like to go another time, don't talk about it.
9. Don't tell everyone you work in crypto. Don't tell people you're rich in crypto. Don't flex.
10. Don't drive around with a Lambo that has the Bitcoin logo on it. Unless you want to get a tax audit and/or into serious trouble. Don't add a mention of Web3 and crypto in your plate number (no *"BTC ROCKS 615"* plate number please).

11. Don't keep all your crypto in one place, but always make sure to have some crypto available in case.
12. Don't stay in a violent or crime-rigged country if you can afford to live somewhere else.
13. Don't assume that if a country is said to be safe, it's safe. Nothing is 100 percent safe.
14. If you're doxxed, don't travel to dangerous countries without professional security.
15. Don't assume people are friends. This includes colleagues, business partners, and community members. People change. Money changes people. Stay politely careful.

16. Don't wear stuff that screams, *"I work in crypto."* This includes Richard Mille watches and necklaces with a big BTC logo on them.
17. Don't use your address to order physical objects linked to crypto projects (whether it's merch from an NFT collection or a ledger wallet). Find other points of delivery.
18. Don't turn on the light and look from the window if someone rings your door in the middle of the night.
19. Don't meet half-gangster people, and don't pretend to be one (it'll only attract the real ones).

Basically, don't make yourself a target!

Assessing Risks and Threats

The following will help you to put threats and risks in perspective and allow you to act accordingly.

LEVEL 1—LOW RISK

The low risk is someone finding your Telegram contact or an email linked to the project and sending threats. Usually, it's empty threats or blackmail. There is no precise or personal information. Nothing about your real identity, geographical location, or personal things (unless you haven't respected the common sense list).

This level of threat is *"normal."*

It happens every day.

An appropriate action could be to talk about it with your team to see if other members have been affected. Block the people. Change your contact details and/or upgrade all your privacy settings on all services and devices.

LEVEL 2—HIGHER RISK

Increased risk happens when you have a growing number of haters and when they organize themselves in a group to hurt or doxx you. **Never underestimate the power of stupid people in large groups.**

If the threats include personal or professional information that is not easy to find, it's also a factor of higher risk. It's good to research how they could have found this information. Most likely you made a mistake somewhere.

An increased number of threats or insults is also a sign to take into consideration.

LEVEL 3—EXTREME RISK

Extreme risk is when things get serious. People threaten you while having very personal information about you—things that were not easy at all to find (once again, unless you didn't respect the common sense list).

People knowing your address is in the *"extreme risk"* category. People having pictures of you or your family that they have taken themselves is also an extreme level of risk. For example, a picture of you taken on the street is something critical.

At this stage, it's worth getting in touch with a professional or talking to the police (if they are trustworthy, depending on where you are around the world). If your address has been doxxed, consider living somewhere else. Adding security cameras and alarms and increasing the quality of your doors is also a good thing to do. **You're in the danger zone. You're in the zone where things can happen.** The goal here is not to put you under pressure. The chances that people can hurt you are low, but the danger is real.

LEVEL 4—MATERIALIZATION OF THE RISK

Level 4 is when people take action against you. It could be showing up at your home, following you in the street, or talking to you in the street. It can be even worse, with real attacks, physical violence, and kidnapping.

These are things you want to avoid at all costs. Go talk to professionals and/or to the police depending on where you live.

How to Get Professional Protection

We know, it's crazy. You got a book about how to sell JPEGs on the blockchain, and now we're talking about bodyguards.

We saw in the previous chapter the risk associated with being a builder in Web3, especially if you're doxxed.

One of the best-kept secrets in Web3 is that a lot of successful entrepreneurs are protected by professionals 24-7. They don't talk about it, but they are. They have to be.

UNDERSTAND YOUR NEEDS

Do you protect only your person or also your family? Do you need to protect your home too? Are you going to travel a lot? Where do you live? If you're in a violent country, your needs are not the same as in Dubai or Singapore. By the way, in case you wonder why so many people in crypto live in Dubai, it's for safety reasons.

THE ISSUE WITH SEARCHING FOR A COMPANY

Here is one of the biggest problems with protection. The business of protection is like Web3: everybody lies. It's hard to trust companies. People who have protection don't advertise it and don't write reviews on Trustpilot.

And in the meantime, it's a very lucrative business not always run by ethical people. Credentials are often faked. Research in your country what the required credentials are to become a bodyguard, and make sure they have them. Maybe there is a government website listing accredited companies. Look for something like this.

Knowing where they recruit and how they train their people is also an issue.

Avoid fishy people at all costs. You have a friend who knows someone who knows someone with a lot of muscles and who deals with weird people. Don't let these people enter your life. You have a higher chance of them kidnapping you than people on the internet looking for a target.

Here are some ideas to get recommendations:

- *Friends in the police forces.* Former policemen often work for private security firms.
- *Business relationships* who raised money from the very rich and famous. Billionaires have security, and you can ask your friend to ask.
- *Expensive lawyers.* They work with many rich and famous people. Some of them might have recommendations to make.

HOW TO START A CONVERSATION

When you start a conversation with a firm or an agent, it's important *not* to disclose everything. At this stage, they don't have to know where you live or where you work.

You can mention the industry you work in, but not your projects or your net worth.

Show them the threat, and ask if they have experience with this kind of issue. More and more people in crypto have security personnel, so it's not uncommon for professionals to work with Web3 entrepreneurs.

During the conversation, it's important to feel if they are trying to increase the fear or the perceived risk or not.

Increasing the stress (to sell something) is a red flag. Being too naive and saying, *"Oh, it's just people on the internet,"* is also a red flag. The green flag is somewhere in between.

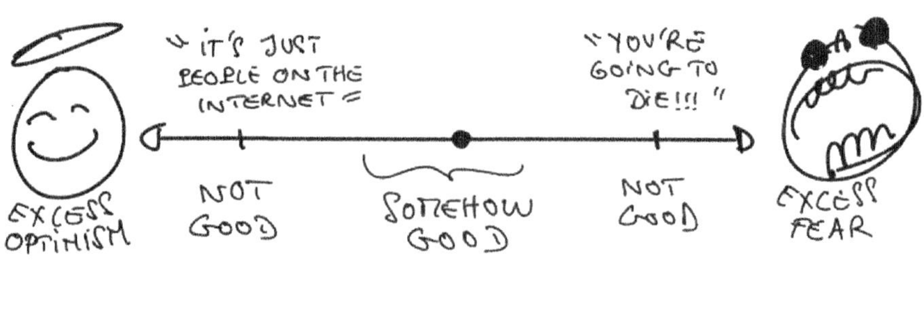

MEET IN PERSON IN A PUBLIC SPACE

When you meet your agents for the first time, do it in a public space, maybe a coffee place or a restaurant. They don't need to know your address at this point.

There are stories of people getting kidnapped by the security team they met to deal with a security issue.

Build first the relationship and the contact in a public space, then move on step by step.

LANGUAGE AND CULTURE

You want to work with people from your language and culture. If possible.

Security is a lot about understanding each other and trusting each other. If language is a barrier or a source of confusion, it might make things either more complicated or even dangerous.

They need to understand you easily, and you need to understand them.

UNDERSTAND THE COSTS

Having protection is very costly. You have to pay for the people, but also their food, their plane ticket if they travel with you, etc.

The cost of a bodyguard will depend on many factors: country, qualification, risks, credentials to carry weapons, and length of the contract.

It's a budget.

A big one.

In the Web2 start-up world, your money is going into the rent you pay in San Francisco. So Silicon Valley landlords end up collecting the money in Web2. Our guess is that in the foreseeable future, a lot of economic value created by Web3 will go to private security firms, especially with the global instabilities we face.

Key Takeaways

- One of the best-kept secrets in Web3 is that a lot of successful entrepreneurs are protected by professionals 24-7. They don't talk about it, but they are. They have to be.
- Apply common sense to the personal information you share publicly. Don't make yourself a target by driving a Lamborghini with a BTC logo.
- Never underestimate the power of stupid people in large groups. Things can get violent super fast.
- Get protection if you feel unsafe or if you live in a part of the world with weak law and order.

The Org Chart

Bro, we're launching this Web3 thing, do you want to run it?

—A rich friend

WIIFM

One of your challenges is creating a team and then turning it into some organization or company. Building in Web3 is exhausting and very intense. Most projects fail at pivoting from a group of friends to a structured company. This chapter will show you the steps to build your Web3 team and crush it.

There are two main categories of Web3 founding teams: some come from Web2, and some come from Web3.

Web2 and Web3 Origin Teams

THE WEB2 ORIGIN TEAMS

The best core teams often have Web2 experience (software, e-commerce, sales funnels, agencies) with a curiosity for Web3. They have access to talents while enjoying years of experience in operating businesses. In crypto, they are investors, holders, and/or enthusiasts.

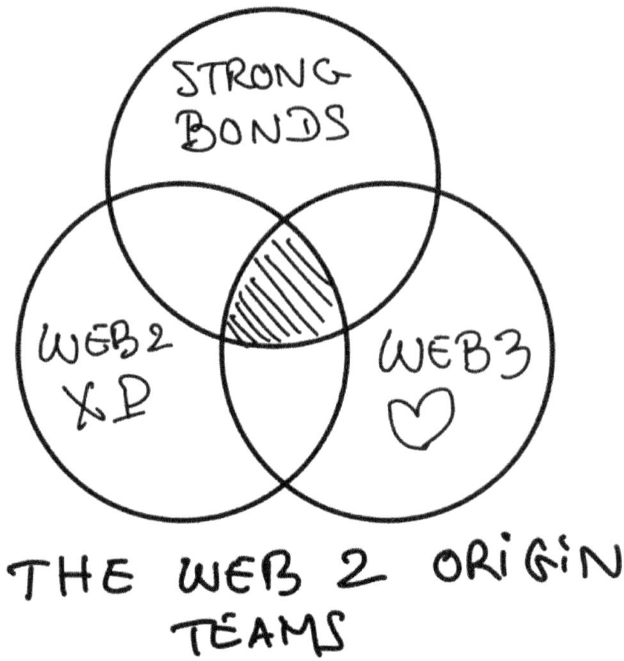

Among the best-performing teams we saw in the 2020–2021 bull run were teams that were already behind small SaaS companies or web agencies that could pivot the whole team in a matter of days to seize Web3 opportunities.

In Web3, speed wins. So the faster the team can launch something, the better. The product has to be shipped to the market as fast as possible before it's too late.

Trends do not last long.

Clones and forks appear overnight.

Whoever is faster wins.

Whoever takes too long to build a team loses.

Moving from an idea to an active community should be done in a matter of days. Creating and deploying the token might take more, depending on the complexity and the marketing strategy, but you don't have time to waste.

THE WEB3 ORIGIN MODEL

Core teams of infrastructures, protocols, and blockchain projects usually come from other infrastructures, protocols, and blockchain projects.

For example, take Gavin Wood who launched the Polkadot ecosystem in 2020. Wood came from Ethereum, where he is credited to be one of the cofounders.

Cardano's founder also came from the Ethereum ecosystem.

The last example is Lukso's founder, Fabian Vogelsteller. He used to work at Ethereum, where he is said to have massively contributed to the smart contract, ERC-20 tokens, and wallet technologies.

Vitalik Buterin, for his part, came from the core Bitcoin community, which he left to create Ethereum.

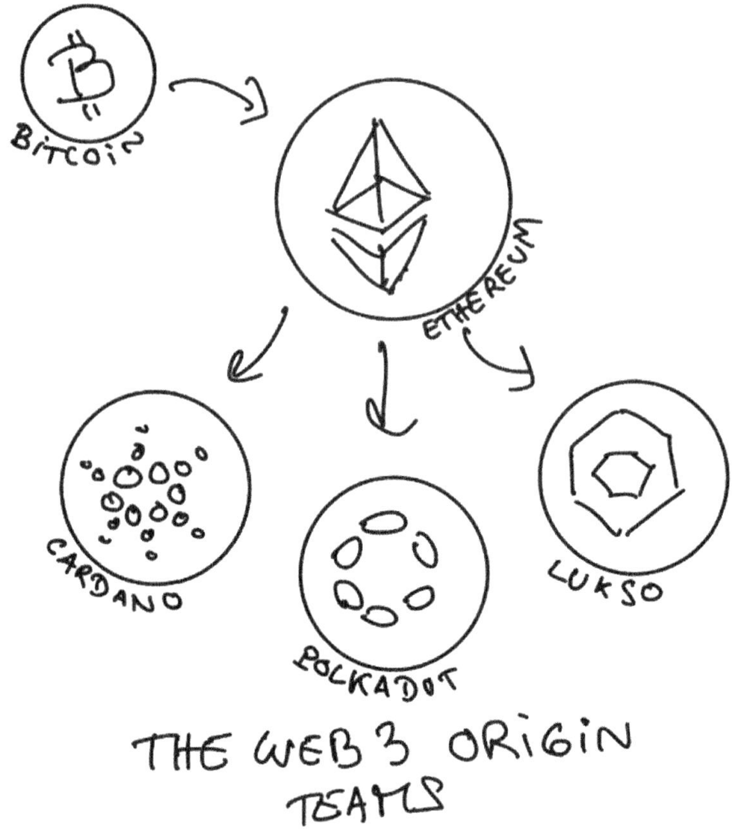

Usually, these founders are not aligned with the technological, ethical, or architectural choices of the project they contribute to. So they part ways to explore other technological hypotheses.

When they start a new project, they already have the network, the net worth, and the reputation. **They are part of the Blockchain Aristocracy.**

Raising funds and attracting talent is not a challenge for them. If you are reading this book, chances are you're not one of them yet.

(But if you are, contact us—it would be cool to make aristocrats friends!)

Going Through Stages

You won't start with a perfect organizational chart. It's a living process that evolves and develops over time. This usually goes like this.

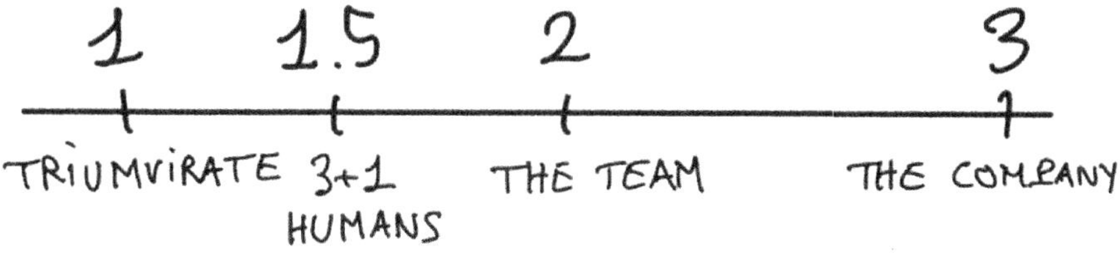

STAGE NO. 1—TRIUMVIRATE

In ancient Rome, a *"triumvirate"* referred to a political alliance or ruling arrangement consisting of three individuals who shared power and authority. Triumvirates were typically established during periods of political instability or crisis as a means of consolidating power and maintaining stability.

(In case you're interested, the first triumvirate was with Julius Caesar, Pompey the Great, and Marcus Licinius Crassus.)

So a good core team is a group of three passionate builders who already know each other. They share a passion for Web3, and the idea of working together stimulates them. They have fun doing it, and they enjoy working with each other. The core team can get stuff done.

Around 70–100 percent of the first version of the project should be done by the core team without recruiting.

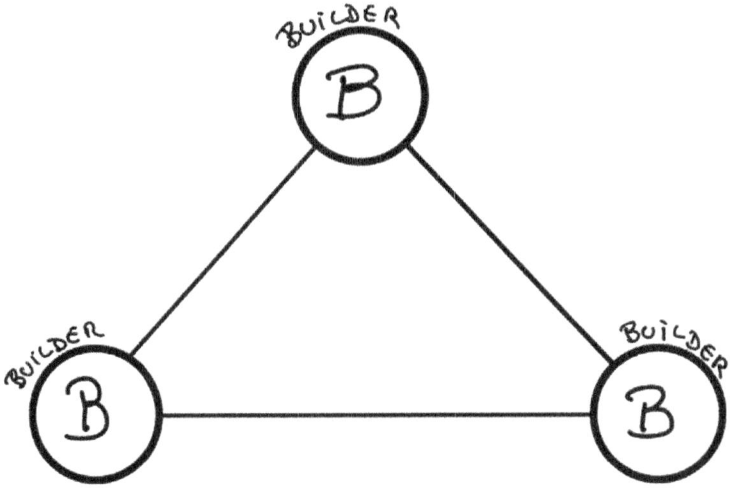

THE TRIUMVIRATE MODEL

Equity is split equally. No overhead costs. This is usually everything you need for the first days and weeks of the projects. Depending on the nature and goal of the project, you will spend this time on building the foundation:

- Branding and visual identity
- Product positioning
- Technological foundations
- Community building (first ten fans)
- Litepaper to summarize all this

> Definition: *litepaper*
> A *litepaper* is a concise, easy-to-digest version of a whitepaper that highlights the important information about your Web3 project. It's an effective way to capture the interest of potential investors and users and give them a better understanding of what your project is all about.

Here you're setting the foundations.

This is an intense sprint time. We recommend doing daily meetings, getting used to not sleeping as much, and getting immense amounts of work done.

If you're in a nontechnical leadership team, wait until all the foundations are set before you start hiring developers.

Usually, the next step is to bring an adviser to the team. This can be somebody from the personal network of the founding team who has been involved in a similar project or is able to bring an experienced set of eyes to the strategy and initial ideas.

- They have been in the space longer than the core team and therefore have a lot of experience.
- They can help with introduction to key influencers or launchpads.
- They give credibility to the project (if doxxed).
- They know how to handle pressure situations since they've experienced them before.

There are some things that a pure Web2 team, or newbie Web3 team, cannot know. A veteran adviser can help the team avoid lawsuits, exploits, or betrayal of team members down the road. Even if they're usually expensive or want a percentage of the project, it's worth it.

STAGE NO. 1.5—THREE AND A HALF MEN

This is a small substep in which you go from a triumvirate to a real company. At this stage, it's you, your buddies, and a seventeen-year-old Indian kid.

Let us explain.

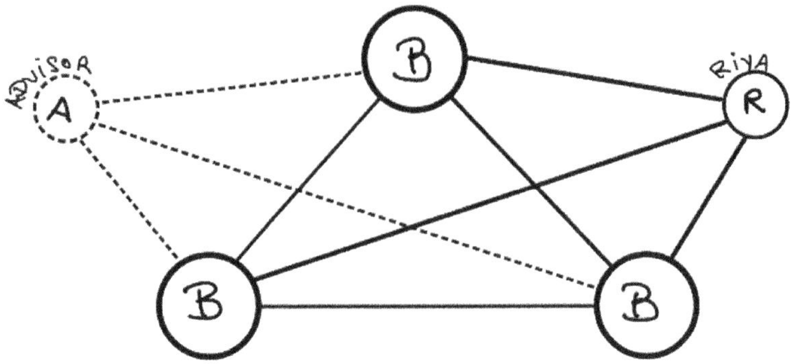

THE 3+1 HUMANS MODEL

By now you've done your research, you came up with some fancy ideas, and you're more than certain that your project will take off.

Now it's time for you to make your most important hire yet.

In our case, let's call him Riya.

Riya spends nineteen hours per day on X.com. He's a collab manager for ten projects and manages six Discord servers, but still only makes around $500 per month (the good months). He truly believes in Web3 and would do everything to drop out of his community college.

Because Riya sees hundreds of Web3 projects every day, he truly understands what works, why it works, and which type of projects have a high likelihood of succeeding.

Riya is probably also going to be the person who will build your Discord server, connect you to the first collab mods, and hire your first batch of mods. He's able to work twenty hours per day and can execute all the simple tasks that you put on his plate. He can be the soldier who completes most of the simpler tasks for you.

He will become your right hand in everything that you do or need. Need a collaboration with this project? Need a Discord server? Need one more moderator in the US time zone? He got it. You will pay Riya somewhere from $1,000–$2,000 per month, with special bonuses and milestones.

He's the feedback and reality check you need to not get *"high on your supply."* It's easy to come up with an idea that seems great in theory but has no chance in practice. Why? There are many things that a rational Web2 brain is not able to comprehend. **A recent Stanford MBA graduate can't explain to you why people like PepeCoin, but Riya understands.**

A piece of advice: Take everything that Riya says with a pinch of salt. Even though he's very confident in the prediction that he's making, he's still only seventeen.

Review and filter through his feedback carefully.

STAGE NO. 2—THE TEAM

Congrats. You're moving from a group of three humans to a small team.

If leadership is nontechnical, you will scour the lands for skilled and ethical developers and get them to work. You hire one or two designers who can take care of the social posts and the user interface (UI) of the landing page and platform you're trying to build.

If your leadership team is purely technical and has trouble creating a website with copywriting that is understandable by regular humans, seek out a marketing adviser who is kept on a token share or monthly retainer.

Simple rule: **Don't work with agencies. Work with individuals who have skin in the game**.

Now your team consists of the following:

- Chief operator (core team member)
- Investor (core team member)
- Adviser (core team member)
- One designer
- One to two developers
- One partnership manager
- One community lead

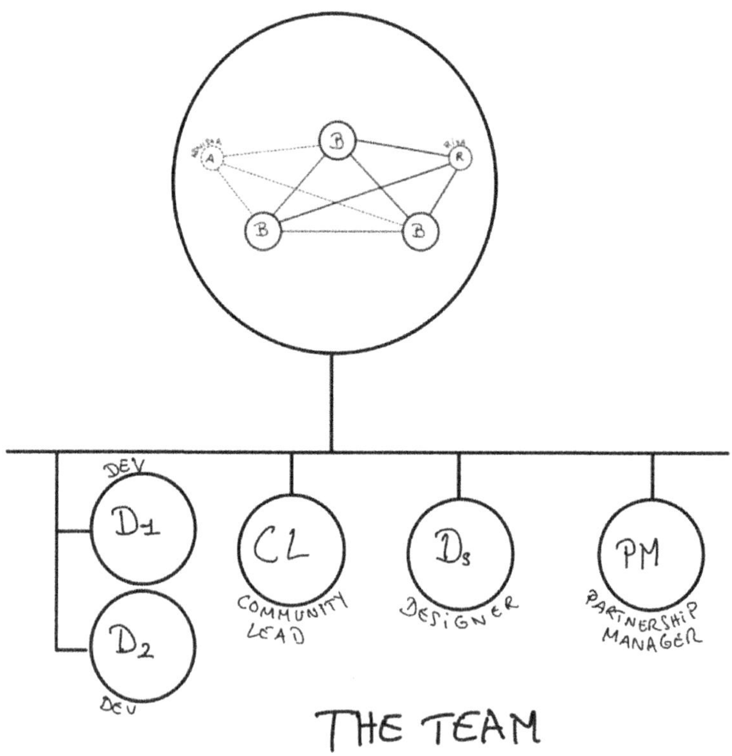

Equity is in the top three.

Developers or tech leads can get profit or token shares. The rest is paid in stablecoins. This might vary, but it's usually the best model to start with.

Keep in mind that once you allocate equity to someone, you cannot take it back. So it's best to pay people and then, when you're sure about their commitment and qualities, offer equity.

Depending on the complexity of the technical aspect, the next step is to launch your community.

Launch it too early—you might lose momentum or interest.

Launch it too late—you won't have enough time to build strong relationships.

TO GET YOUR COMMUNITY OFF THE GROUND, YOU NEED THE FOLLOWING:

- *Community Lead.* Somebody who will take over the leadership of the community, manage FUD, set up clear rules, and manage moderators. Depending on experience, the officer is paid $500–$4,000 per month. It can be an hourly rate in the beginning.
- *Moderator.* While the community lead is asleep, it's wise to have somebody keep an eye out on the chat and what's happening. The moderator is paid $300 per month in a bear market.
- *Partnership manager.* This is a highly connected individual who can arrange the first partnerships that will bring the first couple of community members. The collaboration manager is commission based, since the executor is carrying the end responsibility and most partnership managers are too distracted to carry real responsibility.

Based on how important community is for the success of your project, you can hire more mods and increase expenditure. For example, in the world of profile picture NFTs, community is everything. But in the market for liquid ETH staking, it might be less important.

It's important not to hire too fast or too many people. A small dedicated team is much more efficient than a large group of confused and lowly committed people.

Once the community is live, all leadership teams must be present at the servers for at least one to two hours per day. It's not only important to show your face and connect with early users but to truly connect and understand the people you're building for.

The more you talk and engage with your community, the easier your marketing and product decisions are later down the road.

Connect, get feedback, share progress, and change things based on what you feel and hear from your first fans.

STAGE NO. 3—THE COMPANY

Good. Most don't make it this far. You've crushed the *"team"* stage, and your project is still growing at lightning speed.

You will soon encounter a stage in which employees are starting to burn out, communication lines get messy, and you're spending more time putting out fires than actually building stuff.

It's time for the first version of a real company.

Now you might change from Telegram to Slack. You start using Calendar team invites, and some people are allowed to take the weekend off.

Let's go into more detail on how to find and pay the people who build this stage together with you.

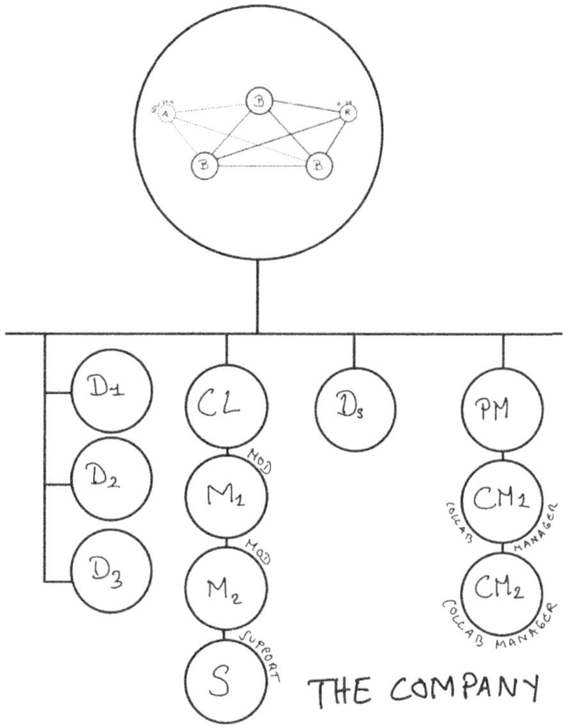

The Talent in the Organization Chart

A quote from Max Levchin, one of the early cofounders of PayPal, says, *"If you're alone, you just work really hard and hope it's enough. Since it often isn't, people form teams."*

That's why you get people around you who are on the same mission as you. As we've discussed earlier in the book already, speed is everything in Web3. Without speed, you won't matter.

That's why it's crucial to find and incentivize the first core employees of your organization.

"THE DEVS"

Devs stand for *developers*. As indicated by their name, they develop and assemble the technology to make the project function. It may be the only one who has the expertise and whose work cannot be compromised or you will fail.

- *How to Recruit.* Usually, the best way is to have one cofounder who understands tech or who has developers to recommend to the project. Hiring people you don't know is super risky. Many rugs and scams come from developers scamming the project without the founders being able to understand or stop it. The worst thing you can do is to hire some anonymous developer on a freelancing gig site like Fiver.com. Just don't do this.
- *How to Pay.* Mostly, pay in stablecoins and bonus or incentive packages in the project's token.

COMMUNITY OFFICER

You have one officer who is leading the community. Look for a person who has some sort of experience with Web3 communities, high energy, and a thick skin. Don't go out seeking them. You will find them organically. Officers help you with writing announcements, posting on X.com, organizing AMAs or events, and thinking about ways to engage the community.

- *How to Recruit.* Select the monk soldiers within the community, who are holders willing to contribute to the project without necessarily getting paid (this is always a green light).

- *How to Pay.* Pay from a mix of your token and stablecoin. Usually, their status in the community is as important as the revenue, if not more. Besides, they usually already own tokens, so they act in their best interest by helping the project.

COMMUNITY MODERATORS

Moderators are the soul and DNA of your community. They are here 24-7 maintaining the hype, teaching newcomers about the product, and onboarding new holders into the culture of your project. Moderators are the first impression that your project gives to newcomers. Therefore, spend enough time teaching about ways of talking and communicating the vision.

They are also here to protect your community from invaders and FUD. They are your most important line of defense. If moderators fail, the project can take a big hit. So manage them closely, and give them a lot of attention.

- *How to Recruit.* Select the most active members of the community.
- *How to Pay.* Pay in stablecoins and airdrops of NFTs or tokens if very committed.

COMMUNITY SOLDIERS

Soldiers are members of the community who are willing to perform tasks to support the project and make the vision happen. They don't really have a job or responsibilities in the project. They're just here and usually happy to help. They can be managed and motivated by the officers. Some people call them junior mods.

- *How to Recruit.* Simply ask for help from the community.

- *How to Pay.* They care more about status than the pay. Give them a Discord role and special recognition. And if you're happy with their job, airdrop them some tokens later on.

MEME ARTISTS

They are the entertainers within the community. They contribute to the culture. Usually, they fit more *"degen"* projects. They share their artwork on X.com, Discord, or Telegram. Ideally, the project should share these creations with the rest of the community.

- *How to Recruit.* Organize meme contests.
- *How to Pay.* Airdrop a few tokens to winners of contests. It's not a job anyway—people do this for free.

PARTNERSHIP AND COLLAB MANAGERS (QUALITY VS. QUANTITY)

They are the sales forces and propaganda machine pushing your vision. You have two types of partnerships and collaboration managers. Professional ones and amateurs. Both are fine.

Professionals are insiders. They spend their days in AMA, talking to founders, in projects, etc. Their job is to know people. Usually, 80 percent of their net worth is in the NFT they use as a profile picture. Having good professionals can make all the difference in the success of a project.

- *How to Recruit.* Get recommendations from soldiers, mods, or other project founders.
- *How to Pay.* Pay with stablecoins.

Amateurs are community members or Web3 enthusiasts from the developing world interested in making an extra income by performing tasks or closing some micro partnerships (usually a retweet from a small community announcement or an invitation in an AMA).

- *How to Recruit.* In bear markets, everybody is an amateur collab mod. They are in your community and X.com DMs before you know it.
- *How to Pay.* Pay with stablecoins.

In the first stages of the project, things are pretty easy. Core founders do pretty much everything (launch stage). Then you start to delegate (delegation stage), and at the end, you use officers to scale (scaling stage).

Web3 Management Secrets

In Web3, you can make a lot of money, very fast. In the last NFT bull run, teenagers without any real business experience raised millions of dollars overnight with no team, business plan, or idea about the future. Most of them had to deal with FUDs, lawsuits, and death threats from cofounders or community members in the following months. Even if you're not a teenager trying to sell NFTs from his basement, the following is a good mental checklist or preparation for what you can expect.

YOU MIGHT DISCOVER COFOUNDERS ALONG THE WAY

If the project you're working on is your first one, don't worry if some skills are missing. A common mistake among beginners is to wait to have the perfect team—the *"dream team"*—with complementary skills to launch something.

The early days of the project are very messy. The most important thing is the motivation, the vision, and the ability to simply get stuff done fast. When the community starts to grow, you can simply and directly ask people if they have skills or connections you might not have. You'll be surprised.

On each project we had the opportunity to participate in, we met people, usually coming from the community of the network of one of the cofounders, who ended up being friends and business partners in further ventures.

DON'T START COUNTING THE TEASPOONS

Don't start a fight around percentages. Don't try to measure the exact contribution of each founder. This is a recipe for anger, district, and disaster. It's usually best to split the equity equally among founders without too much negotiation and overthinking. At the end of the day, when the project succeeds and everyone (hopefully) becomes rich, there will be this feeling that one guy did not contribute much or was maybe somehow useless. That's fine. It's part of the game. Just be happy with what you achieved, and make sure to maintain and push further development of the venture.

DON'T GIVE AWAY EQUITY TOO EASILY

The important notion here is to know who is a founder. If you're missing a skill in your team (let's say community management, for the sake of the argument), and someone is showing up with this skill, don't automatically make him a cofounder. This person, especially if they arrived early, should have a bag of tokens (vested or not) and privileges, but not necessarily the status of founder and equity in the project.

DON'T PAY LIKE AN OIL SHEIKH

Your project is going to the moon. You literally print money. You feel rich. Actually, you are rich. When a Web3 project starts making money, it's a lot of money.

Making $100,000 to several million a day is something common. You feel like a Russian oligarch in Saint-Tropez or an oil sheikh printing cash while sleeping in his Burj Khalifa suite.

That's good. But also not good. At this time it's very common for founders to lose touch with reality. Friends of ours started a Play 2 Earn concept printing $300,000 a day. They hired a manager (whose only management experience was to be a Domino's pizza delivery guy, so not really a manager). They paid him $20,000 a week (or $80,000 a month) to manage the project. Then a random person showed up and convinced them to pay him $1,000,000 to help them *"develop the Brazilian market."* Of course, the Brazilian market never developed, the guy disappeared, and the manager turned against them when the project crashed and when there was no more *"free money."*

While you might find this ridiculous, you might think you won't make these mistakes. We guess that you don't know how your brain reacts when making millions and millions while not having slept in five weeks.

THE HEAD OF COMMON SENSE

Running a Web3 project is exhausting. It's a 24-7 activity. At some point, the fatigue is at its peak, and so are dangers. A wrong announcement, a bad partnership, a coding mistake—and the whole project can go down in flames faster than the Hindenburg over New Jersey in 1937 (it took thirty-four seconds for the Hindenburg to completely burn down and crash).

When you manage a Web3 project, things go very fast. A FUD can happen overnight leading to an 80 percent crash in the price of your token. An inattentive developer can make a mistake leading to a hack.

That's why one member of the core has to sleep at night. You've read it right. While the rest of the team will sleep four to six hours and accumulate fatigue, one member will casually sleep. That's part of his job. In the first three to four days, it'll sound unfair and unnecessary. But at some point, when everyone is getting angry, tired, and lacking lucidity, having at least one person mentally fit and able to exert common sense is critical.

BETRAYAL, BLACKMAIL, AND FUD

Money doesn't buy loyalty. Again, *money doesn't buy loyalty.* Loyalty comes from ethics, mutual respect, and reciprocity. Web3 teams' stories are full of betrayal, blackmail, and FUD.

It's mostly a matter of information. If team members know too much about you, your real identity (while everyone out there has no idea who is really behind the token), they can leverage this against you, accidentally doxx you, and simply be too talkative. You only know who is a *"brother-in-arms"* after the project has survived a first crash or major FUD. Not before. It's an ex post and not an ex ante event. So don't disclose too much to people who are not core team founders.

Conversely, give enough information about projects, updates, and milestones. If there is something that teams hate, it is to discover things at the same time as the rest of the community. They work on the project and expect to be part of the decision-making or at least to be informed before something is in public to know what to do and how to communicate.

Repeatedly bypassing the team will turn them against you. One thing I'd recommend is to have at least once a week a team meeting where the roadmap is discussed.

The team needs a lot of transparency about the project and only a minimum of information about the founders. Not the opposite.

Key Takeaways

- In Web3, speed wins. Whoever takes too long to build a team loses.
- Teams usually start with you and your two friends, grow with an Indian kid who advises and executes, and later expands into a team with clear communication lines.
- Moderators and developers are the most important assets of your project since they are closest to the user experience.
- Money doesn't buy loyalty. Loyalty comes from ethics, mutual respect, and reciprocity.

Web3 Founder as God, Web3 Founder as Victim

The next J. P. Morgan . . .

—Jim Cramer

WIIFM

This chapter is a little bit more philosophical. Here we will teach you what might happen if you succeed too fast and start believing your own propaganda. Enjoy the ride, but remain down-to-earth.

The Web3 space is full of eccentric people, and brilliant innovators but also snake oil crooks and absolute gangsters.

A typical pattern is to see a figure rise to fame and glory sometimes overnight before collapsing in shame and scandals (or even criminal accusations).

We can think of Sam Bankman-Fried (or SBF), who was portrayed as a genius and as the *"new J. P. Morgan,"* until FTX's collapse and his arrest. Celsius's Mashinsky was a Robinhood-style *"unbank yourself"* guru who went bankrupt amid fraud allegations.

In both cases, billions of customers' funds were gambled away and lost.

This rise-and-fall mechanism happens for key figures but also within smaller Web3 niches. **As long as the project grows, founders are idols of the community, but only to become the scapegoat when the price of the token collapses.**

Social media, traditional media, and crowds are part of this complex dynamic where Web3 founders can be gods, only to become victims (sometimes self-inflicted victims) moments later.

It's a story of mimetic desire, a messianic complex, cult of personality, reckless risk-taking, brilliance, and madness.

To write this chapter, we've got from Peter Thiel's CS183 class at Stanford 2012 called *"Founder as God, Founder as Victim,"* which you can find on the website of Blake Masters.

Normies vs. Web3 Founders

Let's have fun and see the distribution and traits in the *"normal population."*

To stay in a Web3 vibe, we're going to call the *"normal population"* normies, or NPCs. All right?

If you look at the NPCs' traits on a Gaussian curve, you get something like this:

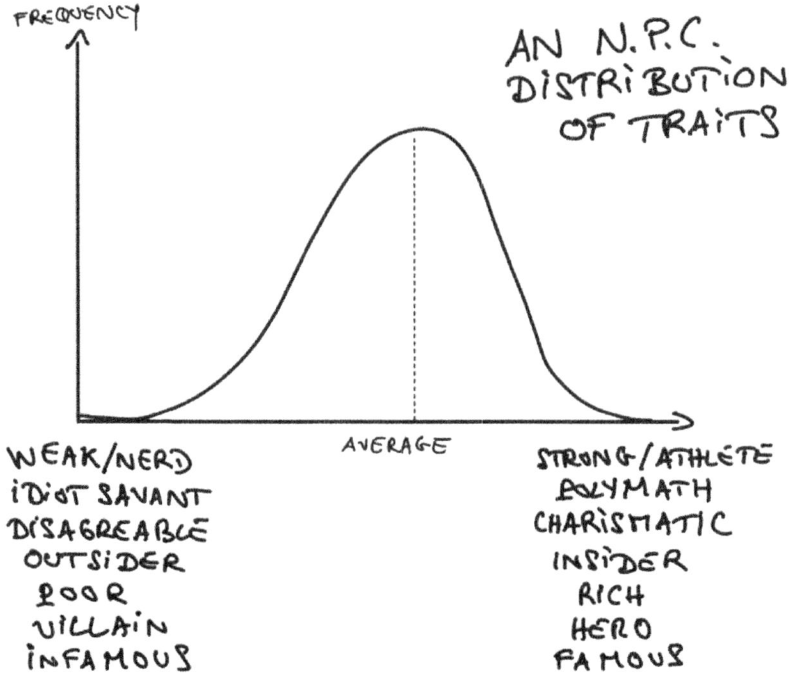

Most NPCs are . . . normal. No extreme traits. The vast majority of normies are not villain outsiders, but also not rich and famous polymaths.

This is a generalization, but you get the point. Extremely negative and extremely positive traits are not very common among NPCs.

When you look at Web3 founders, it's a different distribution.

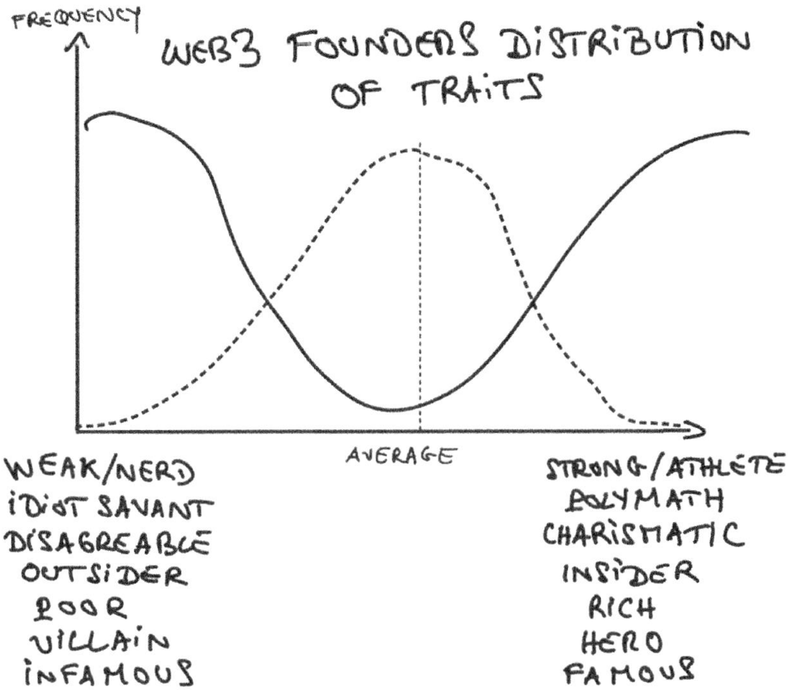

Web3 founders turn out to have an inverted distribution of traits.

You'll see a strong presence of radical traits. Positive and negative. Sometimes at the same time. Occasionally, at different moments. They can be extreme outsiders and extreme insiders.

When the founder is in the spotlight and in a (positive) fame, his positive extreme traits are going to be emphasized (polymath, genius, visionary) while reminding that he used to be a shy, nerdy, outsider weirdo.

PR campaigns will use these contrasts and build an amazing success story around the founder.

But often, as the trend goes, the negative traits will be put forward sooner or later. This happens during FUD and crashes. Suddenly, everyone remembers that founders also have horrible traits and that we should have seen this coming.

Look at Carl

You can think of crypto influencer Carl Runefelt. In his storytelling, he explains being the first poor cashier in Sweden. He was not connected, not famous, and a little bit of an outsider.

Maybe people might have looked at him like an idiot.

A few years later, he became *"TheMoonCarl."* He owns a multimillion-dollar Bugatti and lives in Dubai. Carl shares his extravagant lifestyle on YouTube while designing clickbait thumbnails for his YouTube channels.

A lot of people are mad at him for his financial success. Detractors will focus on the negative traits: *infamous, disagreeable, clickbait idiot.* Some haters might call him a *scammer.*

(That's fine, everyone in crypto had been at least once called a scammer.)

Also, **some traits are seen negatively by the general population while being widely accepted in crypto**. For example, being a *"degen autist on Adderall gambling millions on shitcoins"* is broadly regarded as an acceptable behavior in Web3.

(This is not how Carl describes himself.)

Which leads us to the next big question . . .

Are These Traits Nurtured or Developed?

To quote Peter Thiel and Blake Masters about Web2 founders:

> *There are four basic explanations for such a strange, inverted distribution. The first two reflect the familiar nature vs. nurture debate:*
>
> 1. ***It is natural**. Founders really are different. Max Levchin really has three kidneys.*
> 2. ***It is developed or nurtured**. Cultural feedback makes founders different.*
>
> *However, the "nature vs. nurture" paradigm assumes that the distribution is real. It may be mythology.*
>
> *To the extent that it's fictional, there are two explanations:*
>
> 1. ***It is self-created** (exaggerated by the founders).*

2. ***It is other-created*** *(exaggerated by everyone else).*

Thinking about founders involves thinking about which of these explanations fit and which do not. The complicated answer is that generally, all four apply to some extent. It is very hard to disaggregate them. They all feed into each other in important but complicated ways.

The dynamic might work like this. People start out being different. They are nurtured to develop their already somewhat extreme traits. Those traits become more important, and they learn to exaggerate them. Others perceive that inflated importance and exaggerate in turn.

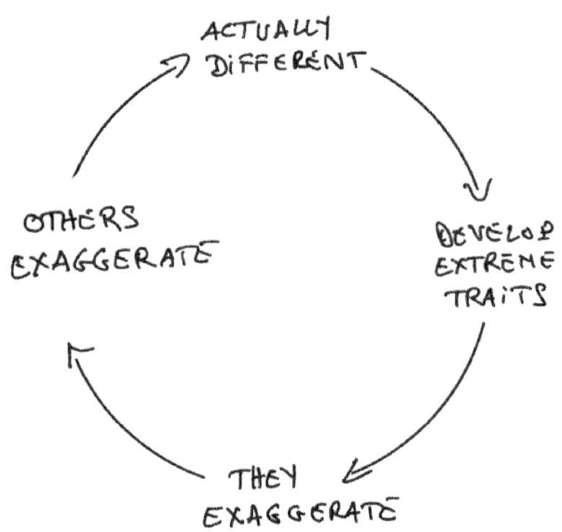

The founders thus end up being even more different than they were before. And we cycle and repeat.

In practice, the arrows could be reversed. Or the interactions might not make a clean circle, and the feedback loop would be much more complicated. The point is that some interactive combination, not just one static piece, drives the process.

Rise and Fall: A Story of Hubris and Nemesis

Let's take a look at Greek mythology to find some analogies.

The story of Icarus revolves around the concepts of hubris and nemesis.

Icarus, the son of the skilled craftsman Daedalus, was imprisoned with his father on the island of Crete. Both managed to escape by creating wings made of feathers and wax. In an act of hubris, Icarus ignored his father's warning not to fly too close to the sun.

His arrogance led to his downfall, as the wax melted, causing Icarus to fall from the sky and drown in the sea.

This tragic outcome serves as a reminder of the consequences of excessive pride and the inevitability of nemesis, or *"divine retribution,"* for one's overreaching actions.

In Web3, it happens the following way:

1. You created something that worked. Congrats, you're now a millionaire. Hundreds of thousands of people follow you. Journalists are publishing stories about your epic rise to success. You're flying very high. Maybe too close to the sun.
2. Now you're taking risks. You're getting cocky. You believe your own propaganda and ignore the Web3 law of gravity.
3. Winds change, FUD arrives, token crashes, and maybe worse things will happen to you.

> Definition: *Web3 law of gravity*
> The *Web3 law of gravity* states that things that go up in value often go down in value much faster than they go up.

Case Studies: Founder as God, Founder as Victim

Let's look at some case studies from Web3 and see if we can find similar patterns in the rise and individuals that were given *"godlike"* status, just before their descent to *"victim"* status.

TERRA LUNA'S DO KWON

Terra Luna's founder, Do Kwon, is a perfect example. He was named among the *"most influential"* people in crypto in 2021 by CoinDesk. They wrote, *"Terraform Labs has built the most successful algorithmic stablecoin yet."*

Don't blame the media for writing positive stories and headlines about it. In retrospect, everything is easy to understand, but things are far from obvious in the context of bullishness and rapid innovation.

Terra Luna raised $1 billion from renowned investors like Jump Crypto and Three Arrows Capital in exchange for LUNA tokens. Mike Novogratz even got a Terra Luna tattoo on his arm.

As of 2021, you could read on Decrypt.co, *"LUNA, the native token of Terra, is setting price records even as the broader crypto market stumbles. What's its secret?"* or *"LUNA looked like the only safety net for investors."*

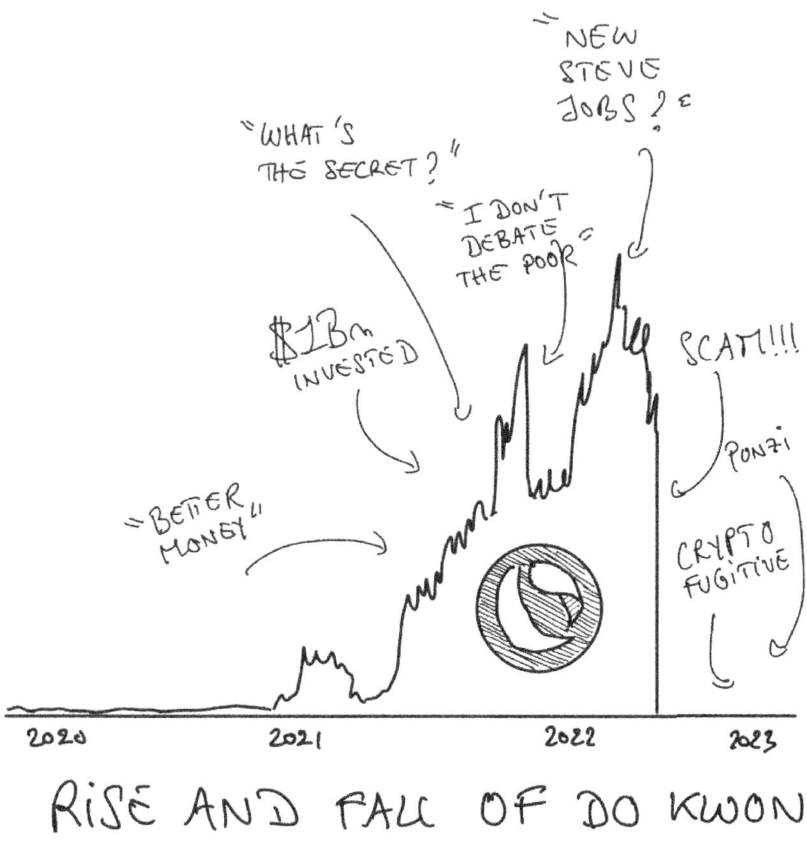

Yahoo Finance asked if Terra's stablecoin UST is *"better money"* while mentioning the comparison made by observers between Do Kwon and Steve Jobs.

In the meantime, one of Terra Luna's products, Mirror Protocol, attracted the attention of the Securities and Exchange Commission (SEC). Do Kwon, now a billionaire, brushed off the concerns of the SEC and refused to subpoena. To critics on the internet, he simply answered, *"I don't debate the poor."*

When Terra Luna brutally imploded, the media outlet that glorified him suddenly became critical.

Now he was a *"villain"* and a *"crypto fugitive."* Interpol emitted a red notice against him, and he was nowhere to be seen for months. Until his arrest in Montenegro while he attempted to board a private jet with a fake passport.

People were cheering for his arrest and hoping the worst would happen to him. As hundreds of thousands of investors lost their money, love and admiration turned into resentment and hatred.

He was a god.

Now he is a victim.

(Maybe a victim from his own making, but still a victim.)

FTX'S SAM BANKMAN-FRIED (SBF)

SBF had a similar story.

From wunderkind to total pariah.

From total insider to total outsider.

FTX was launched in 2019 and became one of the biggest centralized exchanges. They raised hundreds of millions from VC firms like Sequoia Capital. Tom Brady, supermodel Gisele Bündchen, and celebrity investor Kevin O'Leary became spokespersons for FTX.

It was all hype and glam.

SBF was this weird autistic teenager on Adderall, a super genius who previously allegedly made billions in crypto trading and arbitrage through his funds in Alameda Research. He was at the center of Web3, if not *the* center. Through its venture arm, FTX supported hundreds of Web3 initiatives. Solana being one of the most famous examples.

SBF turned thirty and was one of the richest men in the world with $26.5 billion in net worth. As a complete insider, he was also the second-largest donor for the US Democratic Party in the 2020 presidential election.

When crypto entered the bear market in 2022 and companies started to fail and collapse, SBF and FTX were there to bail them out. Jim Cramer called him *"the new J. P. Morgan"* as he saved bankrupt companies like BlockFi and Voyager. The comparison was made with J. P. Morgan's successful bailout of the financial sector in the 1907 crash.

But we all know the end of the story.

FTX was using customers' funds to invest and speculate. Notably, Alameda Research accumulated huge financial losses. The money SBF was spending was not his money, nor FTX's money, but people's deposits.

Many of the tokens linked to FTX had their value inflated to increase the perception of wealth and stability.

The whole thing collapsed in 2022 when Binance's boss started to sell his FTT (the FTX native token) while questioning the solvability of FTX's exchange.

Within a matter of days, FTX became insolvent, blocked withdrawal, and everything fell apart.

Stories started to emerge about SBF's family allegedly buying estate worth tens of millions of dollars in the Bahamas while the leadership of FTX had *"polyamorous"* sex parties and drugs in a $40 million penthouse.

Anecdotes and punchlines from SBF's right hand Caroline Ellison went public. Stuff like, *"Nothing like regular amphetamine use to make you appreciate how dumb a lot of normal, nonmedicated experience is."*

You get the idea.

Caroline collaborated with the Justice Department while SBF was arrested and extradited to the USA.

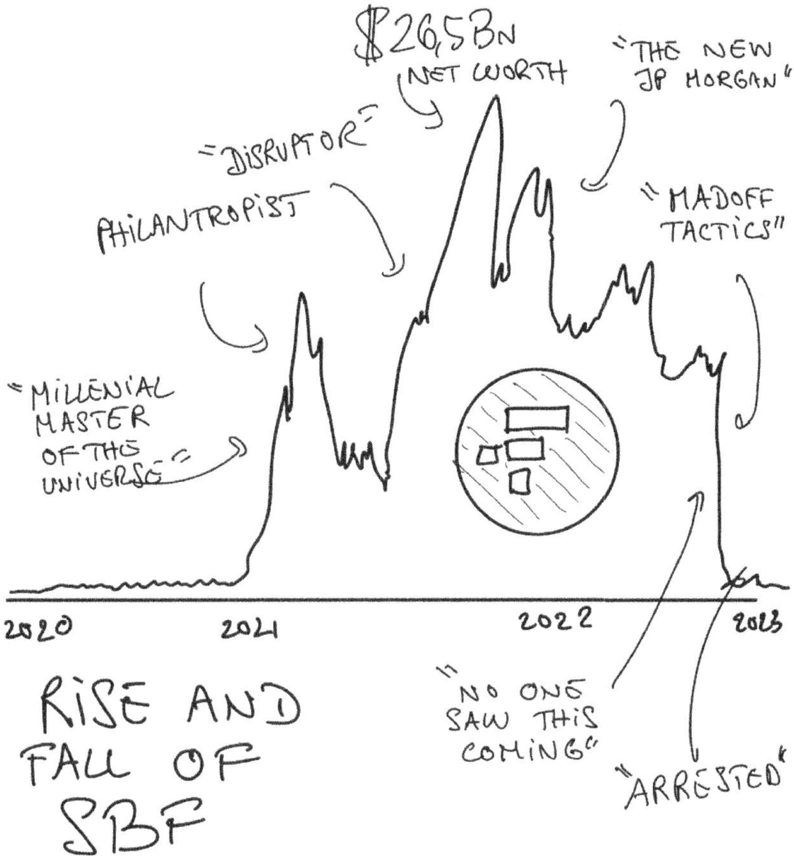

It's fascinating to see how the crypto sphere builds some individuals into legends—into half god, half genius masters of the universe—only to destroy them a few years (or even months later).

It feels literally like Greek mythology.

The Scapegoat Mechanism: Turn the Web3 Founder into a Sacred Person before Sacrificing Him

Let's dig into some philosophy here.

Introducing René Girard's mimetic desire and scapegoat mechanism theories.

René Girard, a French philosopher and anthropologist, introduced the concepts of mimetic desire and scapegoat in his theory of mimetic theory.

***Mimetic desire* refers to the phenomenon where individuals imitate the desires and preferences of others, often leading to intense competition and conflict.** According to Girard, human desires are largely shaped by the desires of others, creating a cycle of imitation that can escalate tensions in society.

The scapegoat mechanism, on the other hand, is a way to release the built-up social tensions caused by mimetic desire and rivalry.

When conflicts become unbearable and threaten the stability of a community, a scapegoat is chosen, and this individual or community is now blamed for all the problems and unrest.

By sacrificing the scapegoat, the community experiences a temporary sense of relief and reconciliation, as the focus shifts away from internal conflicts.

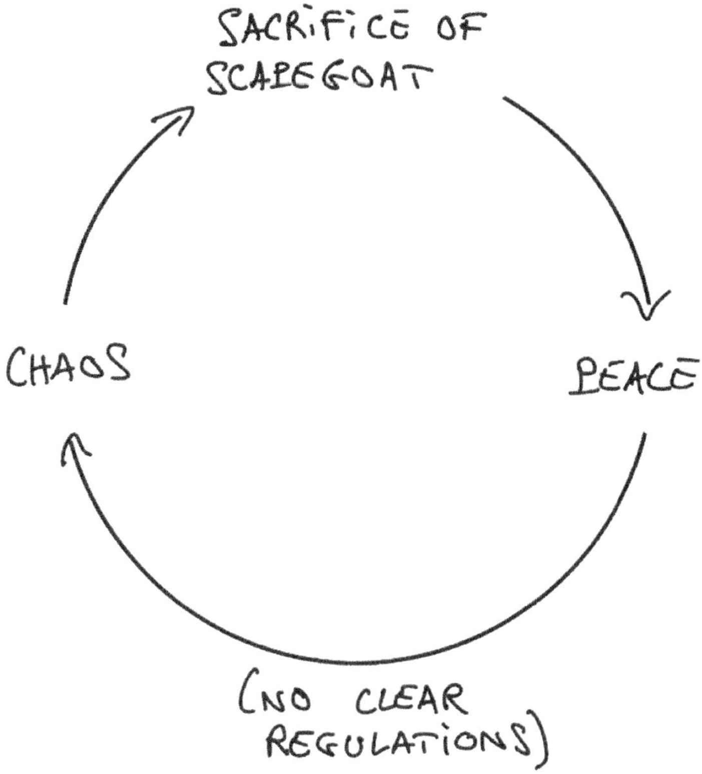

Scapegoats can come from the very vulnerable, weak outsiders and marginalized sections of society. Or from the positive—the powerful, rich, famous insiders.

Girard believed that the scapegoat mechanism is a way for societies to maintain order and unity by channeling violence and blame onto a single victim.

"Scapegoats can turn conflict into peace," **explains Peter Thiel** (a student of René Girard).

However, this process is ultimately destructive, as it perpetuates a cycle of violence and does not address the root causes of the conflicts arising from mimetic desire.

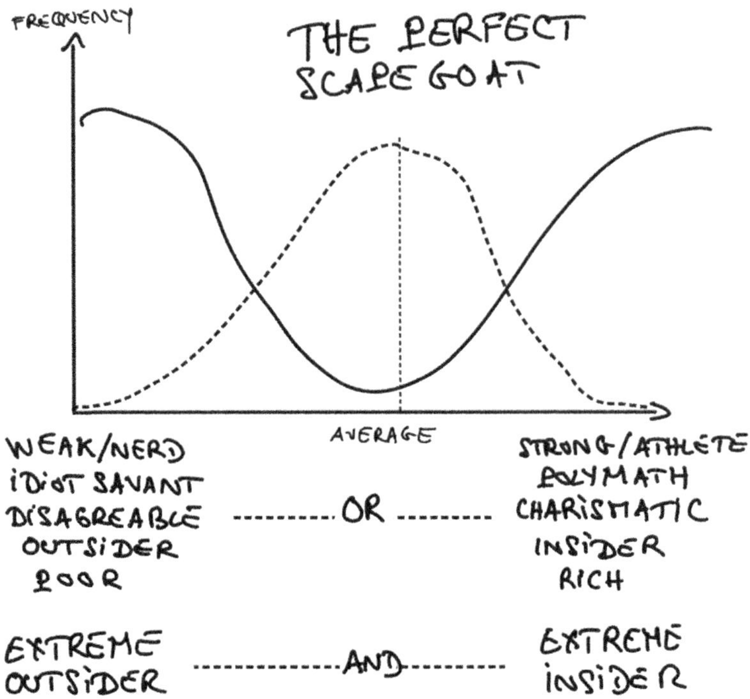

Peter Thiel said:

> *Not all scapegoats were hated all the time. Very often, they would be worshipped before they were sacrificed. People would give the scapegoat a certain amount of power before tearing him apart. That scapegoats were either worshipped or demonized follows from their being all-powerful.*

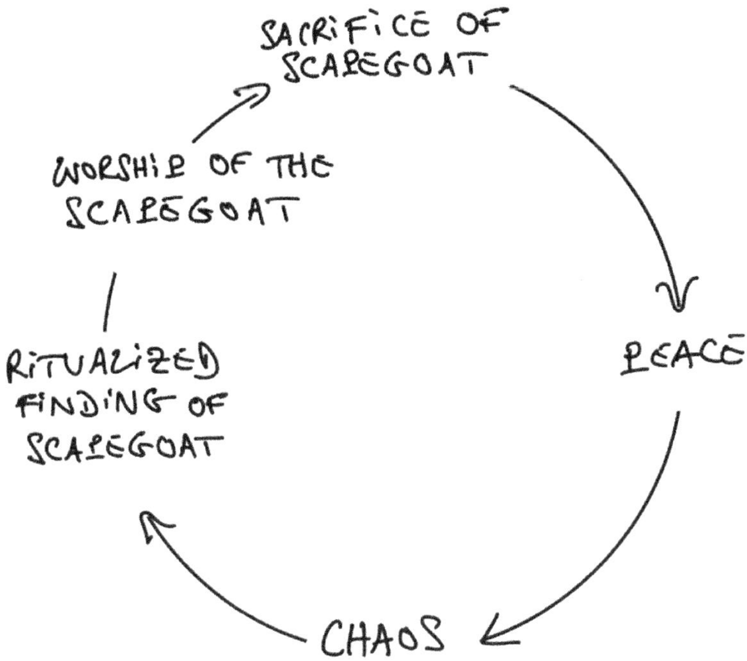

In summary, mimetic desire leads to rivalries and conflicts, which can be temporarily resolved through the scapegoat mechanism, but this process does not address the underlying issues and can perpetuate violence in the long run. Girard's work sheds light on the complexities of human behavior and the role of imitation and violence in shaping societies.

The Lesson: Always Work on Your Doomsday Scenario

First, don't do stupid things so people cannot use you (too easily) as a scapegoat or as a punching ball.

Second, when your Web3 ventures take off, you'll become an overnight celebrity, people will treat you like a rockstar, and headlines are going to be positive. They will call you a genius, a mastermind, a revolutionary innovator, or whatever.

Don't believe the hype. Don't believe the propaganda.

Stay focused on building a good product. Always keep in mind the best interests of the stakeholders.

Once every two weeks, **work on the doomsday scenario**.

Sit with your core team, and imagine everything that could go wrong. Be very pessimistic. Identify all the risks and dangers. **Remember the Web3 Murphy law.** Everything that can go wrong will go wrong at some point and hit you with maximum violence. Understand where you have vulnerability.

- **Check with lawyers** to make sure you're on the right side, and ask for several legal opinions.
- **Check with security firms** about what could be done in case things go wrong and people go after you.
- **Check with your team** on how to communicate if, for any reason, your project crashes and what to do to save it.
- **Check with your moderators** and community if everyone is aware of the risk, if disclaimers are clear enough, and if people understand what they're getting into (they tend to forget risks in times of exuberance).
- **Check with audit firms** to review your code and smart contracts. This is your twice-a-month doomsday checkup.

Key Takeaways

- If the project is on the rise, founders take on godlike figures, like SBF or Do Kwon. Founder figures tend to be both extreme insiders and extreme outsiders.
- Those extreme insider or outsider traits make them susceptible to becoming scapegoats if the project goes from peace to chaos.
- If a conflict arises—for example, the token crashes—the community looks for a scapegoat, who is blamed for all the problems and unrest.
- Before the scapegoat is sacrificed, the Web3 founder is turned into a sacred person, something similar to a god. Sacrificing the god allows the community to shift away from internal conflicts, and the dynamic turns from conflict into peace.
- The lesson—don't do stupid things. Prepare for the downfall when you're on the rise. Talk to lawyers and audit firms, and prepare for the worst.
- Stay humble. And always remember: *"Memento mori."*

SECTION 4

THE CROWD

Madness as a Feature: An Introduction to the Web3 Crowd

Wen Lambo, Ser?

—Someone on Discord

WIIFM

This chapter is an introduction to the Web3 culture. We saw some concepts in the first section of the book (*"Power Triangle"* chapter). You will learn how to understand the irrationality of crowds, the types of people who gather in Web3, and how you can create a loyal army around your future cause.

Let's talk about the crowd.

When you build and market in Web3, you have to navigate the crowd, its emotions, and its desire. It's a roller coaster. **A Web3 strategist understands what goes on in the minds of the individuals within the crowd and the mind of the crowd as a unified entity.**

In this chapter, we'll go deeper into the Web3 culture.

Web3 and Money

In the transition from Web2 to Web3, one of the significant shifts is the involvement of individuals not just as users but also as *"holders,"* or investors, in a project.

This change has profound implications for people's behavior, attitudes, and engagement with the projects they invest in. **There is a psychological ownership and a financial ownership**.

We will see how and why people lose their minds and invest all their savings into Dogecoin or other memecoins.

Elements from the Crypto Crowd Culture

People are drawn to Web3 for a variety of reasons, each stemming from the unique features and possibilities that the decentralized web offers.

CRYPTO CROWD CULTURE NO. 1—*"WEN LAMBO, SER?"*

Most people arrive at crypto with the hope of making some quick buck. Crypto volatility is both a bug and a feature. It's a *"bug"* because a lot of people lose money. But it's also a feature because the price actions are making headlines and going mainstream. The rise and fall of tokens or key Web3 figures are like a sage that millions of people follow.

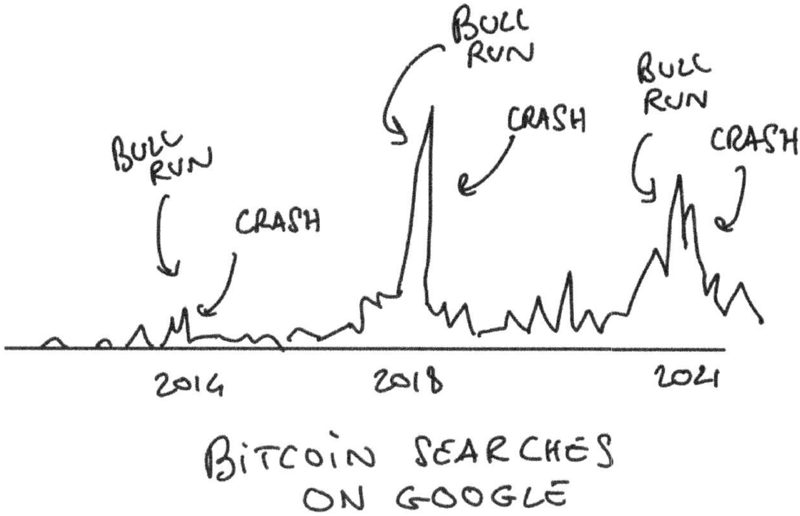

Even die-hard enemies of crypto like Warren Buffett and Charlie Munger are forced to give their (negative) opinions about crypto. Munger calls it *"crap"* while adding, *"I think the people who oppose my position are idiots, so I don't think there is a rational argument against my position." Black Swan* author Nassim Nicholas Taleb, calls it a *"tulip bubble."* But as the saying goes, ***"Bad press is good press."*** People are attracted to crypto for the quick buck.

"Wen Lambo?" is arguably the most frequently used phrase on crypto forums across the internet. It's a well-loved meme, used by people who can't wait for their crypto to finally earn them a lot of money.

By the way, the first documented Bitcoin Lambo purchase happened in 2013, when a 4chan user purchased a Lamborghini Gallardo from a dealership in Newport Beach, California. The buyer, from 4chan's technology board /g/, spent 216.8433 BTC (or $209,995) on the yellow supercar.

In some cases, the Lambo means something even deeper. **A lot of people in Web3 see crypto as a way to prove everyone wrong.** They used to be disregarded, have unfulfilled jobs and boring lives, and they hoped that they were *"one token away"* from proving everyone wrong and becoming the first millionaire in their family or community.

CRYPTO CROWD CULTURE NO. 2—*"I'M HERE FOR THE TECH"*

People come for the free money and then get rekt. Usually, when it's their first ride, newcomers lose 80 percent of their crypto net worth in a matter of weeks during the bear market. Some are panic-selling while others hold their bags hoping it'll *"pump again."*

At this point, people start pretending they are here for the tech and not the quick money. That's why they can give answers they can give to people around them making fun of them. But in some cases, people do get interested in the tech, research it, and start to contribute to the ecosystem. That's the case for the authors of the book.

This and our next point:

CRYPTO CROWD CULTURE NO. 3—*"END THE FED"*

A fraction of the crowd is on a crusade against fiat currencies, central banks, the government, and its agencies. It's about taking down the old world so a new, fairer, more transparent one can emerge.

As Italian Marxist philosopher Antonio Gramsci wrote in his *Prison Notebooks* (*Quaderni del carcere*), "*The old world is dying, and the new world struggles to be born: now is the time of monsters.*"

In the time of monsters, the crypto community is waging a philosophical and technological war against government regulation.

The libertarian vibe is the core of the crypto identity. Bitcoin maximalists, like Max Keiser, who are trying to orange-pill individuals, companies, and countries one by one are on this mission.

Some of these early Bitcoiners started the degen movement. John McAfee promised to *"cut his dick"* if Bitcoin didn't go to $500,000 by 2020. Romanian investor Mircea Popescu, nicknamed *"The Father of Bitcoin Toxicity"* allegedly expressed his view on the government this way: *"It can be said that whatever the government touches it turns to sh——t."*

More positively, there is generally the idea that Web3, by empowering people and enhancing decentralization, is contributing to making the world a better place without government help or interference.

For some people, this will not come from Bitcoin but from more memorable crypto like Dogecoin:

CRYPTO CROWD CULTURE NO. 4—*"NFT BROS"*

Speaking of identity, NFT made it possible for anyone to show their financial status or community membership by displaying NFT as profile pictures. Collections like CryptoPunks and Bored Apes Yacht Club became a status symbol for the rich and famous, or crypto OG. Football player Neymar owns BAYC #6633 and #5269, Justin Bieber owns BAYC #3001, and Jay-Z owns a CryptoPunk.

Other collections like Azuki and DeGods signify an OG or insider status as mainstream opinion never heard of these projects (yet).

CRYPTO CROWD CULTURE NO. 5—CONSPIRACIES

The NFT world is also triggering its drama and conspiracies. BAYC was accused of being of Nazi inspiration.

FROM: GORDONGONER.COM

Anti-BAYC website Gordongoner.com emphasizes the following:

> *The BAYC logo looks very similar to the Nazi Totenkopf emblem, even containing the same amount of teeth in the skull, 18, a number the ADL has identified to mean Adolf Hitler. The logos also both have a ragged edge, something very uncommon in other circular emblems" wrote Gordon Goner. Adding "One of the co-founders goes by Gargamel, a character from the Smurfs who is acknowledged as an anti-semitic depiction of a Jewish person, also a common term used on 4chan to discuss Jews.*

The goal is not here to comment on this issue but to show how the internet culture and the memes are creating social dynamics while driving critics and enabling conspiracy theories to flourish.

CRYPTO CROWD CULTURE NO. 6—*"GM FRENS"*

People come for multiple reasons but stay because of the social interactions they enjoy, the friendships they build, and the team they join. Saying and answering GM every morning on X.com is part of the culture.

Some take a radical approach, and being part of a group is a core component of their existence. Think, for example, about the *"Lunatics"* or the *"XRPArmy."*

The former are the core community behind the now-collapsed Terra Luna blockchain and its leader, Do Kwon. The latter are the believers and supporters of the Ripple XRP. Here are some things the XRP Army does to promote it:

- They create and share positive content about XRP on social media.
- They participate in online discussions about XRP.
- They defend XRP against criticism.
- They promote the use of XRP by businesses and individuals.
- They invest in XRP and hold it for the long term.

Write anything on X.com about one of these projects, and the army will show up!

Are these communities organized by leaders or spontaneous? What can they achieve, and how to build one? This is what you'll learn in this section of the book.

The Talented Monsieur Gustave

Social media made you all way too comfortable with disrespecting people and not getting punched in the face for it.

—Mike Tyson

WIIFM

In Web3, you don't market to isolated individuals. You market and talk to a crowd. Crowd psychology and crowd management are disciplines that started with Gustave Le Bon's work in the nineteenth century. His work is the backbone of any community-building strategy.

Gustave Le Bon wrote his influential book *The Crowd: A Study of the Popular Mind* (in French, *Psychologie des Foules*) in 1895. The book was published in French and later translated to English.

It is considered one of the foundations of crowd psychology, and we love it. **It focuses on the behavior of crowds and the psychological dynamics that emerge when individuals gather in large groups to do stuff.**

An interesting thing is the context in which the book was written. We're in the nineteenth century. Societies back then experienced the Industrial Revolution, the development of big cities, and violent political movements.

It's not exactly Web3, but the core concepts make absolute sense in our space.

Monsieur Gustave's Secret No. 1—The Irrationality of the Crowd

Crowds develop a collective mindset that often overrides individual rationality. They are driven by emotions and impulses.

It's something we all experienced in Web3. Crowds gather behind a project or its founders and get completely crazy. People move from having their own objectives, values, and decision-making processes to adopting collective ones.

You now have the emotion of the crowd (call it the *"vibe"*) and their ideas. Of course, the fact that many members of the community are skin in the game by owning the underlying assets (token and NFT) is making things even more extreme.

A very weird phenomenon is that the larger the crowd gets, the more irrational the people start to behave. Things that they would have not done alone or in a small group are now fine to do.

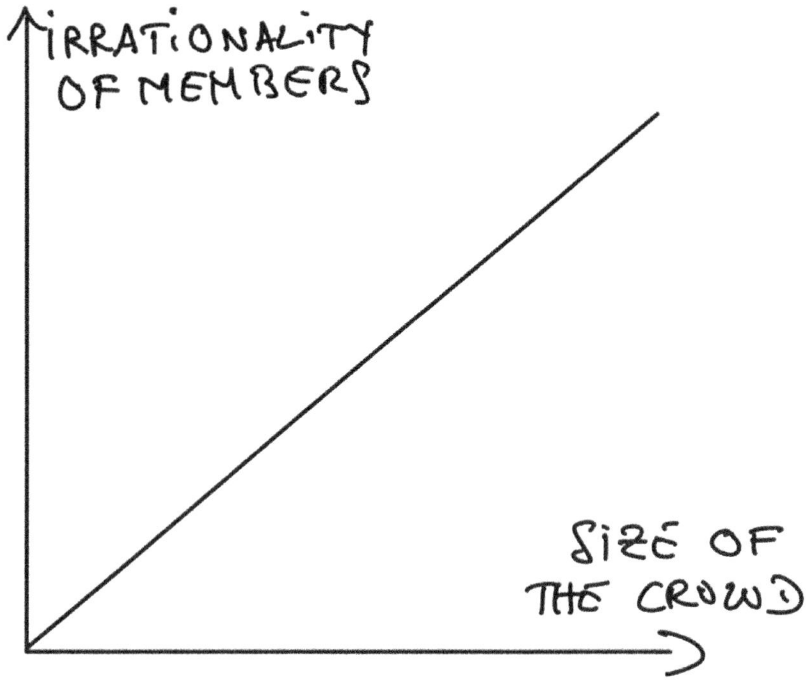

Gamble away their money? Send death threats to the founder? Stay for hours in front of the computer looking at the chart of a token? These things now make total sense.

A group of ten people usually doesn't go as far as an unleashed and unsupervised crowd of ten thousand degens. Now try to imagine forty-five thousand people on a Discord server being completely irrational.

Monsieur Gustave's Secret No. 2— The Crowd's Single Mind

When people join a crowd, their identities temporarily vanish. They adopt a *shared mindset*. Outside the crowd, they have their own beliefs, values, vocabularies, and missions. **When they are part of**

the crowd, they adopt the beliefs, values, vocabularies, and missions of the crowd.

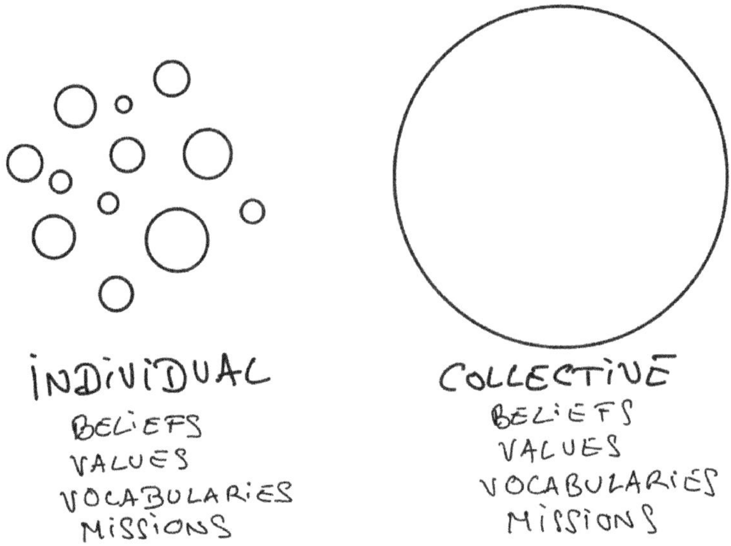

They famously adopt specific languages and memes. Individuals in a Web3 crowd tend to adopt the beliefs and values of the group. From the outside, Web3 communities look like a cult.

Some play with this idea. Cult Dao is a DeFi platform with a token and an ambitious tokenomics. They aim to fight the centralized government and the generalized corruption of its financial system.

You can read in their manifesto:

> *So if you are as tired as I am tired, if you are as furious as I am furious, as scared as I am scared, then join me, you are not alone any longer, the Many should not live in fear of their governments, it is the governments who should live in fear of the many.*

Those are the shared values they are fighting for.

Monsieur Gustave's Secret No. 3—
The Amplification Effect

Le Bon's perspective suggests that crowds often operate driven by emotions and impulsive behaviors, rather than being guided by rational thought.

Emotions spread rapidly in a crowd, creating a contagious state of mind. **A community can collectively move from FOMO to FUD almost instantly.** Not always with valid reasons. Just because the vibe changed.

For a few hours, it was euphoria . . .

Now it felt like the end of the world.

Yesterday the project's founder was their god . . .

Now he is the scapegoat.

A few moments ago everyone loved each other . . .

Now it's a violent anarchy.

There is an amplification effect.

Everything is getting bigger and stronger . . . instantly.

Any good news is making people crazy excited.

Any delay on a feature makes people extremely worried.

Doubt turns into suspicions, fear, and a collective panic attack.

Teasing can turn into desire into falling in love and into gambling the house on a token.

If you don't understand and control the amplification effect, things will go out of control very fast. That's why we insisted on developing a strong Minimum Viable Guru (MVG) in the previous chapters who can lead the crowd, build transparency, and keep things simple.

Monsieur Gustave's Secret No. 4—Anonymity and Individual Irresponsibility

When individuals are anonymous within a crowd, they tend to feel less accountable for their actions, which can increase the probability of impulsive behaviors.

Anonymity on the internet often provides a shield for individuals to express their thoughts and emotions without revealing their true identities. Which is cool.

As Edward Snowden said, *"Anonymity is the great leveler. It allows everyone to have a voice."* That's the positive. Anonymity facilitates open communication, protects privacy, and makes online conversation possible.

But . . .

The absence of real-world consequences can make people feel a little bit too *"comfortable."* Everyone assumes they can get away with everything.

"Social media made you all way too comfortable with disrespecting people and not getting punched in the face for it," argues Mike Tyson after getting too annoyed by keyboard warriors.

Anonymity makes people have behaviors that they would not dare to have in real-life face-to-face interactions.

You can observe this everywhere online from forums to social media. Not to mention the comment section on TikTok!

In Web3, you have anonymous people on X.com and Discord holding a token with no-KYC wallets like MetaMask or Trust Wallet. **So not only do you have Web3 being a crazy place by default, then large crowds of degens being irrational, and on top of this, anonymity makes people a hundred times crazier and more dangerous.**

Monsieur Gustave's Secret No. 5—Charismatic Leaders and Simplistic Ideas

Crowds can be easily influenced by leaders with charismatic personalities or by simple, easy-to-grasp ideas.

Charismatic leaders can capture the crowd's attention and sway their emotions, often leading them in specific directions. Think about Do Kwon or Justin Sun. Think about the infamous Hex.com and PulseChain founder, Richard Heart. He pushed easy ideas while focusing on a lavish and provocative personal brand.

Crowds tend to gravitate toward uncomplicated concepts that resonate with their emotions. It makes them vulnerable to manipulation by leaders who present such ideas, whether they are grounded in reality or not.

In the context of Web3, charismatic figures and straightforward narratives can easily shape the collective mindset and actions of online communities.

Monsieur Gustave's Secret No. 6—There Are Actually Three Types of Crowds

Gustave Le Bon categorizes crowds into three distinct types. Each one is characterized by specific psychological traits.

TYPE 1—IMPULSIVE CROWDS

These crowds are marked by their emotional intensity and impulsiveness. Individuals in impulsive crowds tend to act without much consideration for consequences or rational thought.

Emotions like anger, fear, or excitement can quickly spread through these crowds, leading to impulsive and often erratic behavior.

Such crowds can engage in acts of violence, destruction, or rapid shifts in behavior based on the prevailing emotions.

The Telegram group of a memecoin looks like this.

TYPE 2—SUGGESTIBLE CROWDS

Suggestible crowds are highly receptive to external influences, particularly suggestions from charismatic leaders or influential voices.

Individuals in these crowds are more likely to adopt ideas and behaviors presented to them, often without critical examination.

Suggestible crowds can be swayed by persuasive rhetoric, symbols, or catchy slogans, making them more susceptible to manipulation.

The Discord community of an NFT collection before a mint feels like this.

TYPE 3—ORGANIZED CROWDS

Organized crowds have a more structured and purposeful nature. They form around a specific goal or shared interest, and their behavior is often guided by a leadership hierarchy or preestablished plans.

These crowds are less impulsive and more focused on achieving a particular objective. Organized crowds can include political rallies, social movements, or even professional associations.

This is where you want to bring your community if you want to build and last. In the next chapter, we will see who is in this crowd and how to deal with them.

VeeFriends or CultDAO are great examples of well-organized crowds.

Key Takeaways

- The larger the crowd, the more irrational the behavior of its members.
- Individuals take on the beliefs of the crowd and leave individual beliefs behind.
- Crowds are driven by emotions and impulsive behavior, rather than rational thought.
- Anonymity promotes individual irresponsibility.
- Crowds are easily manipulated by charismatic leaders or simple, easy-to-grasp ideas.
- There are three types of crowds: impulsive, suggestible, and organized crowds.

Typology of Degens

Not all degens are created equal.

—God

WIIFM

Within the Web3 crowd, you have different types of individuals. The whole challenge is to understand the traits and characters of the stakeholders while talking to and managing a crowd. One of the biggest challenges as a Web3 marketer is to create some hype while protecting the people from doing crazy things (like betting all their life's savings on an NFT).

Your job is not to judge them. Your job is to understand them. In their own ways, each one of these degens is crazy and irrational. Our job is to work with them, help them take part in the project, and in some cases, protect them against themselves. **You cannot become good in Web3 marketing if you don't spend enough time in the head of degens.**

Degen No. 1—The Diamond Hand Holder

BEHAVIOR

That's the degree we love. The diamond hand holder is a believer. He is emotionally and socially committed to the project. For him, it's *not* just about money. It's about the community and the message. Being part of this journey means a lot to him. He will be still there even after a 95 percent crash. During the bear market or after the implosion of the project, you'll find him chatting with others on the Discord server and liking your tweets.

HOW TO SPOT

He attends every AMA, he asks questions, he never sells, and he is the first one to trash the *"paper hands"* and push to *"buy the dip."* His intensity is making him easy to spot.

ACTION

Reward him for his commitment (give him a role, airdrop him some free tokens, etc.). But also, teach him about taking some profit along the way and mitigating his risk. Some of them have 80 percent of their net worth in the project's token. This is not healthy.

Degen No. 2—The Monk Soldier

BEHAVIOR

The monk soldier takes matters into his own hands. He wants the project to succeed and takes part. He helps others, he is willing to work, and he moderates and connects you with other projects . . . usually without asking for money.

HOW TO SPOT

He's in the chat for eighteen hours per day. The monk soldier is always in a good mood. He helps without asking for anything. He will make himself easy to spot during FUD when facing critics of the project.

ACTION

You have to **give him insight about the projects and let him know where you need help**. You can guide his contribution. As with the diamond hand, it's vital to show him respect. He has to feel that the team appreciates his work and his person. At some point, he can become a part-time or full-time member of the team. Monk soldiers make also very good cofounders for further projects.

Degen No. 3—The Hyperventilated Paper Hand

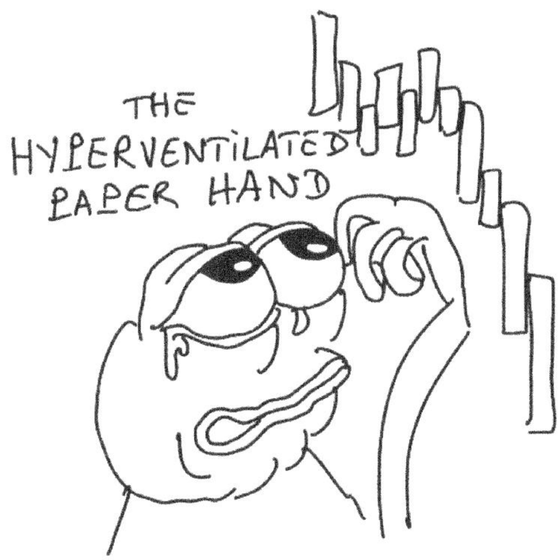

BEHAVIOR

The hyperventilated paper hand is a hard one. He is emotionally unstable. He can't take responsibility for his actions. Holding the token puts him under a lot of pressure. Usually, he sells super fast. Whether it's a little pump or a little dump, he panic-sells. But only to buy back later. He has a special style of Stockholm syndrome. Being a holder puts him in a lot of pain, but he always comes back to it. Usually, he ends up losing money and becomes resentful.

HOW TO SPOT

The hyperventilated paper hand is often spreading FUD and complaining. He will always compare the project to other tokens and more successful projects. He will ask why the team is not doing the same as others without truly making the effort to understand what it means to build and how each project is somehow unique. This degen doesn't offer his help. Just some critiques (which he will call *"feedbacks"*).

ACTION

Your job is to keep him under control. Of course, he is free to air his opinion. But don't let him vent his anger and spread FUD. If he gets too annoying, confront him publicly. Let the diamond hands and monk soldiers deal with him (they might do it on their own anyway). If he starts spreading negative rumors or shills other tokens inside the community, warn him first and then kick him out if he continues.

Degen No. 4—The Degen Parasite

BEHAVIOR

Parasites are by far the worst. The parasite wants to get close to the founder to get insights, free money, access to the next project, and a status role within the community. Basically, he wants to get your attention, resources, and status without bringing anything to the table. The parasite can be sophisticated, and sometimes he might maintain the illusion that he is useful (*he is not*). He will claim he knows important people, has some cutting-edge skills, etc. He has good influence and manipulation skills.

HOW TO SPOT

It's hard to spot him. Parasites can be very efficient. But basically, when it's too good to be true, it's not true. If someone is promising things but never delivers anything concrete, it's a parasite. Whoever claims to know too many people or have done too many great things, without proof, is a parasite. Unfortunately, you often notice parasites when it's too late. At the first FUD, parasites will abandon the ship or stab you in the back.

ACTION

Ignore them. But more importantly, don't give power, resources, and attention too fast to random people. The monk soldier will *first* work then *maybe* will ask for something (usually he doesn't ask, you have to offer). The parasite doesn't do anything. He pretends to do things, to have skills, and to know people.

Degen No. 5— The *"I Have Listing to Sell, Ser"* Degen

BEHAVIOR

You have a project, you're a builder, you're a cofounder, whatever . . . and then suddenly every single day, some people show up in your inbox with great opportunities. Usually, these people offer to get listed on a platform or centralized exchange. They'll offer to give you access to communities of whales. In exchange, they want some

ETH or BNB. They are here to scam you—99.99 percent of them (so just be safe and assume 100 percent of people messaging you with opportunities are scammers).

HOW TO SPOT

He will contact you directly to sell you something.

Easy.

ACTION

Ignore and block.

Easy too.

Degen No. 6—The Mortgage-the-House Degen

BEHAVIOR

The mortgage-the-house degen is the dark and tragic side of DeFi, NFT, and Web3 in general. That's a dangerous profile. This degen usually is a compulsive gambler . . . who doesn't know that he is a compulsive gambler. He just joined the Web3 world and fell in love with it. He'll spend all the money he has on tokens and NFT, without prior research, without risk management, without portfolio management. He just goes all in. Sometimes even with money he doesn't have. He goes into debt to gamble. Most of the time, he ruins himself.

HOW TO SPOT

He is almost impossible to spot. From the wallets, you might think he is a whale. It's really hard. The only way to identify him is during a crash and a FUD. You'll always have a guy who will say that now he is ruined, that he gambled away everything he had, and who will identify you as the responsible person for his suffering.

ACTION

You cannot talk to him directly because he is almost impossible to identify in the crowd. So you have to communicate to the community in general while having the mortgage-the-house degen in mind. **Talk about risk mitigation, talk about taking some profits along the way**, talk about being responsible, and mention the risks (without destroying the hype). You don't control this guy, but it's part of your responsibility to protect him against himself.

Degen No. 7—The Bot

BEHAVIOR

The behavior of a bot is very . . . automatic! Because it's a bot. The bot is not made of flesh (breaking news!)

Some bots are here to trade. It's here to snipe a token—to buy then sell.

Some bots are here to fake engagement in a community. Sometimes founders bring them (bad idea), or sometimes trolls send them to discredit the project (not nice).

HOW TO SPOT

With captcha and verification (phone, email).

ACTION

On Telegram and Discord, **try to block them.**

Regarding trading, you can't do much about it.

Degen No. 8—The Adult-in-the-Room Degen

BEHAVIOR

We call this degen the adult in the room because this degen only wants to multiply his bag by two or ten. Which is very conservative in this space! He's still crazy enough to be here in the first place but not crazy enough to stay too long. He is going to optimize his entry and exit to make a decent 2x or 10x. He has a precise goal and will stick to it. Contrary to the mortgage-the-house degen, this degen will not take unnecessary and crazy risks. He is calculated and rational.

HOW TO SPOT

You can't, and it doesn't matter. He acts like an adult. He is not part of the crowd. He analyzes the crowd to time his actions. He is hard to spot and relatively silent. If you're lucky, he uses his energy to shut down fudders by telling them to get a life.

ACTION

You have nothing to do.

That's fine.

Degen No. 9—The Virgin Degen

BEHAVIOR

The virgin degen entered the space with your project. It's his first rodeo. Everything is new, maybe confusing, but for sure very exciting for him.

He just installed his MetaMask wallet (or another decentralized wallet) and recently created an account with a centralized exchange. Virgins can turn into diamond hands, monk soldiers, or paper hands easily. It's a versatile category. You don't stay a virgin very long in Web3.

HOW TO SPOT

Unfortunately, he gets hacked or scammed pretty fast and asks for help in the community. By his questions and input, the virgin is easy to spot.

ACTION

You have to teach virgins how to use the tech, the blockchain, the wallet, etc. And you have to warn them about the risk. If your project is their first one, it's your responsibility to the industry to **make this first experience as positive as possible. This is how Web3 adoption happens.**

Degen No. 10—The Blockchain Gestapo

BEHAVIOR

That's for the Godwin point. The blockchain gestapo degen tracks all wallets and token movements. He wants to know everything. He is trying to identify the wallets of the team. He wants transparency for others but not for himself. He is prone to fudding and conspiracy. Beware of his sociopathic tendencies. His attitude toward the project and the team is distrustful by default. He will act as if the team works for him.

HOW TO SPOT

The blockchain gestapo degen is easy to spot. He manifests himself very fast by ordering the team to be transparent or by spreading some FUD if any big wallet is moving tokens or selling. In his eyes, the team has no right to privacy. Everything has to be shared with the community (or it's a scam). He has a very negative energy. Sometimes without even being a holder of the project.

ACTION

Be tough with the little gestapo degen. **Don't let him FUD.** Don't let him dictate how things work in your project. You have a duty of transparency, but you and only you have to define its scope. It's critical that you follow the recommendation in the *"Secret of Transparency"* chapter so the gestapo has little room for maneuver. Remind him politely that you don't work for him and that he is free to leave. Ban him from the community if he gets too toxic.

Degen No. 11—The Good Whale

BEHAVIOR

The whale is accumulating a very big bag of tokens or NFT. Whales are big holders and rich wallets. They have the power to make a project pump . . . or crash. The good whale is buying a big position at a smart moment (at launch, during the dip, etc.) and sells bit by bit. He doesn't want to harm the project. He wants things to grow so he can sell and turn a bigger profit.

HOW TO SPOT

From the wallets only, he might not always be easy to spot as he might use multiple wallets. The good whale usually wants to connect with the team to know more about the project and the motivations of the founder. He is letting you know that he has a big bag.

ACTION

Develop a good relationship with good whales. They can be allies, but also they can join your professional network. As the saying goes, your network is your net worth. It's even more true with good whales.

Degen No. 12—The Bad Whale

BEHAVIOR

The bad whale is accumulating a very big bag of tokens but doesn't care to crash the project by selling. This whale just cares about profit.

HOW TO SPOT

He shows up one day and says, *"Now I am become Death, the destroyer of worlds"* (kidding). No, usually, you notice him when it's too late. He sold his bag and the price of your token or the floor price of your NFT just collapsed.

ACTION

There is not much to do about it. **Just stick to your marketing, to your community management, and keep building.** Ultimately, you'll recover from it. A bad whale brutally selling is also a buying opportunity for others. Furthermore, the earlier the bad whale sells, the better for the long-term perspectives of the project.

Degen No. 13—The Web3 Comrade Lenin

BEHAVIOR

As you might have guessed by his name, Web3 Comrade Lenin wants to share other people's earnings. He is very keen on redistribution. *"Community"* has a strong meaning for him. All degens should be equal and founders shouldn't make too much money. This degen is upset to learn that founders are making millions while the little degens don't make enough (according to his very subjective standards). Of course, he is not willing to share the work and effort. The same goes for his money. Only the wealth of others should be redistributed. Surprisingly enough (or not), he gets along very well with the blockchain gestapo degen (you can call this a Ribbentrop-Molotov event).*

HOW TO SPOT

Web3 Comrade Lenin is getting crazy in the chat when learning about how much the team is earning or might be earning from the project. Usually, he shares the *"valuable insight"* of the blockchain gestapo degen. He is keen to spread FUD and conspiracy theories too.

ACTION

First, you have to be patient and understand that you're dealing with some anomaly here. Being a communist in the turbo-capitalism of Web3 is quite something. Reminding him about who is doing all this hard work is a good start. **Ultimately, you can simply invite him to leave the project and do his communist revolution somewhere else.**

* The Molotov-Ribbentrop Pact was a nonaggression treaty signed between Nazi Germany and the Soviet Union in 1939.

Degen No. 14—The Simp Degen

BEHAVIOR

You have a girl on the team, she looks hot in her profile pictures, and you have now to deal with Simp Degens. Simps will start to congregate around her. Even if Web3's irrationality might go beyond what seems possible, it is still surpassed by the irrationality of simps when trying to win the goodwill of a woman. This degen is not an issue. He might just miss the point of the project.

HOW TO SPOT

He interacts with every single post of the female member of the team or influencers.

ACTION

Nothing, it's fine—unless you're running a Web3 female account on X.com or YouTube that is harvesting the attention of Simps.

Degen No. 15—The Angry Grinder

BEHAVIOR

The angry grinder is a degen that only enters and engages with your community to get a quick reward. They're probably in ten other Discord servers in which they paste the same message that they send to yours. If his effort is not appreciated, the grinder degen will get angry at the project and start insulting the team. Most of the time, he is not a holder of the project. He might become one through rewards and airdrop but will sell instantly.

HOW TO SPOT

He copies and pastes messages often out of context. He participates actively in every single opportunity for giveaways or free stuff. Ultimately, he gets angry easily.

ACTION

There is not much to do. **Don't change your course of action for this degen.** It's a good sign that your project is attracting grinding attention.

Degen No. 16—The *"Flat Earth"* Degen

BEHAVIOR

This degen is just looking for conspiracy everywhere. In wallet movements, in design elements, and even in the code of the website. Everything can be turned into a good reason to FOMO (*"they have two lines of code in common with Yuga Labs, so it might be the same team behind the project"*) or to FUD (*"one founder sold $10,21 worth of tokens, they are about to rug the project"*). Most of the time, his contributions are not a net positive for the project, but they might be entertaining.

HOW TO SPOT

He is producing and spreading conspiracies. He might be working hand in hand with the blockchain gestapo, and he stimulates the hyperventilated paper hands to sell everything.

ACTION

When the conspiracy is creating FOMO, you can ignore it. Maybe ask the moderators to ease it up a little bit. **When it's generating FUD, it's important to state facts and provide evidence that contradicts his conspiracies before it goes out of control.**

Key Takeaways

- Web3 participants come in different shapes or forms.
- Some have a positive impact on the project. Some don't.
- Some use crypto in a good way. Others put themselves in danger because of crypto.
- Warning—some are hybrid.

The FU Army

Do things that don't scale.

—Paul Graham

WIIFM

This chapter is a step-by-step masterclass to create and organize your community. It's a long but fun process. Come back to this chapter whenever you're working on community building.

FU Money is your leverage against everything that doesn't go your way in life. **The FU Army is your leverage against anything that goes against your will in Web3.** Do you struggle to build a network? Do VCs and aristocrats ignore you? The FU Army is your answer. FU Armies are the engines behind very successful Web3 projects.

Spectators, Holder, and Soldiers

There are three types of humans, and not all of them are really your *"army."*

THE SPECTATOR

He is in the group but not very active in the community. He is not sure he wants to commit to the project, hold the tokens, and contribute in any form. A spectator is someone who is also checking the project and vibe of the community. He might be in a research-and-curiosity phase. Some spectators ultimately turn into holders and soldiers.

THE HOLDER

A holder is someone who owns the token or NFT. You have many types of holders (as we saw in the typology of degens chapter). Owning the token gives him skin in the game but does not necessarily guarantee that he's active in or outside the group. He is financially committed, but not emotionally or professionally.

THE SOLDIER

He is an active member of the group. He is active inside and outside the group. He is a core believer, and he is part of the army. Usually, he is also a holder, but in some cases, he is not (the token is not launched yet, and/or he cannot afford it for now). You want to have soldiers.

Vertical Relationships, Horizontal Relationships, and Movements

There is a fundamental distinction between vertical and horizontal relationships, each holding unique significance.

VERTICAL RELATIONSHIP

A vertical relationship is formed between an audience and a star. In this setup, all eyes are on the leader who becomes the center of attention. The audience, the followers, engages with the content of the leader. This kind of connection is like a *spotlight shining on the leader*, making him or her the main focus.

This is often the consequence of the successful development of a Minimum Viable Guru (MVG).

HORIZONTAL RELATIONSHIP

The horizontal relationship, on the other hand, is built among individuals within a community. This occurs when people in the same group relate to each other. Rather than one leader taking the spotlight, the attention is spread across the entire community. The strength of this type of relationship lies in the *interconnections* and *collaborations* among members of the community.

Communities like NounsDAO or Dogecoin, before Elon Musk hijacked the project, were typical horizontal relationships.

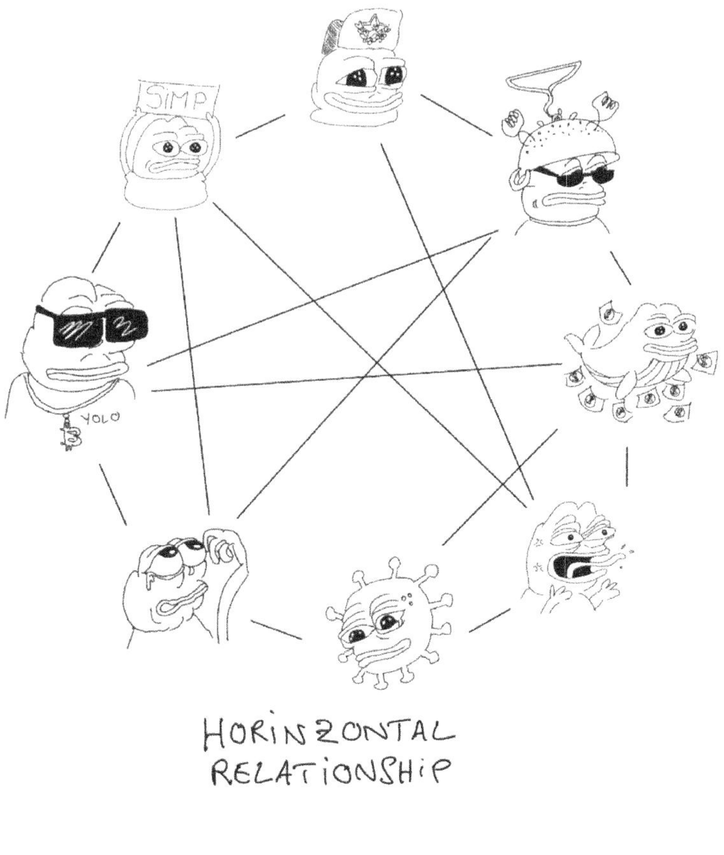

AUDIENCE AND COMMUNITY

Having a vertical relationship means developing an audience. A horizontal relationship is a community.

These are not the same concept, even if people mix them up. You don't turn an audience into a community that easily.

What you want to develop is a mix of both. Your Minimum Viable Guru (MVG) has an audience of followers and fans. These people gather and communicate with each other within your project's Discord or Telegram. Then somehow a community is emerging from it.

THE MOVEMENT

For a community to be efficient and turn into an FU Army, you need to create a movement . . . not just gather people online to talk about stuff or gamble on an NFT.

A *"movement,"* according to Russell Brunson's *Expert Secrets* book refers to a powerful and collective drive toward a shared vision or idea.

In Web2, a movement is not just about promoting a product or service. It's about championing a transformative message or cause that resonates deeply with a group of humans.

Brunson explains that movements start when an individual becomes a **charismatic leader or a *"cause crusader."*** This leader passionately communicates the vision, rallying others to join in and support the cause.

The goal of a movement is to create a **community of like-minded individuals** who believe in the cause and are inspired to take action.

In our case, this person is our MVG. The key to a successful movement is to focus on the **core message** and values that the movement represents. It has to resonate. It has to spark an emotional connection. With more connection and value, the movement gains momentum as more people are drawn to it.

In Web3, the movement is a mix of three components.

First, you have the **Minimum Viable Guru**. Maybe he was created before the project, maybe during the launch of the project. Sometimes he emerges from the group.

Second, you need a **new opportunity**. The vehicle for transformation and success. The vehicle is the project, the tokens, and the product.

Third, you have the **vision**. *"We are going to achieve some big things together."* The vision signifies that we're all part of something bigger than us. It's stimulating.

How to Grow Your Movement

Every movement starts with a small group of people who are thoroughly convinced about one core belief. By implementing the following steps, you will make sure that your movement gains strength with scale and that current members keep inspiring newcomers.

STEP 1—THE MOVEMENT IS YOU AND YOUR FRIENDS

You start the journey here.

You have one channel for chatting (for instance, Telegram) and one for announcements (for instance, X.com). Don't spread the coming spectators, holders, or soldiers in too many directions. You don't need to have Discord + Instagram + Telegram + TikTok when you start.

Focus.

In the group, the closer people are to each other, the better. It's like throwing a party with ten people in a room designed for a thousand. You want first to have a small room (and just one) and then get a bigger room when more people will join.

In this group and at this stage, you don't need to disclose everything about the project. It can be simply some teasing and hints to increase the curiosity and desire to be part of the journey.

STEP 2—START DESIGNING YOUR MISSION WHILE WELCOMING MORE MEMBERS

The mission is more important than the new opportunity (aka the project) at this stage. The mission gathers people and gives them a sense of purpose. It can be serious (*"We're building a first decentralized xyz to give power back to the people"*) or more degen (*"Let's shake the industry and ignite a new bull cycle thanks to some crazy shitcoin"*).

Take for instance Cult Dao's mission about decentralization:

> *The purpose of Cult is to empower and fund those building and contributing towards our decentralized future. Our society is built to make it as difficult as possible to break away from societal, economic, and other norms.*

At this stage, you welcome more members in the movement, and you have a huge unfair advantage over bigger more established audiences, communities, or movements.

How is this possible?

Your advantage is called the *"Olson paradox."*

It suggests that the smaller a group is, the higher the probability that members would be engaged to achieve a common mission. Conversely, the bigger the group, the fewer people are going to be active (while hoping other members will be active).

That's why big CEOs are better at getting what they want from the government than a union with millions of workers.

If the union organizes a demonstration and you don't show up, it won't make a big difference. So you don't show up. So most people don't show up. As a consequence, the movement gets weak.

If there are 20 people in a group and 5 do not show up, the group loses 25 percent of its leverage. If there are 20,000 people in a group and 5 do not show up, the group loses 0.0125 percent of its leverage.

Small groups are more efficient. Their members are more engaged. They can gather and act better than large crowds of people.

Your small group of 50 degens might be more efficient and, for sure, better organized than a group of 100,000 people.

STEP 3—DO THINGS THAT DON'T SCALE. TALK TO FIVE PEOPLE PER DAY

"Do things that don't scale" is a concept put forth by Paul Graham, a cofounder of the start-up accelerator Y Combinator and an influential figure in the start-up world.

The idea is the following:

At the early stage of a start-up (or in our case of an FU Army), don't try to scale stuff, **don't try to automate and growth-hack things.** Just do things yourself, manually. Do this for some time. It helps you collect information, understand customers (or members in our case), and become better at what you do. Once you achieve this, and only once it's achieved, you can start thinking about scaling things.

In your case, the *"things that don't scale"* consist of talking individually with each new member, getting to know them, and establishing your ***"OG CRM."***

Each time you or your moderator meets with someone, you have just one single goal: to uncover the deepest desire of this person, to understand what they want and cannot have. The one little dirty thing they won't tell anyone about.

The name of the game is, *"What do they want?"*

You can achieve anything in life if you first understand what people want and secondly help them get it (or give it to them if you can).

It's the same here when building your small community. You need to know people to help them improve their lives and get what they want.

This is what friends do.

But you have to talk to them.

Each one of the early core team and moderators should talk with five people each day and remember five things about them. You put all this information in a CRM, which we nicknamed the OG CRM.

You can simply take a Google Sheet and separate it into the fields of *"Name," "Special Thing 1," "Special Thing 2,"* and so on. Then every day you enter your own findings and manage to stay up to date about new community members by reading the entries of your mods.

If done well, you can create first a group of ten OGs, then twenty-five, then fifty, etc.

You grow while not losing in quality of relationships and engagement.

STEP 4—MAKE PEOPLE TALK TO PEOPLE

Another step, another small theory.

This time it's **Metcalfe's law**.

Metcalfe's Law is a principle from the field of network theory that states that the value of a network is proportional to the square of the number of its users.

In other words, the key thing is *not* only the number of people in a network (here, in an FU Army) but the number of **connections** people have with each other in the network.

The more users are connected within the network, the stronger your network becomes.

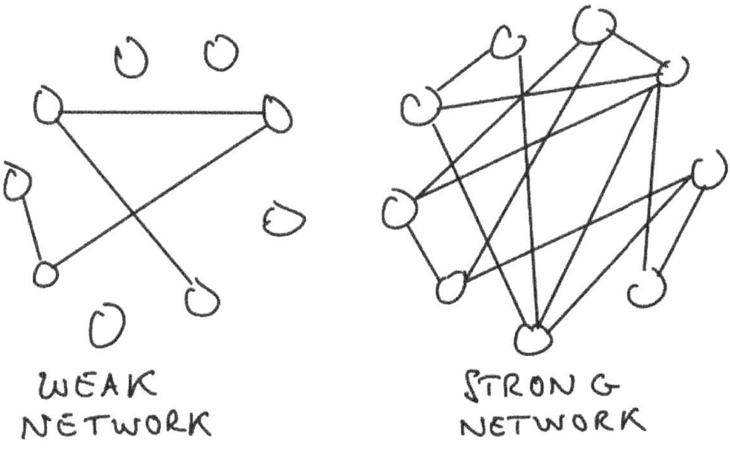

The job of moderators in the group should be to talk to people, include more people in the conversation, and ask other members for their ideas, input, and feedback. **Make them talk to each other, and start conversations inside and outside the group.**

With Side.xyz, we introduced something called the *"accountability partner,"* community members face weekly goals and challenges on their path to becoming Web3 content creators. In the first week, we connect them with someone who is in a similar niche and similar place like them. They set goals together and hold each other accountable. This leads to extremely strong network connections inside the community.

Besides this, members meet every day for AMAs, give feedback on each other's content, and present their work in the *"Sider Story"* workshops every Friday. The goal is that every user has multiple deep-rooted connections with others. This creates a very stimulating energy inside the community.

Which leads us to the next step . . .

STEP 5—INSPIRE AN IDENTITY SHIFT

You have an identity shift when you change your perception about yourself. Your self-perceptions, beliefs, and sense of belonging evolve.

You move from one identity into another. The same goes for your mindset and values. People's internal narratives change. It's something we saw in the *"Talented Monsieur Gustave"* chapter.

Members of the group will move away from some personal beliefs and values to adopt the one of the group. Of course, the project has to promote positive values and beliefs.

So how do we engineer an identity shift?

You use several leverages. Among them are the following:

- A polarizing MVG
- A common jargon and vocabulary
- Insiders' jokes
- An anthem (you don't have to, but it might be fun)
- A manifesto and clear shared values
- A common enemy
- A shared visual identity
- A nickname for members of the community

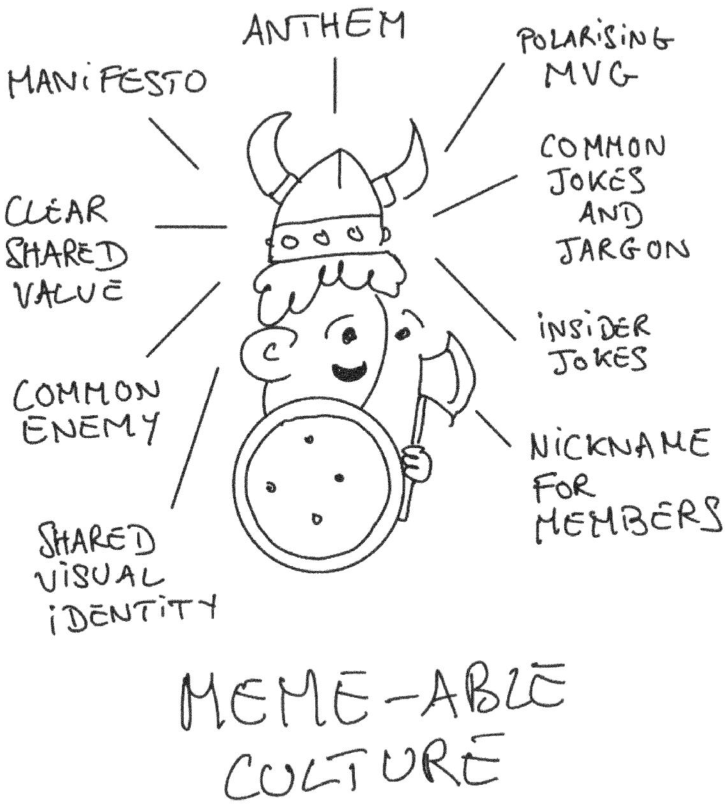

Take for instance Bored Ape holders. Then they define themselves as *"Apes,"* use their NFT as profile pictures, and tweet about *"standing*

with Yuga Labs?" Yuga Labs being the parent company of the NFT collection.

You know that the identity shift is completed when a member can say, *"I'm a ______."*

For instance, on Side.xyz, we have *"I'm a Sider."*

STEP 6—CLARIFY ROLES AND RANKS

An army needs ranks and roles. Without them, it's absolute chaos. An organized army doesn't need an external enemy to collapse. Internal power struggles and confusion will cause its fall.

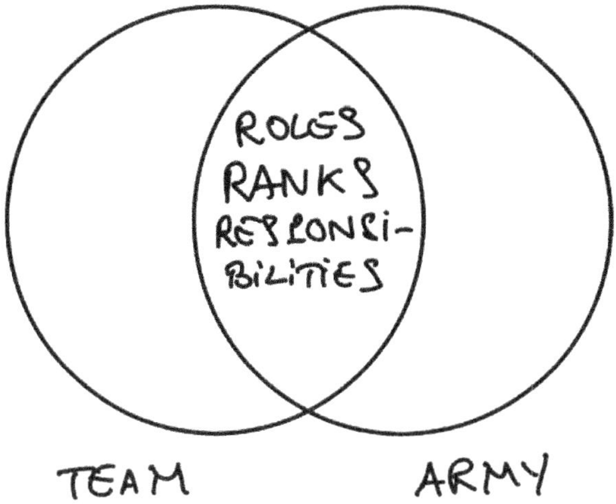

When you develop the FU Army, the frontier between the army and the team becomes blurry. And it's fine. It's like Web3 to add to the core team, active soldiers, and holders.

Here is the hierarchy:

1. Founders
2. Officers (OG, key soldiers, moderators)
3. Troopers
4. Soon-to-be troopers (aka simple holders and spectators)

We saw this in-depth with the *"Web3 Organization Chart"* chapter.

A fraction of holders and spectators will become soldiers. The goal of community building is pretty much to achieve this.

The project should sometimes put the spotlight on the officers so the troopers can fully identify them and pay them respect (or simply ask them for help). The hierarchy should be transparent and visible on the group chat. People have to feel that if they participate, they'll be rewarded and recognized for what they are.

Ranks are about privileges and status (people crave this), but it's also about roles and responsibilities.

In contrast to the current world where leaders get privileges while never endorsing any responsibilities, **in Web3, officers are responsible for specific actions and domains.** For instance, they can be responsible for managing the moderators, being in charge of onboarding, helping newly arrived users on the project, etc.

This is the condition to go to the next step:

STEP 7—SCALE FU ARMY GROWTH

You've done things that don't scale and organized your crowd into an army with strong bonds to each other and a shared culture.

Now it's time to scale.

Scaling and growth strategies are developed in depth in the last section of the book.

Basically, here we are moving from an army of a few dozen people to a few hundred and then to thousands. Projects that reach the first page of CoinMarketCap or become blue-chip NFTs manage to reach a critical mass of holders and soldiers.

Among the strategies, we can mention the following:

- *The Berlin Techno Club*—making sure the music is always playing so that new and old members are stimulated alike.
- *StepN invite link*—creating an allure of scarcity and exclusivity around you by only allowing *"Invite Only"* access.
- *Bribe it until you make it*—bribing users in ethical ways to switch over to your opportunity.

- *The viral loop*—implementing features that are so loveable and shareable that your marketing team has no way of messing up.
- *The Tugan Method*—inspiring your FU Army to create mass content for you and spread your vision for basically no cost.
- *The Apollo Juggernaut Method*—bribing your way into the location of your perfect customer avatar and scaling the operation by hiring hundreds of gig workers.

Scaling implies usually hiring more people (staff members, officers), having a 24-7 high-precision monitoring of the FU Army, and developing multiple communication channels. Coordination and proper communication within the team and with the community are of paramount importance.

STEP 8—THE ULTIMATE *"FOUR SEASONS"* CHALLENGE

Imagine the moment you're entering the lobby of the Four Seasons.

The lobby boy opens the door for you. Two seconds after you enter the lobby, a charming receptionist takes your hand luggage and assists you with your check-in.

By some miracle, they already know your name, and they have all your details. The only thing you need is to sign, and after thirty seconds, you're in the elevator off to your room.

Over the next couple of days, everybody in the hotel remembers your name, your preferences, the museums you went to, or the restaurants you dined in.

You're on a first-name basis with everybody from the barista to the general manager.

After four days, you leave the hotel with a heavy heart. It has started to feel like home, a place you belong in, and a place where you are truly appreciated.

You can compare this experience to the local Holiday Inn, where you get lost looking for the reception. The check-in takes ages. The staff makes sloppy mistakes and you feel like nothing more than a room number.

We truly believe that no matter which business you're in, you're in the business of selling experience. *"Magical internet experiences,"* as Frank DeGods puts it.

Your job as a community owner is to make sure that every new member that joins your space is welcomed, remembered, appreciated, and can't wait to come back once he leaves your sacred halls—just like at the Four Seasons.

The challenge is to do this . . . at scale!

The Community Canvas

Ninety percent of communities fail.

Why?

First scenario—founders are not intentional in what they are building.

Second scenario—founders fail at scaling the team and building a community.

Information gets lost, roles are not clear, and new newcomers don't understand the culture and the mission of the project. Everything gets confusing. The team gets tired. Some moderators don't even show up to stop FUD from spreading.

The Web3 community canvas, which we stole from Alea.eth, is one proven framework to increase your odds of success when building a community.

(You can follow Alea.eth on X.com and Anna Kamp LinkedIn. Credit for Web3 community canvas is hers. Errors and omissions are ours.)

The canvas looks like this:

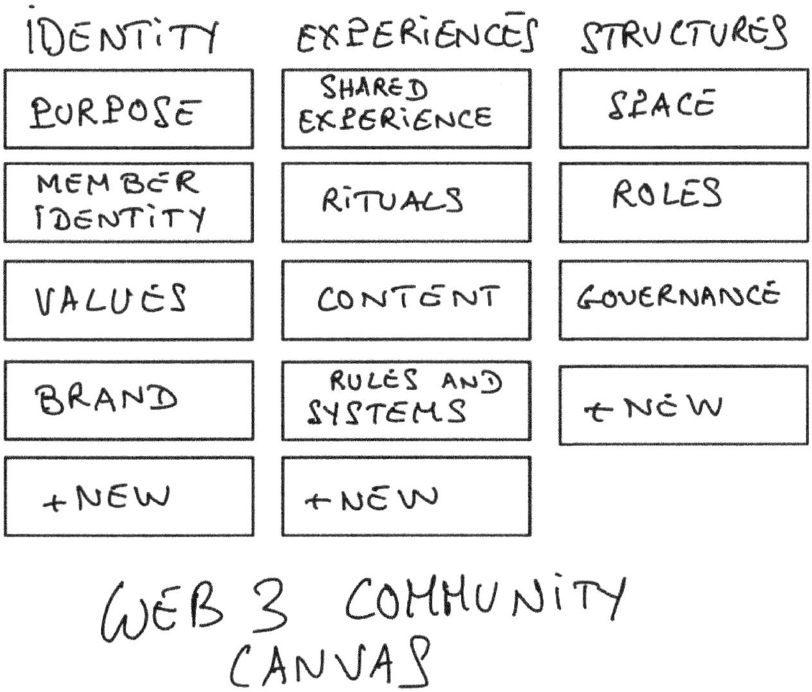

Basically, it's a folder—or an organized document (for instance, using Notion)—that gives everyone all the information they need at any time.

This document can be public for the community or kept private for the team. Both are fine. It'll help you train your team and organize operations regarding community building.

IN THE FIRST PILLAR, YOU FIND EVERYTHING RELATED TO THE IDENTITY

- *Purpose.* What do we want to achieve? What is the cause? Are we fighting something or someone? What is the mission?
- *Member identity.* Whom is this community for? What is the ideology? What kind of identity shift do we want to achieve? We want to transition from purely individual identities to a shared positive identity (at least when we're in the project's Discord server or Telegram group).
- *Values.* What is important to us as a community? Values provide a North Star for the community. Embed them into the community's rituals. Make them tangible with stories, principles, or a manifesto.
- *Brand.* How does the community express itself? A strong brand unites members, as the members collectively own and proudly share it. Make sure to tell the same story across touchpoints. Use symbols and language to anchor and reflect values, and rituals

IN THE SECOND PILLAR, YOU FIND EVERYTHING RELATED TO THE EXPERIENCES

- *Shared experiences.* What experiences do members share? Is it purely online, or do they gather in real life (for instance, during events)? Experiences have to be consistent and reliable. The community should be involved in the designing and improving of these experiences.
- *Experience funnels.* Design process for the moderators and them. When X happens, you do Y. This is typically how the Four Seasons hotels manage the scaling of experiences.
- *Rituals.* Which rituals enhance the community experience? Rituals (even small ones) create a sense of belonging. They can mark some members' milestones. Rituals should have meanings.

- *Content.* What content creates value for members? Relevant content strengthens bonds and shapes members' experiences. This creates trust, learning, exposure, and inspiration. Make sure to incentivize members to create content, share stories of members, etc.
- *Rules and systems.* What incentives help us reach our purpose and represent our values? They make interactions easier and more stable. Make sure to use incentives and not simply strict rules.

IN THE THIRD PILLAR, YOU FIND EVERYTHING RELATED TO STRUCTURES

- *Space.* Where does the community meet? Every community needs a place where they can congregate. Make sure to create a place where members have immediate access to information, other members, and the team. At the same time, do not bombard members with too much information.
- *Roles.* What roles can members play in our community? Smart communities provide different roles catering to needs throughout the member experience. Make sure to reward early supporters and the most engaged members. Roles give rights but also duties. It has to be clear.
- *Governance.* How do we make decisions? In the early days, decision-making is top-down. As the community matures, it becomes more decentralized (with a DAO). Make sure to document how decisions are being made. Over time, have a smooth transition to a DAO by aligning on purpose and tools.

Key Takeaways

- An FU Army is the answer to everything that doesn't go your way in life (networking, VCs, aristocracy).
- Communities are either horizontal or vertical relationships. In horizontal ones, everyone is equal and shares decision-making power. In vertical ones, you have a clear leader on top whom individuals follow and aspire to become.
- The word *community* is used wrong in most contexts. It's either vertical or horizontal relationships. A vertical relationship is an audience-fan relationship, while a horizontal relationship is built among individuals within a community.
- A movement does not circle your product a service. It's inspired by a transformational message that deeply resonates with your audience.
- Every FU Army goes through a distinct series of steps that needs to be monitored and managed closely.

How to Manage a FUD

I'm no in danger . . . I am the danger.

—Walter White aka Heisenberg
(But also any anon in the community)

WIIFM

A strong FUD can kill a Web3 project. First-time builders have no idea how to manage one, and they do stupid things. Read this chapter now, and check it again whenever the vibe of the community starts to evolve in the wrong direction. You'll thank us later.

Let's discuss something that will happen sooner or later: the FUD. It stands for *"fear, uncertainty, and doubt."* A **FUD is an accumulation of anxiety and frustration in your community. It's the step before the sh——tstorm.**

We apologize for the profanity of our vocabulary, but if you experienced one, you know that our words are still way below the level of madness of what can happen.

How Do FUDs Happen?

FUDs can happen for many reasons. Most of them you don't expect.

The main cause is usually **the team getting tired or not paying enough attention, the communication getting sloppy, and the price of the token tanking.** FUD almost never happens when the token price is cruising to a new all-time high.

WE CAN NEVERTHELESS IDENTIFY SOME CAUSES:

- The project is not making enough progress fast enough.
- There are conspiracy theories about the real intentions of the founders.
- The team is not communicating enough with the community.
- There is confusion regarding the roadmap and the introduction of a new feature or token in the ecosystem (especially prior announcement and teasing).
- The price of the token or NFT simply going down in the context of confusion.

- Whales are selling, and the price is dropping.
- Founders are selling (it doesn't have to be much to create a FUD).
- The team is changing, or some members of the team are leaving the project.
- There is a hack or a major bug in the platform or smart contract.

The reasons are plenty. The issue when you manage the crowd is to **distinguish the signal from the noise.** Every day some holders or community members will act negatively. That's part of life. Maybe they have a bad day or maybe they are part-time psychopaths. All the options are on the table. Having a deep understanding of the typology of holders will help you identify borderline behaviors.

THE CHALLENGE IS TO KNOW WHEN A FUD IS STARTING AND SPREADING.

Usually, it's around one specific core issue. If you notice a growing dissatisfaction or frustration around a specific topic and this topic becomes a growing concern in the community, you might have the first sign of a FUD. Also, the reaction of the community will tell you if it's a FUD. If people who act normal on a daily basis start to give credit to the negativity and take a slight part in it, you might have something that you should look at. If people who are usually positive are not taking the defense of the team, it might mean that they are agreeing with the fudders.

What You Should Not Do

Here is what you should not do: ignore angry people, ban the people spreading FUD, and continue business as usual.

This will make things worse. Also, by banning more and more people, you'll make someone credit conspiracy theories or be seen as someone afraid of *"the truth"* and who has something to hide. It won't work in your favor.

Don't get me wrong—it's okay to sometimes kick out and block super toxic, useless, and irrational people who hurt the project. **But banning too many people raising concerns during an early FUD is bad**. Also, the worst you could do is to ban people who are moderately frustrated but still polite.

Moreover, banned people might gather somewhere else, create their own Discord server or Telegram group, and go completely crazy in their own echo chamber. We have experienced this in several projects. In these echo chambers, fudders are even banning and blocking moderated people! Hence increasing the madness of the crowd.

Defamation campaigns, death threats against founders (and their families), and manhunts usually emerge from these groups.

Don't underestimate the stupidity and naivety of stupid people in large groups (and don't forget what we learned from Monsieur Gustave in the dedicated chapter).

How to Manage a FUD

Benjamin Franklin was right when he said, *"An ounce of prevention is worth a pound of cure."* The following are a set of weapons that will help you avoid or at least protect yourself from a FUD.

WEAPON NO. 1—FOUNDATIONS AND TRANSPARENCY

First, you manage the FUD by having a strong foundation, especially regarding transparency. People will complain mostly about money, volatility, risk, team, team's ability, and intention. All this has to be put on the table at the beginning of the project. If it hasn't been done enough, it's the team to emphasize all this. It's not the time to promise things. When a FUD starts, the promises of the founders sound like those of desperate politicians. It doesn't work. And keep in mind that politicians are actually professionals when it comes to handling these situations. So focus on transparency.

WEAPON NO. 2—MOBILIZE THE COMMUNITY

You put the focus on all the good things that have been achieved collectively as a community. Founders need to give credit to the team members and community for all the things that have been done. The crowd has to feel the commitment of the team.

Keep in mind that fudders are always a very vocal minority. The majority might still be on your side or on the brink of changing sides. You need to reassure the silent majority and ask them to also be vocal about their satisfaction. Push them to engage with fudders. After all, you're all in this together, and Web3 is about decentralization. Make the *"happy people community"* work for the project and support a positive mood (it's in their interest too since FUD usually affects the prices of digital assets).

WEAPON NO. 3—FACE FUDDERS WITH COMPASSION AND STRENGTH DURING AMAS

Start an AMA and ask the angry people to come to raise their complaints. Always stay very polite but firm. Fudders are enemies. Treat them with respect and destroy their arguments.

Before the AMA, ask your team to gather all the complaints and prepare answers for each point. Identify arguments and proofs. If some failures have happened, don't dismiss them, but remember that building in Web3 is about testing things and making mistakes.

Ask fudders how things should have been done. Usually, they can't answer this question. If your transparency foundations are strong, you should be able to have an answer to anything. The AMA is usually the joker to reverse the trend, take control of the narrative, and build up a positive vibe.

WEAPON NO. 4—SPOIL YOUR MODS

Last thing. FUD is always hard on the moderators because they are on the front line. Also, they are humans, and they might agree on some point with fudders. You need to have a daily meeting with moderators, to give them talking points and arguments to answer the public. Listen to them, ask them how they feel, and ask them for advice about how the project should communicate about the ongoing issues.

It's very important to thank them for their work, give them credit for helping the project, and give them bonuses. This is how countries avoid revolutions.

In France, when a vast nationwide protest movement started with the *"yellow vests"* in 2008, the government gave bonuses to the police to keep them happy. This and hundreds of plastic bullet ammunitions shot at the population saved the government.

Revolutions always happen when the police join the protest. Moderators are your police. If they join the fudders, it's game over.

Key Takeaways

- Common causes for FUD are a tired team, sloppy communication, not enough attention, and the tanking price of a token.
- Banning fudders and ignoring angry holders will only make things worse.
- To manage FUD, have a very strong transparent foundation, mobilize the community, and face fudders with compassion and strength during AMAs

Horizon Stacking

The Next Episode.

—Dr. Dre

WIIFM

Horizon Stacking is a fun strategy that we came up with while trying to turn a short-term hype into a long-term commitment to a project. As you'll soon see, creating hype is not very hard. Maintaining it, though, is almost impossible . . . if you don't know the Horizon Stacking Method!

Effective community and project management involves handling incentives and expectations. It resembles a captivating series. After each episode, there should be a prevailing desire to know more and continue watching.

While having some idea of what might unfold, the anticipation of witnessing it firsthand keeps you engaged. So you eagerly click on to . . . the next episode!

In Web3, retaining participants, their commitment to the project, and their daily presence signify momentum. **The present relies on the future being projected and the community's vision. People take action today based on what they foresee on the horizon.**

Controlling what lies on their horizon is crucial. Therefore, mastering the narrative surrounding your project is essential.

Introducing: The Klaus Schwab Method

Klaus Schwab is the head of the World Economic Forum (WEF)—an opaque and nondemocratic organization often accused of running the world and pushing narratives.

Here is what you have to understand:

Running the world and overseeing a crowd of degenerate token holders may seem unrelated, but they share more similarities than meets the eye. In both scenarios, you find yourself faced with an irrational crowd whose actions and behaviors can be unpredictable.

There are narratives you control and narratives you don't control.

Managing a crowd requires narrative control. You must control debate topics, attention, and focus. Don't let the crowd alone decide. While it may sound somewhat Machiavellian, the reality is that you need to choose and control the narrative, both present and future.

This is a critical aspect of crowd management.

Let's consider two examples to illustrate this point:

- Example 1: *"We will reach X million in market cap by this date."* Unless you personally have millions to invest, you cannot exert control over this narrative. If the community fails to achieve this goal, it may lead to fear, uncertainty, and doubt (FUD).
- Example 2: *"We will conduct a $X airdrop next Friday for token holders above Y amount."* This narrative is within your control. You can determine the date and the criteria for eligibility, and you can position yourself to carry out the airdrop.

The second example is the kind of small narrative that you want to communicate about. You control them. It's not random. It's not about some force outside your control. People will have a sense of clarity and trust because you deliver what you talk about.

This is precisely what the World Economic Forum, politicians, and figures like Klaus Schwab are doing.

In your scenario, it involves unveiling a deliberate sequence: starting with an airdrop, followed by announcing a significant partnership, and culminating in the release of a new feature. More importantly, both the partnership and feature are prepared in advance, under your control. You shape what the next episode holds.

This is a promising beginning, but it's not the final destination.

Your next move is . . .

The Horizon Stacking

Horizon Stacking is a strategy for maintaining engagement, arousing curiosity, and generating anticipation.

The key differentiator lies in the nature of these elements and their timing.

In mature and technologically advanced projects, the time horizon tends to be longer, emphasizing the importance of consistency. Users seek stability in such cases.

Conversely, projects driven by excitement and hype attract a more short-term focus. Users here crave immediate stimulation.

To effectively manage your project, it's crucial to have short-term, mid-term, and long-term narratives in place at all times. **The seriousness of the project determines the length of these horizons.**

	SHORT	MID	LONG
TECH	3 WEEKS	3 MONTHS	3 YEARS
HYPE	3 DAYS	3 WEEKS	3 MONTHS

Crucially, the community should maintain full awareness of project developments, upcoming events, and ongoing construction.

This transparency keeps them engaged and excited, providing them with a compelling reason to remain involved and hold the token. It's a clear signal that significant developments are on the horizon, ensuring their continued commitment.

People know something big is coming.

It looks like this:

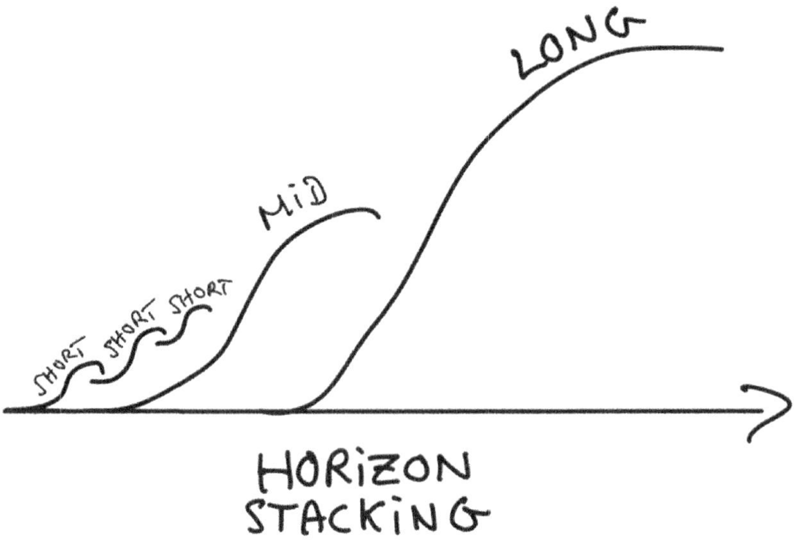

The process involves stacking short-term horizons on top of each other, with a mid-term horizon in place, while quietly advancing the long-term horizon in the background.

This accumulation of developments enables you to control what the community perceives on their horizon.

Without this structured approach, a project can seem inconsistent, appearing to generate random ideas without a clear direction. Such uncertainty invites criticism and undermines the project's credibility.

Horizon Stacking transforms amateurs into planners with a structured approach. It manages expectations and brings a sense of control.

While complete control may not be achievable, you establish foundations and structures aligned with agreed-upon goals. Depending on your governance model, the community can also participate in this planning process.

The Zappos Secret Hack

In his bestselling book *The Personal MBA*, Josh Kaufman introduced a notion that's going to be very useful for us.

It's called the *"anticipation effect."*

To quote him directly:

> *A customer's perception of quality relies on expectations and performance. After a purchase is made, the performance of the offering must surpass the expectations for the customer to be satisfied. If performance is better than expectations, the perception of the offering will be high. Do whatever you can to*

provide something that unexpectedly delights your customers.

He takes the example of Zappos, the shoe-delivery company. Zappos was launched in 1999 by Nick Swinmurn and Tony Hsieh. The company was acquired by Amazon for $1.2 billion in 2009.

Zappos had a secret weapon back in the day to delight customers and surpass the expectations of customers. As Kaufman wrote, *"When you order from Zappos, it's very likely that you'll receive a pleasant surprise: your shoes will arrive the next day, several days ahead of schedule."*

This strategy can benefit any Web3 project. **By providing a buffer in your timeline, such as announcing a twenty-day delivery for a feature that takes ten days, you create a win-win situation.**

If everything proceeds as planned, you'll exceed expectations by delivering ahead of schedule, which delights the community. On the other hand, if unexpected challenges arise, you still have a good chance of meeting the deadline and maintaining trust and confidence within the community.

The two criteria to take into account are the expectation and the performance. You can imagine a formula like this:

QUALITY = PERFORMANCE – EXPECTATION

If the expectations are higher than the performance, the score is going to be negative. **It takes a long time and a lot of work to improve performance. But expectations are easier to manage.**

Which leads us to the following point . . .

The Case for a Flexible Roadmap in Web3

In Web3, a paradox emerges when it comes to roadmaps. Many token holders and enthusiasts desire a detailed plan for the months or even years ahead, yet they often disengage from the project long before any substantial progress is made.

Traditionally, projects would outline their roadmap on their website or whitepaper, essentially making commitments to what they intend to build.

This approach has its pitfalls:

- *Inflexibility.* A rigid roadmap can hinder a project's ability to pivot. Any deviation from the stated plan may be perceived as a breach of promise.
- *Legal risks.* Roadmaps can be used against project developers in legal proceedings if they fail to deliver on what was *"promised."*

This inflexibility is problematic because the Web3 environment is dynamic. Things evolve: technologies, market preferences, and project needs change over time.

A more adaptive approach, such as the Horizon Stacking Method or a DAO-based variant, provides a solution. It combines clarity and flexibility, allowing projects to innovate and adjust until they find a product-market fit.

You can feature this Minimum Viable Roadmap on your website, a Medium post, or a big announcement in Discord.

This approach aligns with the ever-changing Web3 landscape, where adaptability and responsiveness are the keys to success.

Key Takeaways

- In Web3, controlling what lies on their horizon is crucial, so it is essential to master the narrative surrounding your project.
- *Horizon stacking* is a strategy for maintaining engagement, arousing curiosity, and generating anticipation. It involves stacking short-term horizons on top of each other, with a mid-term horizon in place, while quietly advancing the long-term horizon in the background.
- By providing a buffer in your timeline, such as announcing a twenty-day delivery for a feature that takes ten days, you create a win-win situation. This is the Zappos secret hack.
- The flexible roadmap approach is more adaptive to the Web3 environment as it combines clarity and flexibility, allowing projects to innovate and adjust until they find a product-market fit.

SECTION 5

THE GROWTH

Formula One: An Introduction to Growth

Let's start tweeting and go viral.

—*Every Web3 "Agency"*

WIIFM

This is another *"common sense"* chapter. Before building up crazy growth and going *"to the moon,"* you need to check that the foundations are strong. It's quick. Let's do this.

Web3 is entrepreneurship on speed. It's like driving a Formula One car.

It's very fast, very profitable, very stimulating . . . but any mistake can be fatal.

Foundation of Growth

The foundation of growth therefore is a checklist that you should not avoid. It will make sure that your car won't break apart, once you start pushing on the gas pedal.

THE TEAM CHECKLIST

- Do you have an active MVG?
- Do other members of the team have active MVGs or minimal online presence?
- Are roles clear among the team?
- Do you have advisers?
- Do you know who you could hire if you need help?
- Is your schedule empty for the next two months (at least)? Clearly, it's not the time for traveling, honeymoon, or summer vacation. The core team has to be fully available.
- Where does communication happen (Slack, Telegram, WhatsApp)?

THE PRODUCT CHECKLIST

- What is the new opportunity that you're presenting to the market? Both a seasoned Web3 veteran and a five-year-old need to understand.
- Is your first version of the product simple enough? Do you keep your option open to add more features?
- Are all components of transparency clear for everyone?
- Have you done basic legal research about your product?

THE CROWD CHECKLIST

- Who are the target audience and users for your product? Where do these people gather?

- What are the competing projects? Who could be allies? List twenty projects.
- Can you list twenty influencers or MVGs in your niche?
- What are people upset with existing products?
- Where do you want to communicate and gather the community?

What Are the Stages of Growth?

Even a Formula One Car needs to accelerate before it reaches full speed. You start pushing on the pedal, you start accelerating, and you reach the top speed limit. Now another problem arises: you have to keep driving at top speed without crashing. The following steps will illustrate how you can survive each phase without driving the car against a wall.

STAGE 1—PRELAUNCH

Prelaunch is everything that happens *before* the launch. It's the checklist, networking, research, development. Depending on the growth and launch strategies that we will discuss in the coming chapters, the prelaunch might or might not include the development of a community and the teasing of the product.

In 90 percent of cases, we do this during the prelaunch while making sure to keep a lot of dry powder for the next stages. The prelaunch is not about scaling anything. It's about doing things that don't scale, identifying the first OGs, talking, and bonding with as many potential holders as possible.

You have to get in touch with other MVG and projects. People have to know that you're there. You exist. That something is coming. The level of teasing and information at this stage depends on the strategies you will adopt.

STAGE 2—LAUNCH

It's the big day. You launch. Something will fail. You'll experience some bugs and some mini FUD. That's fine. Launches in Web3 are almost always messy. With the launch, you experience the first volatility.

Suddenly, the team has to be on board 24-7. If you have a lot of traction, you might start considering hiring people. The launch is in a very short time frame of a few hours to a few days. It's worth mentioning that most projects fail their launch and never recover from it.

STAGE 3—SHAKE 'N' CRUISE

You survived the launch, and let's assume things worked almost fine. Now everyone in the community says, *"And now what?"* At this stage, part of the holders will simply dump their bags if they have turned a profit, while some others who are not profitable will already lose hope and move on to the next shiny object. It's going to shake.

The value of your token might drop by 30–70 percent in trading volume. Hype in the community and the clarity of the vision will make all the difference. The growth strategies you'll discover in the coming chapters will be useful here.

In the shake-'n'-cruise stage, the goal is to move from emergency management (panic mode, shaking) to steady management (cruising). At this stage, many projects die too because the team gets exhausted and commits too many mistakes. Transitioning to cruising under high pressure requires some serious entrepreneurial skills.

STAGE 4—HYPE MAINTENANCE AND PRODUCT DEVELOPMENT

Now you enter the long game, blue-chip projects are at this stage. They got their hype, they got crashes, FUD, and volatility, but they survived it and entered a phase of longer time windows. Instead of hyping the community about the announcement that comes in twenty-four hours, you set for them a longer vision while keeping strong energy and culture in the community.

You take the time to develop the product and make the project more complex if it started simple. It's now about managing your team and the expectations of the community. Key project developments should be around scarcity management, adding more comprehensive utilities, and establishing long-lasting partnerships with key players, and if possible, Blockchain Aristocrats.

You have to plan and strategize. Choose what makes sense for you when and why. But always make sure that you have dry powder. By *dry powder*, we mean product releases, announcements, features, news, and partnerships. There always must be something going on. Web3 marketing is about staying relevant and being a constantly evolving landscape.

Should You Launch before or after Having a Product?

There is no hard science regarding the question of the launch time. This question also assumes that you do have a product to build (a lot of tokens don't have).

But here are our two cents.

IF YOU'RE IN A BULL MARKET, LAUNCH THE TOKEN BEFORE THE PRODUCT IS READY.

It makes sense because of the ability to raise huge amounts of funds during a bull market. By the way, this is not financial advice, but don't trade or hold with all the money you raised. Keep most parts in stablecoin or fiat to be sure to have the financial resources to pay the staff during the next bear market.

Be transparent about the delay in launching the beta version or the Minimum Viable Product (MVP). Don't overpromise. Do technical research about the difficulty and time required to achieve what you want to achieve. Let your community know that the product strategies and features might change. Be transparent about the fact that if a bear market appears before the product is ready, it might affect the price of the token without altering, of course, the motivation of the team to build the product in question.

You can justify the launch of the token for funding, for governance (decisions about features or strategies), and also to kick off the marketing (since each holder now has skin in the game).

IF YOU'RE IN A BEAR MARKET, LAUNCH THE PRODUCT BEFORE THE TOKEN

During the bear, it's very hard to raise funds for a Web3 project. All VC *"smart money"* was invested around the ATH and got rekt. Retail investors mostly left the place or a dollar-cost-averaging Bitcoin. Raising money is simply hard. Crypto is not cool anymore. People start saying there won't be a bull market for five or ten years, and that we will maybe never see the ATH. Even foundations behind blockchains are getting reluctant to give away grants. It's all doom and gloom.

In this case, it might make more sense to stay super lean and cost-efficient and build the product and the community without launching a token. One thing you can nevertheless do is reward contributors and active community members with soulbound tokens attached to no fiat value (*"soulbound prelaunch"*). They are just *"points"* that people can accumulate in their wallets and that might be turned into real tokens later on.

If you do this, make sure not to promise future value and not to commit completely to a specific tokenomics. Keep your options open, and stay a little bit vague on the token while being very precise and diligent regarding the product.

The Berlin Techno Club

I haven't slept in the last three days, and all the people around me are strangers.

—A Web3 participant, or somebody in Berghain

WIIFM

We're not really party people, but this analogy is quite good.

Managing hype is like running a techno club in Berlin. **You pretty much have two jobs: bring people inside the nightclub and make sure they have fun.**

Some nightclubs stay open twenty-four hours a day during the weekend, and at any time of the day and night, the hype is at the max.

IT IS VERY SIMILAR IN WEB3 MARKETING AND GROWTH

- You need a flow of new people to keep the nightclub full. Keep in mind that at every hour, some people are leaving, and you don't want the dance floor to be empty.
- New arrivals want to feel a big hype and atmosphere. If everyone is tired after twelve hours of partying on acid, some people are asleep or puking on the floor, newcomers will leave instantly and not even try to dance.
- People who are already there need to be stimulated about something new. The DJ's best sound cannot be played again and again, or people will get bored. But at every hour newcomers arrive, hoping to hear the DJ's best sound. So you need many good sounds.
- People enjoying themselves might tell their friends to join the party.

If you translate this into Web3 marketing, you have internal and external marketing.

Internal Marketing vs. External Marketing

A nightclub has two sorts of marketing jobs: **attract people from the outside to come in and make sure that the people inside stay as long as possible.** Here's how this works.

EXTERNAL MARKETING IS OUTSIDE THE COMMUNITY

It's about bringing new people to the projects and the community. It's about growing your crowd and FU Army. It's about creating a conversation about you in the ecosystem.

INTERNAL MARKETING IS INSIDE THE COMMUNITY AND THE PROJECT

It's for the people who are already there and are using the product. They need to be constantly hyped with kept promises and new ideas. They need to feel that the future is much bigger and much more exciting than what has already been achieved.

Many Web3 marketers fail at combining these two forms of marketing.

Let's assume your project is cruising, the community is strong, the community was hyped during the first days by AMAs from the founders, and there's a strong vision and shared experience. This is very strong. But newcomers never experienced this. They have no idea about the culture and about the crazy things that they've missed. They've just arrived very late to a party where a lot of people are getting tired and want to move on. By *tired*, we mean, they are less active, less joyful, and often selling the token. Yet no one in the team is offering these newcomers the experience and rituals that the early adopters got. As a consequence, the newcomers are confused and bored very fast. They leave the project without really interacting with the community or trying to hold the token or NFT.

This happens when the founders and marketers don't understand that the audience, the crowd is multiple, and not everyone has the same temperature.

Degens' Temperature

"How likely is this user going to buy what we offer?" To answer this typical Web2 sales question, you can separate your audience into *"cold," "warm,"* or *"hot."* In order to *"warm up"* leads, you can show them more content, give them more care, or show them other smaller offers.

This is how this looks like in Web3:

COLD DEGENS

They are those who have no prior knowledge of or interaction with a project. They don't know the founders or their MVG. Cold degens understand Web3, but they don't know you or necessarily the niche you work in.

WARM DEGENS

They are those who have some level of awareness of your project but have not yet taken any action, such as participating in the community or buying the token or NFT. They are there but passive. You can also call them tourists. They are here, but that's pretty much it.

HOT DEGENS

They are those who have already taken some action, such as making a purchase or actively taking roles and becoming soldiers in the community. They are typically the most engaged degens and are the most likely to convert into diamond hand holders or monk soldiers.

Project Phases and Degen Temperature Allocations

All these groups have to be addressed for viable growth. Always think about your allocation of marketing efforts and growth actions among these groups.

DURING THE PRELAUNCH STAGE

- 80 percent for cold degens
- 20 percent for warm degens
- 0 percent for hot degens

As you're building the community from scratch and the project is not launched, the focus is very clear. You don't have hot degens yet, just cold and warm.

DURING THE LAUNCH STAGE

- 20 percent for cold degens
- 70 percent for warm degens
- 10 percent for hot degens

With the launch, some warm degens turn into hot degens. You need to take care of them, but not too much for now. They are super happy to be holders now and to see that the project is live. It's also not a priority to have a high allocation to the cold degens as you already have a community. The core of your effort is around the warm degens that you need to convert.

DURING THE SHAKE 'N' CRUISE STAGE

- 20 percent for cold degens
- 40 percent for warm degens
- 40 percent for hot degens

The number of hot degens is increasing, so is the care for them percentage-wise. Warm degens are still a strong priority, and as some people are exiting the project, you need to maintain a reasonable flow of new cold degens.

DURING THE HYPE MAINTENANCE AND PRODUCT DEVELOPMENT PHASE

- 30 percent for cold degens
- 10 percent for warm degens
- 60 percent for hot degens

The project has reached a milestone and is somehow recognized. So warming people is not that critical. On the other hand, cold degens have so many alternatives to you, and maybe they prefer to enter a project that is younger and smaller as the perceptive upside is bigger than yours, which is a bigger, more established project already. The retention of hot degens is key to success. They are your OGs. They are gathering to face FUD and build the brand. They have to feel that they are the priority of the founders.

Key Takeaways

- Managing hype is like running a techno club in Berlin. Your job is to bring people inside and make sure that the club is always full and that the people inside never get bored.
- External marketing is about bringing new people to the project and creating conversations about you in the ecosystem.
- Internal marketing is about making sure that the people inside the project are enthusiastic about the future.
- We differentiate between cold, warm, and hot degens and who needs different levels of attention during each phase of the project.

Stuff That Doesn't Work

Vitalik just burned half of the circulating supply. Very bullish.

—The Shiba Inu community in May 2021

WIIFM

Simply a list of stuff you shouldn't waste time and resources on.

All right, let's go over all the *"strategies"* and *"tactics"* that simply don't work when it comes to Web3 growth. We mention them here so we don't have to talk about this ever again.

Deal? Let's go!

Stupid Idea No. 1—Spamming Elon Musk

Elon won't drop Dogecoin for your memecoin. Yes, he tweeted once about CumRocket. But that was it. Don't harass him. It makes your project look desperate and cheap. Spamming the X.com accounts of other celebrities or important Web3 players won't work either.

Stupid Idea No. 2—Airdropping Wallets for Famous People

No, they won't care about your project if you do this. It's even worse. It will make your token or NFT look like a scam (because that's what scammers and hackers usually do). Some think that airdropping a celebrity and then claiming to the community that this person *"owns"* some tokens and NFT from the project is not factually wrong. It's just profoundly misleading. Remember, it's always about having the best intention in mind that you need to do things.

Stupid Idea No. 3—Promising Crazy Stuff That Will Never Happen

Pilling up items and crazy (empty) promises in your roadmap doesn't work either. Not only no one believes them but holders might use this to sue you if they lose money on their *"investment"* that never lived up to the initial promise.

Stupid Idea No. 4—Raiding Other Communities

Raiding a community works the following way:

You ask your dozens or hundreds of holders to join a different community, enter the general chat, and start screaming about (1) the greatness of your project and (2) all the bad things of the other project to attract attention and lure new holders onboard. It's not only annoying for the other community owner, but it will also make you look like a scammer and only result in negative reactions.

Stupid Idea No. 5—*"We Run Ads, Senator"*

This is only half stupid. It might work. But it's not great. Ads signal too often that you're a Web2 marketer trying to make a cash grab in Web3. Good Web3 products, NFT collections, and protocols don't spend on ads. They spend on the community, and the holders take care of selling the vision.

Stupid Idea No. 6—PR Agencies

PR agencies in Web3 are very expensive, and they won't help you attract new users, nor will they make the current community feel hyped. Pretty much everyone knows that PR rhymes with BS when it comes to growth. So don't spend money on PR hoping to grow your project thanks to this.

But it doesn't mean it's useless. Most projects should do a little bit of PR, but for different reasons. Projects always get haters. If you don't have high-ranking content on Google about your project or your person, haters' content will arrive first (hence hurting your reputation and making the compliance process more complicated with institutions).

Key Takeaways

- Any shortcut is going to hurt in the long run.
- Don't waste your time on questionable marketing techniques, and focus on building beautiful internet experiences instead.

Typologies of Launches for Tokens

Not financial advice but . . . we're going to the moon

—Anyone launching a token

WIIFM

Welcome to the most technical chapter of the book. There is no way around it. If you ever launch a token, read this chapter. Then read it again. Make sure to understand the concepts and dynamics. *(Disclaimer: The part about the liquidity pool is quite a headache. If you want to launch an NFT-based project, move on to the next chapter.)*

You have many ways to launch a token. In this chapter, we will go through four key strategies:

- The Presale/ICO Strategy
- The DEX Fair Launch Strategy
- The DEX Stealth Launch Strategy
- The Token Soulbound Prelaunch Strategy

Let's go!

Token Launch Strategy No. 1—Presale/ICO

Both token presales and initial coin offerings (ICOs) are methods used by Web3 projects to raise funds for their development and operations.

They involve selling tokens to investors before the token's official launch on decentralized (DEX) or centralized (CEX). Usually, we have a presale and then an ICO.

TOKEN PRESALE

A token presale, also known as a private sale or pre-ICO, is a fundraising round that occurs before the official ICO.

It typically involves selling a limited number of tokens to a small group of investors, often institutional investors, venture capitalists, or high-net-worth individuals.

HERE'S HOW A TOKEN PRESALE WORKS

- *Select investors.* The project team identifies and approaches a select group of investors who are interested in supporting the project's development. Usually, these early investors have a strong network or a brand or who can add something to the project. Crypto VCs like to enter at this stage.
- *Agreed terms.* The project and the investors negotiate the terms of the presale, including the price of the tokens, the amount of tokens each investor will receive, and any bonuses or discounts offered.
- *Funds raised.* Investors contribute funds (usually in cryptocurrencies) to the project in exchange for the promised tokens at a discounted price.

- *Vesting and lockup.* To align the interests of the project team and investors, there might be vesting periods or lockup periods, during which the tokens cannot be immediately sold or transferred.
- *Use of funds.* The funds raised in the presale are used to further develop the project, create the platform or product, and potentially market the upcoming ICO.
- *Public ICO.* After the presale, the project may conduct a public ICO where tokens are offered to a broader audience at a higher price.

INITIAL COIN OFFERING (ICO)

An ICO is a public fundraising event where a Web3 project sells its tokens to the general public. ICOs gained significant popularity during the cryptocurrency boom and were used by many projects to raise funds.

HERE'S HOW AN ICO WORKS

- *Announcement and promotion.* The project announces its ICO, detailing the purpose of the token, the problem it aims to solve, the team behind it, and the project's roadmap. Marketing and promotion play a crucial role in attracting potential investors.
- *Token sale.* During the ICO, investors can send cryptocurrencies to the project's designated wallet address and receive the corresponding amount of tokens based on the ICO's exchange rate.
- *Token distribution.* Once the ICO concludes, tokens are distributed to the investors' wallets. Some projects might have lockup or vesting periods for the tokens.
- *Listing on exchanges.* After the ICO, the project aims to get its tokens listed on cryptocurrency exchanges to enable trading.

- *Use of funds.* Funds raised during the ICO are used to develop the project, hire team members, conduct marketing, and achieve other milestones outlined in the project's roadmap.

It's important to note that while token presales and ICOs can be legitimate ways to raise funds for blockchain projects, they also carry risks.

Due to the lack of regulatory oversight and regulatory clarity, offering or participating in ICO is very risky. For investors, scams are many. We can think about the ICO mania of 2017–2018 where projects raised tens of millions before simply disappearing with the money.

For builders, ICOs are challenging due to the uncertain regulation. Is the investment an investment contract? Is it passing the Howey test? Meaning, *"Is it a security or utility?"*

Usually when doing an ICO, you simply perform a KYC process while blocking investors from the USA and sanctioned countries to avoid most of the problems. (None of this is legal advice. Consult a lawyer.)

HOW DOES IT TURN OUT? (IN MOST CASES)

The project raises a lot of money. During presale and ICO, people can get the token at a discounted price in comparison to the listing price during the future launch.

So for instance, people in the presale will get the token at $0.01 but are vested over 3 years, and during the ICO, people get it at $0.5 with a 6-month vesting. Then the token is listed at $1.

In theory, people from the presale have already made 100x their money (it's good to be an insider !) and ICO holders 2x their money. But they cannot sell immediately.

It's all depending on the vesting schedule and model.

- *Cliff Vesting.* In the cliff vesting model, there is a predetermined period called the *"cliff period"* during which no vesting occurs. After the cliff period expires, vesting begins, and a portion of the assets becomes available at regular intervals, usually on a monthly or quarterly basis. If an individual leaves the project or organization before the cliff period ends, they typically receive no vested assets. After the cliff period, they might receive a prorated portion of the vesting.

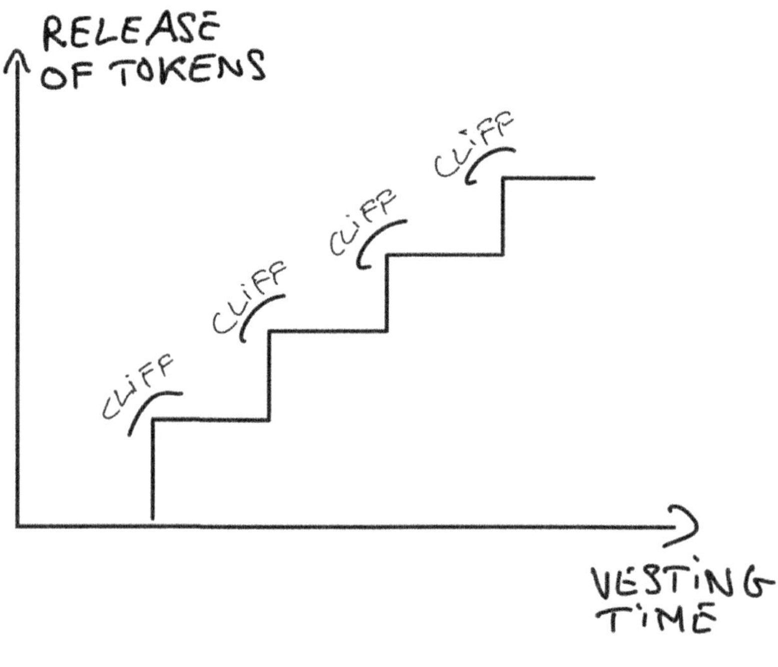

For example, consider a situation where an employee has a one-year cliff period and a four-year total vesting period with a monthly vesting schedule. After the first year, they would have a 25 percent ownership stake, and then an additional 1/48th (about 2.08 percent) would vest each month.

- *Linear Vesting.* In the linear vesting model, vesting occurs gradually over the entire vesting period without a cliff period. This means that assets become vested in equal portions at regular intervals throughout the entire vesting period.

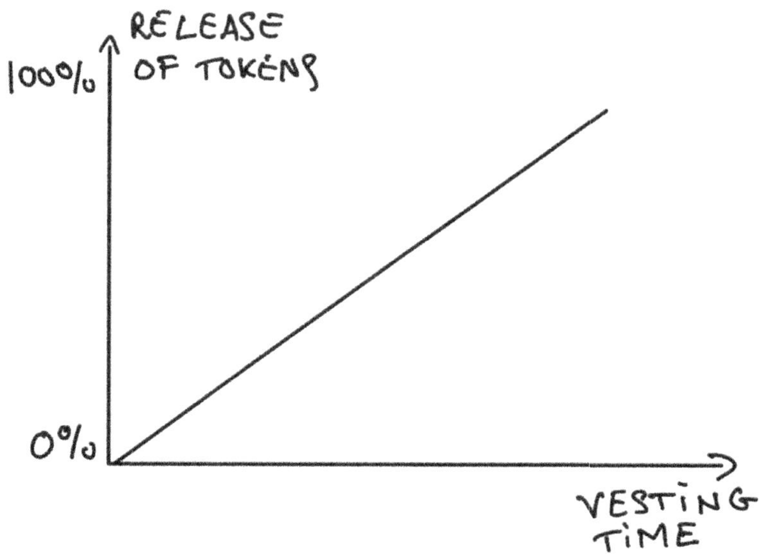

For instance, if an employee has a 4-year vesting period with a linear schedule, they might vest 25 percent of their assets each year. This differs from the cliff model, where there would be a waiting time before any vesting begins.

THE IDEAS ARE THE FOLLOWING:

- In the presale/ICO model, it's all about vesting. The cheaper you get the token, the longer you're vested.
- Vesting time, schedule, and cliff will affect the chart of your token. Whenever there is an unlock, you might see a huge dump.
- Insiders and VCs will always negotiate custom and preferential vesting schedules to have more flexibility to dump on other investors (you want to avoid this).
- Usually, it's expected that the team itself will be vested so the team cannot dump on the face of other vested holders.

Token Launch Strategy No. 2—DEX Fair Launch

A fair launch of a token, often referred to as a *"DEX fair launch,"* involves the introduction of a new token on a decentralized exchange (DEX) in a manner that aims to ensure fairness, accessibility, and transparency for all potential participants.

The big difference between the presale and ICO models is that with the DEX fair launch, investors don't buy the token from the project (or its founders) but from the decentralized exchanges. Founders and projects cannot control or know who buys the token.

This process is designed to prevent centralized control and manipulation, which can occur in traditional token launches or initial coin offerings (ICOs). A DEX fair launch seeks to align with the principles of decentralization and community-driven development.

Everyone will have the same chance to enter at the same moment on a coin. There is no VC allocation, no presale where insiders could get a better price, nothing. Just pure fairness (in theory).

THE COMMON FRAMEWORK

- *Build community and momentum.* You attract potential holders, gather them in Discord or Telegram, communicate on X.com, and book influencers to shill the launch.
- *Design.* You design your token, token name (or ticker) tokenomics, blockchain, etc.
- *Deployment.* You deploy your smart contract. Now your token is almost live. It exists, but it's not on a decentralized exchange, so no trading is possible for the moment.
- *Liquidity providing.* You provide liquidity on the DEX so it's possible to buy and sell the token. (More about this later.)
- *Announcement.* You announce it to the community while providing all the relevant links.
- *Trading.* The token pumps super hard because the liquidity is small in comparison to the trading volume. So the token can get up to 5x to 50x in a matter of minutes before having its first correction.

WHAT HAPPENS IN REALITY

- *Bot and tax.* In reality, bots are faster than anyone, and they buy instantly when you add liquidity. Then they dump on the holders coming from your community. A way to prevent this is to keep a buy tax super high until the announcement to the community. This way, most of the money bots invest goes to you. But you have to be sure you remove this tax before your community arrives.

  A friend of ours forgot to remove the tax on time, and the community got wiped out while he collected $4.9 million in fifteen minutes from the tax. Ultimately, he paid back the people, but the confusion and anger were huge.
- *Founder cronyism.* Founders usually try to enter before and/or give the contract address to their close friends before

sharing it with the community, giving them a time advantage over others.

- *Ultimate dump.* The danger with the fair launch is to have everyone buying and using their dry powder in the first minutes, then dumping. When the token starts to dump, panic spreads, nobody has the dry powder to *"buy the dip,"* and the token crashes. Once a token crashes by 90 percent (and especially in a ten-minute time span in a thirty-minute existence time), no one wants to buy it. You had a pump-and-dump. Now you're dead.

That's why we prefer the next strategy when it comes to launching a token the DEX fair launch way.

Token Launch Strategy No. 3—DEX Stealth Launch

This is our favorite strategy by far to launch a token.

THE STRATEGY IS VERY SIMILAR

1. *Design.* You design your token, token name (or ticker) tokenomics, blockchain, etc.
2. *Deployment.* You deploy your smart contract. Now your token is almost live. It exists, but it's not on a decentralized exchange, so no trading is possible for the moment.
3. *Liquidity providing.* You provide liquidity on the DEX so it's possible to buy and sell the token.
4. *Announcement.* No announcement.
5. *Trading.* Little to no trading (just some bots trading against each other).
6. *Build community and momentum.* Attract potential holders, gather them in Discord or Telegram, communicate on X.com, and book influencers to shill the launch.

The problem with the fair launch strategy is that all the marketing ammunition, all the dry powder, is accumulated before the launch. Everything is released at the same time, and fatally, the tokens pump-and-dump. When it dumps, there is nothing to save it, and that's the end of the token.

When the charts look like this, no one wants to enter:

What do people want?

A chart like this:

That's what you have with the DEX stealth launch strategy. You launch your token, and you tell . . . no one. Or very few people. Maybe you can let advisers or trusted members of your PayPal Mafia or loyal monk soldiers from a previous project know. Tell them to stay quiet and only buy a maximum of $1,000 (in several transactions). Don't get them excited. Tell them that the marketing will start in a week or so.

It's very okay to have nothing going on for a day and little to no trading volume. Then you start building the community, telling people about the product and the mission.

People will come progressively, buyers and holders both. There is no big hype, but people can feel that something is coming.

From now on, you deploy your marketing ammunition, day after day, and you make sure that you always have ammunition for the next few weeks. You don't rush things. You enjoy the fact that the community is still small enough to build a real culture and a shared vision about the project.

The DEX stealth launch combines the spirit of decentralization of the blockchain with a healthier approach to the token.

Token Launch Strategy No. 4—Token Soulbound Prelaunch

A soulbound token is a token that you cannot trade, sell, or transfer. It is there in your wallet, but there is not much you can do.

So what's the purpose? There are many purposes. For instance, to attribute characteristics or information about a wallet (by linking it to your CEX account and letting the IRS know that this decentralized wallet is yours).

In a friendlier fashion, the soulbound token is a way to reward early community members or users without having to think too much about tokenomics and commit to anything. You let people know that the soulbound token will give the wallet the right to buy or claim for free the real token when it's launched.

Why is it so interesting? Because token ownership makes people care about your stuff. People have skin in the game. They want to accumulate this token (especially knowing that they are early so the future upward price action might be life-changing).

DeFi protocol Morpho.xyz used this strategy. Users and contributors were rewarded with a soulbound token.

This strategy maximizes both the commitment of the token and the flexibility of the team. The team keeps the option open about strategy, tokenomics, choice of blockchains, etc.

Then it can do a presale and ICO model or a DEX launch. The DEX stealth launch is not an option since the awareness around the project is already huge at this point.

The Notion of DEX Liquidity Pool for Token (LP)

When people buy and sell on a DEX, they don't literally sell and buy to each other directly. As this book is about marketing and not super-deep technical automated market makers (AMM) things, I'll explain them quickly in a complicated way and less complicated way:

THE COMPLICATED WAY

In the context of decentralized exchanges (DEXs), liquidity pools and automated market makers (AMMs) are fundamental concepts that enable trading without relying on traditional order books and centralized intermediaries. They are key components of how DEX functions, allowing users to exchange cryptocurrencies directly with each other.

- *Liquidity pool.* A liquidity pool is a collection of funds (cryptocurrencies) locked into a smart contract on a decentralized exchange. These funds are used to facilitate trading by providing the necessary assets for users to trade against. Liquidity pools are essential because DEXes don't have the concept of a central order book like traditional exchanges. Instead, they rely on liquidity pools to match trades between users.

  When you provide funds to a liquidity pool, you are essentially becoming a liquidity provider. In return for providing liquidity, you earn a portion of the trading fees generated by the DEX. Liquidity providers deposit pairs of tokens, usually one of which is a stablecoin (like USDT or DAI) and the other Ethereum token they want to trade.

- *Automated Market Maker (AMM).* An AMM is a mathematical formula or algorithm used by DEXes to determine the price of assets in a liquidity pool based on the ratio of each token in the pool. The most common type of AMM is the constant product AMM, often associated with the formula $x \times y = k$ (where x and y represent the quantities of two tokens and k is a constant).

  When a trade occurs on a DEX that uses an AMM, the algorithm automatically adjusts the token balances in the liquidity pool to ensure that the constant product remains the same. As a result, larger trades cause more significant price slippage—meaning, the price of a token changes as the trade size increases due to the changing token ratios in the pool.

In summary, in a DEX using an AMM, the following can be observed:

- Users provide liquidity by depositing token pairs into a liquidity pool.
- Liquidity providers earn a share of trading fees.
- Trades are executed against the liquidity pool using the AMM's algorithm.
- Price is determined based on the constant product formula.
- Larger trades experience more price slippage due to changing token ratios.

AMMs and liquidity pools democratize trading by allowing anyone to participate as a liquidity provider and enabling decentralized trading without relying on a centralized order book. However, it's important to note that price slippage and impermanent loss (when the value of tokens in a liquidity pool changes over time) are inherent risks associated with providing liquidity to these pools.

THE LESS COMPLICATED WAY

- You need a liquidity pool on a DEX to trade a token. If you remove the pool, then trading becomes impossible, and people stay with their bags of tokens impossible to sell (it's called a rug). It's common for project founders to use a function to *"lock"* the liquidity pool to make the rug impossible.
- This pool is composed of a pair of two tokens: yours and a blue-chip token (usually ETH on the Ethereum blockchain, BNB on the Binance Smart Chain) or in some cases a stablecoin (USDT, for instance).
- The price of the token is determined by the pair in the liquidity. Let's say we have 1 token and 1 ETH in the pool, then your token is worth 1 ETH. Another example, we have 100 tokens and 100 USDT, then your token is worth $1.
- People trade against the pool, not directly against other people. The pool adapts to the buying and selling. If now we have 50 tokens and 100 USDT, the new price of your token is $2.
- The bigger the pool, the more stable the price is. If there is a pair of 1,000 tokens and 2 ETH on a pool and someone wants to buy 20 ETH worth of tokens, the price impact will be huge (so the price will skyrocket and the buyer will get fewer tokens than he usually thought).
- Anyone can become a liquidity provider for the pair of tokens composing the pool in the DEX. When you provide liquidity to a pair, the DEX gives you LP tokens. You can transfer and do many things with these LP tokens, but if you lose them, you can't remove your tokens from the liquidity pool. While you provide liquidity, the DEX is paying you for your contribution (part of the trading fees are going to you).

In case you wonder, you don't have this problem with NFTs. Tokens (with LP), you can always sell. NFTs, you need somebody to make you an offer or buy them instantly.

How to Get Listed on a Centralized Exchange (CEX)?

Centralized exchanges are places like Coinbase, KuCoin, or Binance where people can send fiat money (aka stuff printed in unlimited amounts by the government), buy, and trade tokens. They offer a much easier user experience than a DEX. Also, they usually have a lot of liquidity, so price changes are lower and people with more money can easily buy.

For traders and whales, they also offer the benefit of less transparency. You cannot track individual wallets on a centralized exchange.

CEX also offers the possibility to founders to sell tokens more discreetly than on a DEX, where the community can track any movement. It's common for founders to have deals with CEX to sell tokens for them.

Finally, being listed on a CEX is a strong sign of credibility. CEX does due diligence before listing anything. Surprisingly enough, people in the decentralized world are super happy when a centralized institution (a CEX) validates a project. It means to them that this project has legitimacy and is probably not a scam.

So how do you get your token listed on a CEX?

OPTION 1—YOU PAY

The first option is quite straightforward. CEXes are service providers. They earn money on trading fees.

But adding tokens means compliance, costs, and risks. So if your token doesn't have massive traction, CEX will ask you to pay to get listed. It can go from $50,000 to $1 million, depending on market conditions (it's more expensive during bulls) and the traction of your project (numbers of holders, trading volumes, etc.). There are agencies specialized in getting your project listed on a CEX.

OPTION 2—YOU HAVE MASSIVE TRACTION

Let's assume now that after reading all the chapters of this book, your token has a huge success, daily trading volumes are in millions or tens of millions, and everyone is talking about it.

Then you might wake up one day with your token listed on Binance or another major CEX without you having any knowledge of it. It happens. But it's not common.

WHAT ABOUT INCUBATORS AND SUPPORT PROGRAMS?

It's common for CEX to have programs to support new and promising Web3 projects. Usually, it's a CEX that owns their blockchain like Coinbase with BASE, Binance with the BSC, or Crypto.com with the CRONOS.

They want to attract as much liquidity and traction as possible to their chain. So it makes sense for them to support projects with huge potential. Nevertheless, being supported and helped by these programs doesn't mean they are going to list you on their CEX. It can help, but don't expect it.

HOW TO RANK CEX?

There are no official rankings for the best or the most serious CEX. They don't operate in the same jurisdiction nor have the same strategies. But here is a list that is commonly accepted:

TIER 1	TIER 2	TIER 3
COINBASE	BITFINEX	YOBIT
KRAKEN	HUOBI	BITMART
BINANCE	BITTREX	COINEX
GEMINI	KUCOIN	GATE.IO
	OKEX	EXMO
	BITSTAMP	HOTBIT
		COINBENE
		LATOKEN
		CEX.IO

Key Takeaways

- *The Presale Strategy.* Early investors and team members get tokens at a discount in exchange for being vested (they cannot sell immediately). The public buys the token once trading is live and hopes the insiders are vested long enough to make a profit.
- *ICO Strategy.* Investors can send cryptocurrencies to the project's designated wallet address and receive the corresponding token amount based on the ICO's exchange rate. Risks are little regulatory oversight, and participating can be very risky.
- *The DEX Fair Launch Strategy.* You build momentum and announce your token launch. This is a high-pressure environment. If your community runs out of powder to *"buy the dip,"* your token chart might be ruined forever.
- *The DEX Stealth Launch Strategy.* Our favorite launch method. You launch in silence with no hype or no announcement. Now you can slowly deploy your marketing strategy to build up the token.
- *The Token Soulbound Prelaunch Strategy.* Soulbound tokens are nontradeable. It allows you to get the project going without overthinking about tokenomics while rewarding early users.

Typologies of Launches for NFT

I connected my wallet, and it got drained.

—Somebody spreading FUD during your NFT mint

WIIFM

In this chapter, we will go through the different launch strategies for NFTs.

NFT was one of the big stories of the 2020–2021 bull run with the world discovering this technology and the art associated with it. Millions of people saw these little BAYC monkey JPEGs or CryptoPunks.

Most people haven't grasped the transformative nature of NFT, but millions, if not tens of millions, got a free awareness campaign about NFT.

Sadly enough, NFT scams or batched NFT projects brought more people to crypto and DeFi than blue-chip projects and serious Web3 educators. Instagram and TikTok influencers made NFT go mainstream whereas DeFi and tokens stayed too niched and hard to handle.

The three big NFT launch strategies are the following:

- The Big Mint Day
- The Dutch Auction
- The Nouns Auction

NFT Launch Strategy No. 1—The Big Mint Day

The traditional Big Mint Day is the following:

One specific day, at a specific hour, mint is open. The supply is limited (4,000 to 10,000 NFTs). Hype is (hopefully) huge. Mint price is high ($500 to $2,000 per NFT). The NFT collection is sold out in a matter of minutes. And founders buy Lambos, Richard Mille watches, and real estate in Dubai the next morning. Sort of.

SO HOW DOES IT WORK?

1. *Community building.* Everything starts with a strong community, core values, and codes. Art is teased, roadmap is teased, utilities are teased. The goal is to gather tens of thousands of potential buyers in a Discord server.

2. *Pressure accumulation.* When you do a Big Mint Day strategy, you need to sell out the whole collection on the day of the mint. To achieve this, FOMO has to be at its peak.
3. *Whitelisting process* (optional). In some cases, some users are whitelisted to be able to mint before the other one and hence have a 100 percent certainty of people able to get one NFT. To be whitelisted, users have to perform tasks for the project (referrals, for instance).
4. *Big Mint Day.* The big day has arrived, pressure is huge, FOMO is absolute, and the whole community is focused and waiting for this moment. Future buyers hope to get their hand on the new Bored Ape blue-chip NFT.
5. *Hype maintenance.* The mint was successful, and now everyone is asking, *"Now what?"* You need to deploy your marketing, roadmap, and partnership and start shipping things before the hype cools down.

THE RISKS

- *Not selling out.* If the collection is not sold out on the day of the mint, the launch is seen as a failure, and everyone leaves the project faster than when they arrived. The project becomes suddenly radioactive. There are a few cases where a project failed on the mint day due to technical issues and was rescheduled to achieve success. The fact that it's a technical failure and not a lack of demand is what saves the project.
- *Pump-and-dump.* All the buying pressure is released at a specific moment (like a bottle of champagne that you vigorously shake before opening). Most people came to buy and flip the NFT to earn a quick profit. The price of the NFT goes to the moon before collapsing while further demand fails to catch up, and the expectation of believers is way higher than the ability of the team to deliver something big in time.

To conclude, it's very profitable to launch this kind of NFT if the market conditions are fine, but usually, it ends rapidly in blood. As we saw in the chapter *"The Science of Scarcity,"* a supply of 5,000 or 10,000 NFT is in most cases too large for sustainable future growth.

NFT Launch Strategy No. 2—The Dutch Auction

The Dutch Auction is quite similar to the Big Mint Day, but it plays with people's nerves. The steps are similar, and so are the risks. What's interesting is the mint mechanism.

In a Dutch Auction, the starting price for the NFT is set very high, and it gradually decreases over time until a buyer is willing to purchase the NFT at the current price.

HERE'S HOW A DUTCH AUCTION FOR NFTS WORKS

- *Start price.* The auction begins with a high starting price that is typically above the expected market value of the NFT.
- *Descending price.* The price of the NFT gradually decreases over time. This can be done using a predetermined schedule or algorithm.
- *First bid wins.* The first bidder who is willing to buy the NFT at the current price wins the auction and obtains ownership of the NFT.
- *Dynamic timing.* Dutch Auctions are time-based. The auction ends either when a bidder accepts the current price or when a predetermined time limit is reached.

No one wants to buy first because it's more expensive. But no one wants to wait too long and not get an NFT. Rich people will go first (like on the *Titanic* when it comes to getting a lifeboat, but I'm not sure the analogy is helpful) because they can afford it and don't want to wait.

The risk here is to price the NFT too high at the beginning and have the community reject the offer and label it as a cash grab. Also, it's complicated, and complicated things often don't work or face problems (technical for instance). More broadly, people might have the feeling that you're playing with their nerves, and this mint model might have to be justified. At the end of the day, if the hype is huge, it'll work.

NFT Launch Strategy No. 3—The Nouns Auction

Let's move to our favorite NFT collection and tokenomics of all time. We mentioned it already in the chapter *"The Science of Scarcity."* This model is a perfect harmonization between the interests of the community and the founders while offering the potential to be long-lasting.

HERE IS THE MODEL:

- Each day, one and only one NFT is auctioned. The highest bidder is minting the NFT.
- All the money goes to a treasury managed by the holders through a DAO (i.e., money does not go into the pocket of the founders).
- Founders make money by receiving one NFT every nine mints. They are incentivized to maintain and grow the project over time because there is no magical Big Day Mint money here.
- Each new holder can join the community and engage with current holders.
- The project can build the community day after day along with daily mint. You don't need to accumulate a lot of pressure before a big mint. You simply build up the demand and pressure while developing the project. The money arriving (almost) each day on the DAO is offering financial resources to spend on marketing.

  The risks are quite limited here. It's just less appealing for people who are here for the fast money and the quick buck (whether they are founders or speculators).

These are not the only strategies. Many other scenarios could be thought of. Ultimately, it's the job of founders and marketers to come up with ideas and concepts that very few people have thought about before them.

People crave novelty and stimulation. Doing new things is expected in the NFT world if you want to stay relevant.

As Frank DeGods said in a conversation with Kevin Rose on the PROOF podcast, *"The name of the game in NFT is capturing attention and building 'magical internet experiences.'"*

Key Takeaways

- Big Mint Days can generate a lot of money in one day if you manage to generate a lot of hype. If not, then your project is dead the next day. If there is enough hype, you need to be fast enough to maintain hype, ship features, and try to make holders happy, in order not to drown in a FUD.
- Dutch Auctions are very similar to Big Mint Days. The price gets lower over time until the collection is sold.
- The Nouns Auction (our favorite method) is a perfect harmonization between the interests of the community and founders while offering a long-lasting potential. Every day you mint one NFT, the highest bidder wins, and ever tenth NFT goes to the founders' wallet.

Influencer Marketing in Web3

Hey, bro, just send me 10 ETH, and I will help you to sell out.

—Wannabe Web3 influencer

WIIFM

Long story short: influencer marketing doesn't really work. But there are a few powerful moves you can make. Read now.

Web3 opened a new chapter in the history of influencer marketing where influencers were pumping and dumping coins, shilling NFT, and amassing millions of degens ready to buy anything they mentioned.

But . . . what's influencer marketing? A company looks for an individual who enjoys the trust of the masses and borrows the trust in the hope of generating more sales.

Rolex did this for the first time in the 1920s when they put a watch around the wrist of Mercedes Gleitze, who became the first British woman to swim the English Channel.

Later, Phil Knight was the first one to roll out a series of exclusive endorsement contracts with key athletes such as Michael Jordan, LeBron James, Christiano Ronaldo, and many others. Knight created Nike.

But . . . why not influence people directly? Paul Lazarsfeld developed a study that answers this question in the 1940s called *"two-step flow of communication."* It states that communities are influenced by trusted opinion leaders (or influencers) and not mass media directly. Whatever the opinion leader says is true . . . is true. So if you want to reach or change the opinion of communities, you first need to convince the opinion leaders.

Let's look at how this works in Web3 and how you can use influencers to your advantage.

The Web3 Influencer Paradox

Let's get straight to the point here.

There are two kinds of Web3 influencers:

FAKE INFLUENCERS

Influencers who accept to get paid $500 to promote any stuff. But after a while, everyone knows that they are just paid to shill stuff they don't believe in. As a consequence, their word is worth nothing, and paying them is useless. Most of their audience is bots anyway. Engagement is faked to continue scamming rookie founders into paying $500 for a tweet or a story. Let's call them *"fake influencers."*

REAL INFLUENCERS

The paradox is that you can't pay them to promote your stuff. It's because they refuse to promote stuff that they stay credible. Their audience is loyal to them because of this.

They genuinely can influence people, thanks to the trust they have accumulated. You can't pay them to promote your Web3 project. Usually, they prefer to talk about projects they love, use, or are part of (as a member or as an insider investor).

THE FAKE INFLUENCER STRATEGY

So you might ask, why are projects still paying influencers to talk about their project?

That's very simple. You hire influencers to show to your existing community that the project is hot, that people with large followings (or bots) are talking about it, and that it's big. **Most of the influencer marketing spending is about keeping the existing members hyped. It's not bringing directly new members**. Nevertheless, hype and enthusiasm are contagious. So the energy in your community and around your project will bring in new members.

It's 80 percent hype maintenance and 20 percent indirect growth.

The key lies in the indirect growth element. Even if the influencer is fake, there still might be part of his audience that is somehow qualified for your offer.

If you offer sticks, people will start talking about it, recommending it to your friends, and eventually, a real influencer might notice you and reach out to you.

Strategy No. 1—Make Your PayPal Mafia Say, *"By the Way, This Is Cool."*

Remember a few chapters ago when we were discussing your PayPal Mafia (aka your network of builders, entrepreneurs, creators, and all sorts of crazy but capable people)?

Well, now that we've understood that working with influencers is kind of a dead end, we turn to the most valuable asset in Web3. Your network.

But you don't ask them to shill or talk about your project.

Instead, you do the following:

- Ask for feedback about the products, the tokenomics, and the strategy. If the person is interested and stimulated by your project, maybe they will offer to become a strategic adviser.
- Airdrop or offer whitelists to your network to advertise the generosity of your project.
- Check if their community or network would have a use for your project, if it might resonate with them, or if it might contribute to their work and project.

Basically, you don't ask directly for money. You don't ask for exposure. You don't ask for anything (except feedback). Instead, you offer, you give, you contribute.

The more people you help, the more useful you are, the better you can leverage your network. **Building a network is all about giving a lot and asking very little**.

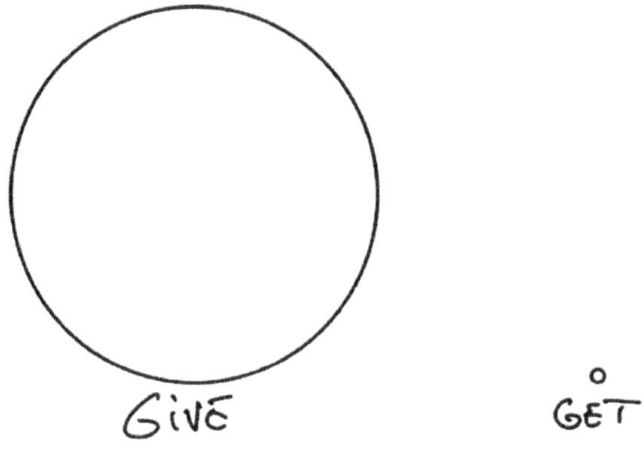

So when the time comes to get some help, introductions, feedback, and traction, people are indebted to you. Which brings us to the **prin-**

ciple of reciprocity. It's a psychological concept popularized by Dr. Robert Cialdini in his book *Influence: The Psychology of Persuasion.* It refers to the social norm and tendency that humans have to want to repay or reciprocate favors, gifts, or acts of kindness that they receive from others. In essence, when someone does something nice for us, we often feel a sense of obligation to do something nice in return.

YOU HAVE A THREE-STEP PROCESS:

1. You pay it forward every week with or without a project. You just increase your reciprocity balance.
2. You introduce your PayPal Mafia to your concept and get them excited about it (see *"The Science of Common Sense"* chapter for instance).
3. You turn them into long-term soft supporters of the project.

What is a long-term soft supporter of a project? It's someone with an audience that is mentioning the project without shilling it. It could be something like, *"Oh, by the way, use the tool X to do Y."* It is much more impactful to have a legit person say, *"By the way this stuff is cool"* (without any link) than to have a professional shiller getting paid to copy and paste some message for an audience of bots.

The more you have credible people just mentioning your project or product without sales vocabulary (*revolutionary*, *new*, *extreme*, *profit*, etc.), the better.

The goal here is for the key individuals in your network to just enjoy what you do and have skin in the game (by holding tokens for instance). Then they'll naturally support it, maybe mention it, or at least make some introductions for you.

Strategy No. 2—Turn Small, Excited Content Creators into *"Orbiting Influencers"* (or Orbiters)

We developed the notion of orbiting influencers by looking closer at Terra Luna when the project was still cruising to the moon and something caught our attention. A small group of specialized influencers were growing at the same pace as Luna. They were people on X.com and YouTube discussing the project, the DAO proposals, the votes, the innovations, and the tokenomics.

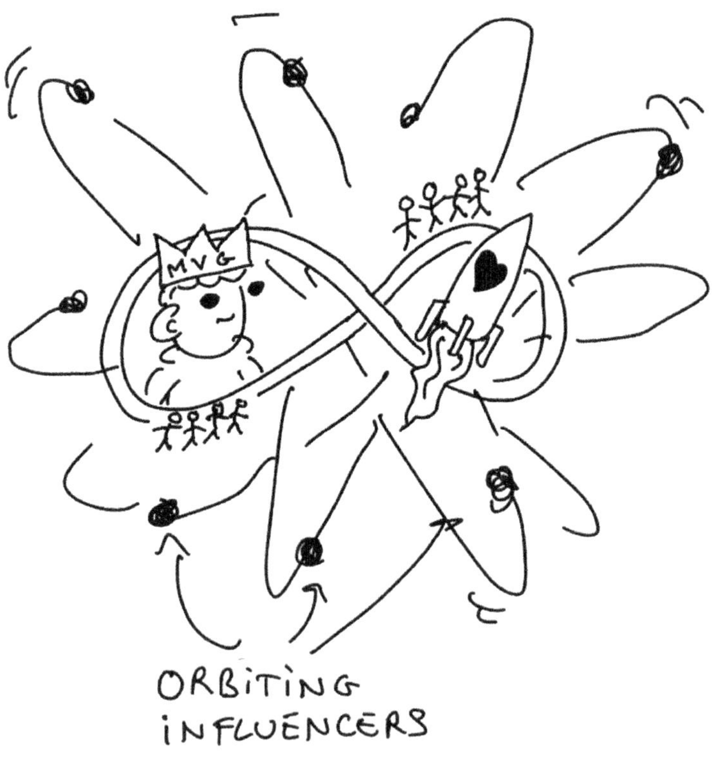

Ninety percent of their content was about the Terra Luna ecosystem (Terra Luna, Anchor Protocol, and other projects). They would invite and interview each other and talk for hours about voting proposals for Anchor Protocol and technical matters. Very soon, the best way to understand and get fresh updates about Terra Luna was through these influencers and not through the official channels of the project. These people also contributed to gathering and bonding the community behind Luna, better known as the *"Lunatics"* (one of the most vibrant and degenerate Web3 communities out there . . . even after the collapse).

This is how we came to this concept of *"orbiting influencers."* The important notion here is that the MVG behind the project, the project, and the orbiting influencers are growing all together hand in hand.

HOW YOU CAN ATTRACT ORBITING INFLUENCERS FOR YOUR PROJECT: THE ICBM METHOD

1. **Identify** a list of small content creators and MVGs in your niche. Try to find thirty to forty. Don't focus on the number of followers. Look for small creators with a good vibe and good values.
2. **Connect** with them, and pitch them the project. Don't ask them to mention or shill the project. Don't treat them like an influencer to pay. Talk about building a relationship and getting feedback from them and their community. Talk about helping and building together. Share your passion and your vision. See what you can bring to their community.
3. **Bond** with those who click with the project. Give them weekly updates and insights, and airdrop them some free tokens. Try to call them instead of simply writing. Interview them in front of your community (if it's relevant) to give them some traction and recognition. Retweet and share a

lot of their content to your community. Give more than you want to get from them.

4. **Multiply**. If your project is relevant and well designed, a percentage of these creators will first mention your project here and there. Then they'll update the community more often about your recent developments. Ultimately, they have updates and content about your project every week of the month. Your community will come to them to get information about your project. You invite them for AMA sessions and take into account their ideas for the project.

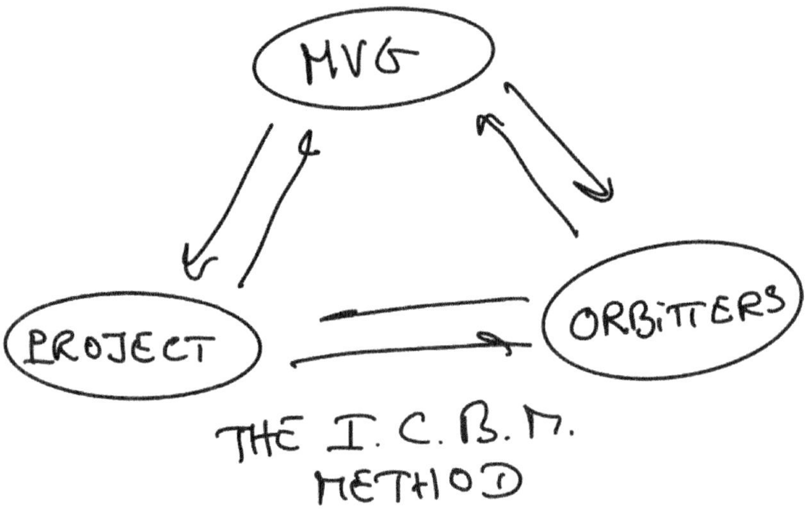

Your MVG account, the profile of your project, and the orbiters will all grow together.

Strategy No. 3—Become *"So Good (and Loud) They Can't Ignore You"* (Leverage FU Army)

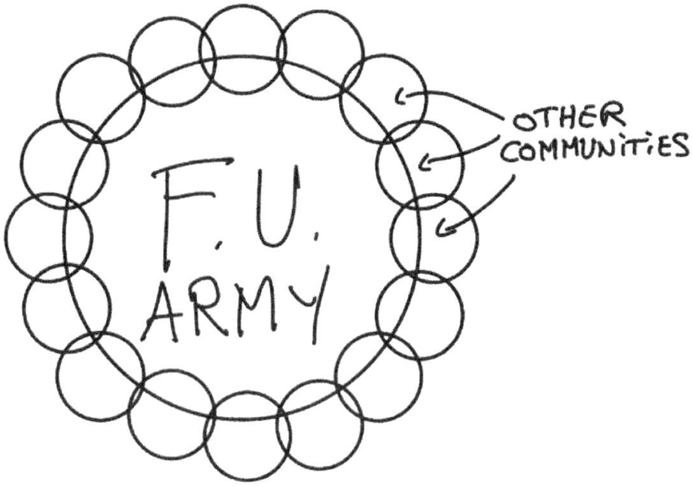

The third strategy is the most simple but the hardest to deploy. Your product and the FU Army around you have to be so good (product) and so loud (army) that it's impossible to ignore you.

Understand this: People in your FU Army who also follow other projects and MVGs collectively interact with hundreds, if not thousands, of people daily. They are also followed or viewed by community members, holders, and founders of other projects. Sooner or later, they'll notice you.

We know that enthusiasm is contagious. The more you innovate and grow, the better you market. The more efficiently is your FU Army organized, the harder it will be to ignore you.

There is this famous sentence in the propaganda business: *"**You can't decide what people think, but you can decide what they think about.**"* You can make sure that they think about you. We're in the attention economy. As Frank DeGods would say, *"The name of the* *game is capturing attention."* You have to become the most discussed topic in your niche.

Strategy No. 4—Small Is Beautiful

If you decide to walk down the road of community collabs or influencer collaborations, prioritize working with small groups.

Usually, the smaller the group, the bigger the commitment to the leader. Remember the Olson paradox? In Web2, people also call these microinfluencers. In Web3, this usually comes in the form of small, and very niche, alpha groups. A Telegram alpha group with ten users can be much stronger than a Discord channel with over ten thousand. Therefore, look at the subtle places.

The big players are usually too arrogant, expensive, or annoying to work with anyhow.

Go for the crumbs to secure partnerships at lower costs and with a longer time horizon. How do you find them? Ask your soldiers and mods which communities they are a part of or which ones they love.

Key Takeaways

- The influencer paradox—you can't pay real influencers to work with you. Opinion leaders only talk about projects they love or that they're part of.
- Fortunately, your fate does not depend on influencers who are selling their souls for a couple of tokens. Have your PayPal Mafia talk about the project. Attract *"orbiting influencers."* Or be so good and loud that they can't ignore you.
- Most of the influencer marketing spending is about keeping the existing members hyped. It's not bringing directly new members.

The Tugan Method

Yes, I gave it my own name. Deal with it.

—Tugan Bara

WIIFM

The Tugan Method was thought of as a method to make money in Web3 without investing your own money. Basically, help and contribute to existing projects in exchange for tokens. But it's also something you can leverage as a founder to create a little army of die-hard fans promoting your project and spreading your vision.

The Tugan Method has been invented as a way to train hundreds of people to support a project while giving Web3 enthusiasts a less risky way to make money.

The letters in the Tugan Method come from *target*, *understand*, *grow*, *advocate*, and *negotiate*.

Let me explain the method not from the perspective of a founder but as a Web3 enthusiast.

BEFORE WE START, HERE ARE SOME DISCLAIMERS:

- *Disclaimer 1. In case you wonder, yes, naming the method Tugan while being called Tugan is a casual ego trip. Now that it's been said, let's move forward.*
- *Disclaimer 2. The following is written from a user perspective but can be adapted easily from the project owner's perspective.*

T for *Target* . . . Many Projects

You start with researching Web3 projects that fall under the following criteria:

- Less than 1,000 holders
- A market cap below 50 million (if it's a token)
- With an early product release or active development
- Target tech projects, platforms, or protocols answering a demand, or solving a problem, because these will thrive (and you will make money) in the long run

No short-term *"shitcoin"* or *"profile picture NFT"* with zero innovation. Play the long-term game. Contribute to a better world, not to a cash grab. It's okay if it's a fork of a popular project on a different blockchain (usually it's a good target).

You can research these projects using Coingecko.com, Mobula.fi, Producthunt.com, or Smoothie.so.

At the end of this stage, you must have identified and targeted ten to twenty-five projects fitting these criteria. You mustn't jump on the first idea.

U for *Understand* . . . In-Depth

For each target project, join the community and understand the culture, the things they stand for, and the big things that add to the world. Same for the founding team. Ask them why they do what they do. Whom are they competing with?

Understand the vibe of the community and the needs of the project. Ask yourself these questions: Are they good at marketing? Are they missing to address a key segment of the target demographic? Are they missing out on some communities, languages, and audiences? Identify their communication channels and the communication channels that are not developed.

Check also the tokenomics and the whitepaper. Make sure to understand the stage of development they're in and if the team can build things.

At the end of this stage, you choose from one to three projects to work with and contribute to.

G for *Grow* . . . Hard-Core

The core idea here is to grow while you help grow. Create social accounts, or use your current ones (if they don't doxx your real identity or personal information about you). Build your MVG following the rules of the dedicated chapter in section 3 of the book, and be present on multiple networks (X.com, TikTok, YouTube). Make sure to have the same profile picture on all social accounts so people know that it's you.

From now on, the game is to be hyperactive, to participate, and to create even more. The goal is to give some love and traction to the project. Capitalize on the *"exposure effect,"* which suggests that the more we are exposed to something or someone, the more likely we are to develop a preference or positive attitude toward it to become a known figure within the community. Create your profile page on Side.xyz, and add it to your bio or under (or at the end of) your content.

SOME TACTICS TO HELP THE PROJECT GROW

1. Be present each day in the Discord or Telegram group of the project, and contribute. People have to see your face and your name.
2. Write a Medium.com article after each AMA to summarize the key points (you can translate it into different languages using ChatGPT).
3. Write a thread after AMAs to summarize the key questions asked and the team's answer.
4. Record videos (even without showing your face) about product updates, vision, and milestones. You can use Loom.com for free and post on YouTube.
5. Create short-form videos from the videos and interviews of founders (if applicable), and post them on Instagram or TikTok.
6. Record your screen while discussing X.com threads and official posts from the project or its founders.
7. Retweet founders and the project. But don't retweet only giveaways.
8. Follow and interact with as many people as possible who interact with the project on social media. Become their friends. Ask questions.
9. Translate marketing content and update announcements (even whitepaper) in different languages. One of the strategies is actually to become the go-to guy for everything about the project in a specific language.

But **do not shill and promote aggressively (or stupidly) the project.** Don't write everywhere that it's a *"revolution,"* that it's *"new"* or *"better,"* that everyone will *"make money,"* or that it'll *"go to the moon"* unless the team is okay with this. Don't talk negatively about competing projects and communities. Don't just copy and paste links to the project below other people's posts.

You have to create and contribute to a good vibe. **You need to add value and not only be loud**. You have to teach people why the project is going to be huge but without exaggerations and extreme vocabulary that will make you sound like a shiller or some early 2000s internet scam.

A for *Advocate* . . . For the Project

At this stage, anywhere the people of the community go, they see you. Founders and teams start to build a relationship with you. **Slowly, you've become part of the team. Community members check your content to stay updated about the project.** Most projects suck at marketing, and you're reading this book right now, so you're probably better than most of the marketing teams of Web3 products.

If you push a little bit harder, you will become the indirect spokesperson and ambassador of the project outside the community. People outside the community looking for information about the project will arrive and maybe ask you questions directly. Especially if founders are not easy to reach (usually they're not). You advocate for the project.

At this stage, **usually, the team offers you a role in the project**. For instance, to be a moderator. It's not huge, but it's a good start. It is a sign that they have identified you and they trust you. Depending on your skills, the goal would be to have a more active role in the project. Don't ask for it too fast. You build your following and content. Now you need to build a relationship with the founders.

At this stage, **don't ask for money, don't be greedy.** Give before you get it.

N for *Net Worth* . . . Because Someone Has to Pay the Rent

The endgame is, of course, to get paid in tokens of the project. The more you can accept tokens, the better. Use all the stablecoins you have to pay for your lifestyle and accumulate bags silently. If it's during the bear market, it's even better (but we have no idea in which market condition you'll read this book).

Let's take a few examples. Let's imagine you successfully applied this strategy with the Fantom (FTM) blockchain during the 2018–2020 bear market:

Getting paid, let's say, $4,000 worth of tokens over a few months during the deep of the bear market would have been worth around $500,000 at ATH. If you contribute a lot, you can expect to get more than $4,000. Let's say $10,000 over the year (exclusively paid in token). It would be around $1,250,000 at the ATH.

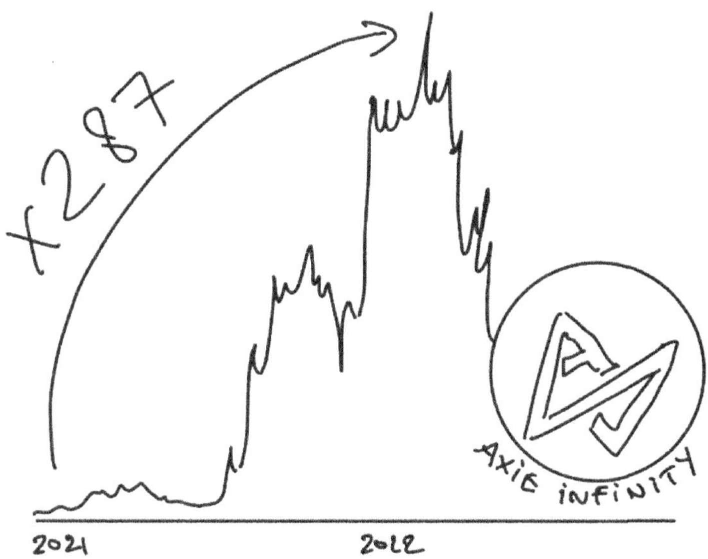

$4,000 in Axie would have been $1,150,000 at the ATH.

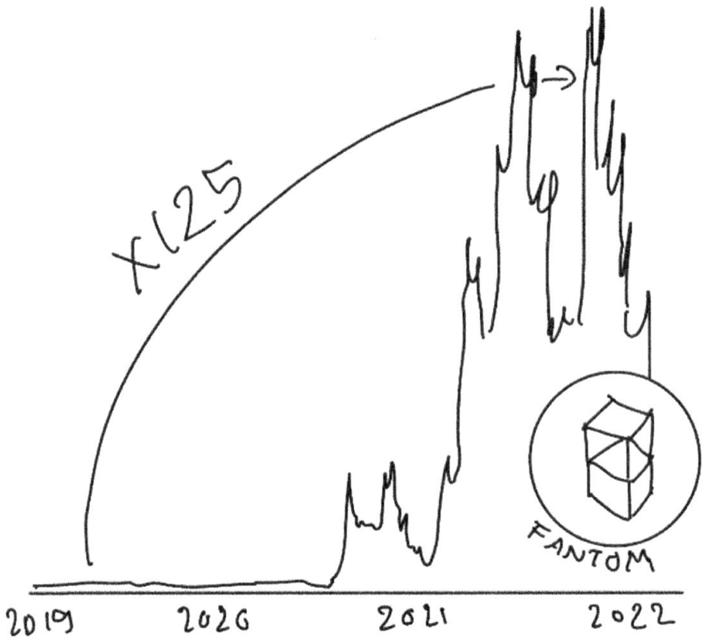

$4,000 in $CHZ would have been $330,000 at the ATH.

Don't get me wrong, the Tugan Method is tough. It requires work ethics and consistency (something 99 percent of people in the world lack). **It's about understanding the long game, the fact of giving and building before getting** (and actually without the certainty of getting anything one day).

You're risking your time on a project, and time is valuable. But building your MVG and skills while connecting with communities and founders sounds like a good investment of some of your time.

How to Leverage the Tugan Method as a Marketer and Founder

Basically, you take your existing community and start at stage *G* (for *grow*). In Web2, it's called UGC (for *user-generated content*). So how do you organize this from a project's perspective? I'll show you how we did with our *"Siders"* on Side.xyz.

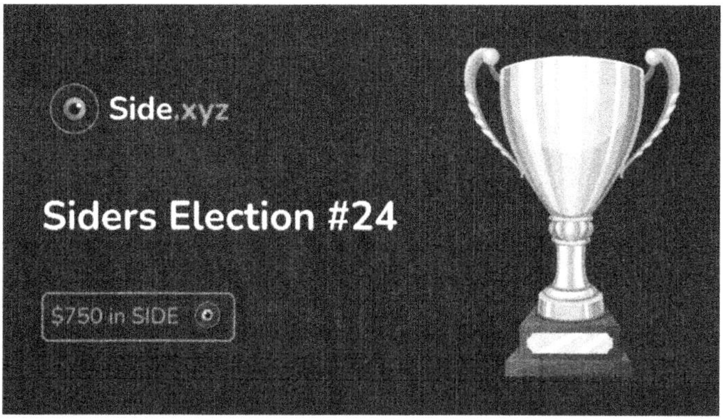

FIRST, DEFINE A VERY FAIR AND TRANSPARENT INCENTIVE STRUCTURE

For instance, how much token you're ready to give to contributors and why. On Side.xyz, we started with $250 worth of tokens to be shared among ten Siders every week at the start. Then while the number of Siders grew, we increased this number week after week.

At this stage, you need to clarify two things:

- Yes, the number of tokens you're giving is not much, but the project has a chance if we work all together to do a 100x or more in the future (this is not financial advice). A chance is not a certainty. Be precise and transparent about this. Never overpromise, or your contributors will turn against you.
- Yes, special MVG having a higher contribution to the project could get some custom deals in the future. It's important that people know that if they grow fast and big, they can get much more. But first, they have to put in the work.

We also added special bonuses (paid in $Side tokens) to Siders reaching specific numbers of followers or completing the one-week boot camp to build their MVG.

SECOND, SUPPORT AND SHOW APPRECIATION TO YOUR CONTRIBUTORS

With the Siders, we're doing one live call a week to give feedback on their work, update them about the project, and teach them Web3 marketing.

We also have one full-time person coaching the team and answering their questions. A graphic designer is also hired by Side.xyz to create professional visual identities of Siders. Active Siders are also getting free access to my copywriting tool Tugan.ai.

Contributors have to feel that even if they're beginners, you value their work and contribution. **You have to show your appreciation.** For instance, the project can share or retweet content done by the contributors. It's a way to push them forward while recognizing their work publicly.

THIRD, PROVIDE THEM WITH MARKETING MATERIAL, WEEKLY CONTENT, AND PRECISE TEMPLATES

Each week you can give them talking points and ideas about content creation. You have to give them ready-to-repurpose templates and ideas for content creation.

Don't assume they'll come up with ideas on their own. Some will, but most won't. Something we've noticed is that most people don't have an instinct for good content ideas. They don't naturally know what to talk or to write about. Nor do they know what is really interesting and what is not.

To solve this, the project's team has to **provide them with materials and templates** they can use. There are two kinds of content:

- *Contextual content*—shipping on a new feature, DAO vote, bipartnership announcement, etc.
- *Immutable content*—things that stay true week after week, for instance, the vision, the mission, the tokenomics, information from the whitepaper, and details about the art or the business model.

Key Takeaways

- Microinvestors don't get rich by investing. They get rich by using their time.
- From a user perspective, the Tugan Method works the following: target projects with a market cap of less than $50 million and less than a thousand holders.
- Understand the community, culture, whitepaper, and what the team stands for. Choose one to three projects to work with.
- Grow by being active in the community, summarizing AMAs, and writing threads about recent developments, RT founders, and the project.
- Advocate for the project. Become an indirect spokesperson or an ambassador for the project.
- The goal is to get paid in the token of the project. Instead of accepting stablecoins, ask for a token airdrop. Four thousand dollars in Axie would have been $1,150,000 during the bull market.

The Viral Loop

Most people buy NFTs that they get referred to by someone they trust (friend, group chat, influencer, etc.)

—Frank DeGods

WIIFM

The notion of virality is where you separate the businessmen from the wannabes. Every newbie thinks, *"Oh, you just need to go viral, and then everything else is easy."* But you don't decide what goes viral and what doesn't. Nevertheless, this chapter will give you a few keys to spread faster.

You cannot decide if a product or a piece of content will go viral. Virality is not something you decide by decree. It's something that happens to you.

"Viral content" or *"viral growth tactics"* are buzzwords that are thrown around by every online marketer and agency owner. And **while there are ways to increase the odds of virality, it's not something you can predict.**

Nevertheless, your goal here is to **create a cycle where existing users bring in new users, who then, in turn, do the same**. This continues until you reach viral growth.

In some cases, they love the product and community so much that they talk about it without thinking about any rewards. In other cases, there are incentive mechanisms to invite people. We will see in this chapter how referrals usually backfire in Web3.

Before we get started . . .

Agencies cannot do on-demand viral marketing. **Anyone who tells you that they are a *"viral marketer"* and can blow up your idea by adding a *"marketing feature"* is lying to you.** A viral product is built by product decision. The product's core use case must be inherently viral.

Viral Loop and K-Factor

A viral loop is a mechanism that enables exponential growth of a product, service, or idea through word-of-mouth and social sharing.

Virality is a complex concept that is hard to grasp or visualize. One metric that comes close to giving a satisfactory result is the viral coefficient (K-factor).

$$K = N * C$$

K-factor = (number of invitations sent by each user) × (conversion rate of invitations)

A K-factor greater than one indicates that the content or product has the potential to go viral because each user is bringing in more than one new user on average.

Crypto Is Virality by Default

Web3 is a gigantic marketing campaign.

Non-crypto holders think an average day in this universe looks like this:

Some token with a strange name goes up 10,000% and turns a seventeen-year-old teenager from Nigeria into a multimillionaire.

Five minutes later, somebody loses access to his Bitcoin wallet that he created in 2007 and therefore loses access to hundreds of millions of dollars.

You probably know the quote *"There is no such thing as bad publicity."* Even if Bitcoin goes down 30 percent because of the tweet of Elon Musk, the media keeps talking about it, which in turn brings more eyeballs to Web3. **The more the price goes up, or down, the more Web3 wins.**

CURRENCY AND VIRALITY

The good news is that virality is one of the core features of crypto. If you think about crypto as currencies and not assets, a currency is social by nature. A currency bonds people and enables transactions.

Whenever someone asks, *"Do you accept Bitcoin?"* he is advertising crypto. It's creating new awareness, interest, and adoption.

The currency feature, even if imperfect, is expanding the Web3 ecosystem and making crypto more viral day after day.

PRICE ACTION AND VIRALITY

The virality force within crypto is its volatility. As we saw together in the previous chapters, the volatility of crypto is not a bug but a marketing feature. The roller coaster with ATH, crashes, bankruptcies, scandals, and overnight millionaire stories is core to the crypto's virality.

It's not something that was designed purposely but something that happened to crypto. Once again, you don't decide virality by degree. It's something that happens to you.

"US VS. THEM" DYNAMICS AND VIRALITY

The cultlike behaviors of people in crypto are also a contributing factor to its virality. It's an *"us vs. them"* mentality, akin to recruiting members into a fervent following. Bitcoiners, for instance, actively engage in *"orange-pilling"* people, drawing them into the cult of Bitcoin maximalism. Max Keiser's podcast, *"The Orange Pill,"* is one among many examples. To *orange-pill* means to convert someone to Bitcoin and convince this person to abandon fiat currencies.

"PUMP MY BAG" CONSCIOUS OR UNCONSCIOUS BEHAVIORS

Holders of a token are keen to spread the word about their token. The reasons are multiple. Maybe they just want to share their enthusiasm. Maybe they want to spread the mission and vision behind the project. Or maybe, consciously or not, they want more people to join and buy so the price of the token goes up making current holders *"richer."*

Crypto and Web3 communities are inherently viral.

The Limits of Referral Systems in Web3

Referral and affiliate programs are among the best-performing growth tactics since the beginning of the internet. The invitation system on PayPal in the late 1990s is one key contributing factor to their exponential growth. Airbnb and Uber also used referral codes to grow their user base. It has been one of the best-performing marketing strategies in Web2 for almost twenty years.

Designing a referral system for a Web3 project is tempting.

Some crypto companies are managing to leverage it, but they are not decentralized products. For instance, a centralized exchange like Binance offers referral rewards in its native token. Ledger hardware wallet is also rewarding affiliates with a commission on sales of physical wallets that they generate.

When it comes to decentralized products and Web3 communities, it's getting trickier.

First, because of a tracking issue. Some information are on chain while others are off chain. You cannot easily bridge these two worlds (even if some start-ups are working on this issue). There are also different forms of conversion. You can measure Web2 actions, like inviting someone to a Discord. It's getting trickier to track the referral of the purchaser of a token on a DEX.

Then let's say you figure out a way to track the conversion and reward it with tokens. What will happen instantly is an **army of bots will invade your projects**. You can add all the antibot features you want. One way or another, airdrop farmers will find a way to work around your limit to try to extract value from your project.

Once a project is completely invaded by bots, it makes it look like a scam, and a growing number of potential holders or users will avoid it.

The StepN Activation Code Method

When we were first introduced to StepN, we were told, *"If you want, I have an invitation code."* It was the first time that we saw this mechanism working efficiently on a Web3 project. StepN also seeks to create a Web2.5 experience where people could get into a blockchain product without too much hassle.

It was also an easy product to describe: *"You're getting paid to walk."* (People forgot to mention, *"But first you have to pay to buy their shoe*

NFT!") StepN managed to gather up to 500,000 daily active users and 2.3 million monthly users. Which makes it one of the most successful Web3 projects ever.

The great thing with StepN in its beginning was that **you couldn't join it unless you had an invite code**. Hopefully, the person who told you about it might have one available. Active members could get activation codes, but in very limited supply and just one at a time.

You could also try your chance on the Telegram group or Discord of StepN where the team was making daily invitation code giveaways.

This wait-and-ask mechanism made people completely obsessed with the project.

Besides introducing **scarcity** to the project, it also allowed StepN to manage the hype of the project and avoid a quick pump-and-dump of the token.

Instead of tens of thousands of new buyers and users today, they were able to manage the influx of new holders.

Instead of begging people to come, you block people from joining unless they have an invitation. They were tapping here into the scarcity effect. It's a classic psychological mechanism that consists of making something scarce and not easily achievable to increase the desire.

The Gryffindor Method

"Five points for Gryffindor!"

Remember how in *Harry Potter*, each member of a house had to wear almost at all times some sign of the house—whether it's the scarf or the logo of the house on their robe?

If you don't want to go too deep into referral or invitation features, at least **make your community *"wear your colors."***

It simply means that you ask your community to add in their bio on their social profiles the name of your token (for instance *"$Side holder"*), add the name of your community *("member of the Side.xyz Army")*, and/or use some visual elements of your project in their banner or profile pictures. If your project has a profile picture NFT, it's even better. You should ask them to display all this on their individual Side.xyz page.

You can **randomly reward community members who wear your colors to incentivize others to join**.

With the Gryffindor Method, you can achieve passive promotion and indirect referral without designing a referral program or asking anything complicated from your community.

Key Takeaways

- Virality is a part of product design, not marketing.
- The good news is that crypto, together with its volatile price actions, is viral by default.
- Do it like StepN: Add a layer of exclusivity and allure around your project by making it *"invite-only."*
- Referral features are good in theory, but impossible to protect from bots in practice (for now).

Bribe It Until You Make It

Fake it until you make it.

—Someone wearing a hoodie and raising funds in Silicon Valley

WIIFM

The *"Bribe is Until You Make It"* method is the most common growth tactic used in Web3. It works . . . but it often backfires (especially if you don't read the end of the chapter).

We're not talking about bribing government officials to get a diplomatic passport. We're referring to a famous motto in Silicon Valley, *"Fake it until you make it."*

In the context of Silicon Valley start-ups, the phrase *"fake it until you make it"* describes a common strategy where early-stage companies project an image of success and growth, even when they are still in the early phases of development

Sometimes it works well and creates billion-dollar businesses. Sometimes it creates companies like WeWork or Theranos.

What Is *"Bribe It Until You Make It"*?

In the context of Web3, **a famous strategy consists of offering *"free money"* in the form of tokens to bring people to your project.**

It's widely used by decentralized exchanges (DEX). A DEX needs to attract a large amount of liquidities to be viable. A DEX is relevant if you have a lot of liquidity to make transactions and trading smoother.

That's the idea.

So when a blockchain or a DEX launches, they offer a lot of *"money"* to people bringing their liquidity there. Of course, they're paying with their token, and people immediately sell the token when they receive it.

Usually, the charts end up looking like this:

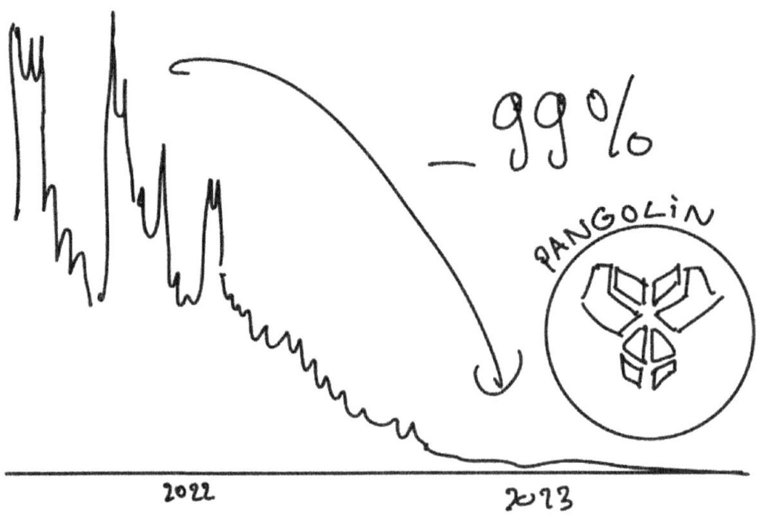

This is the chat of the PNG token of the Avalanche-based DEX Pangolin. Even if Pangolin is a fairly successful DEX, the use of the token in a *"bribe it until you make it"* strategy annihilated it. The token is down 99 percent from the launch.

The problem with the *"bribe it until you make it"* strategy is that you'll attract liquidity farmers who will come to siphon your free money then leave as fast as they arrive. You'll hope that a small percentage will stay.

> Definition: *liquidity farmers*
> *Liquidity farmers* are people who lend or stake cryptocurrencies into a liquidity pool to receive rewards.

But . . . this strategy has proven to be efficient in attracting attention, holders, and liquidity to your project.

The Blur.Io and Terra Luna Case Studies

Let's look at two case studies that attempted this approach and see if they succeeded.

BLUR.IO

Blur.io completely disrupted the NFT marketplace business model by bribing users. The bribe was double.

The first bribe is the absence of fees (while the main competitor OpenSea is charging fees). It's a typical start-up textbook strategy. You raise funds (Blur.io raised $11 million in a round led by Paradigm), you grow super fast (it's called *"blitzscaling"*), and you wait to have a monopoly to monetize your platform. This works if you have external sources of funding to pay for the team and development.

The second bribe is the airdrop of Blur tokens to traders. The more you trade, the more you get free tokens. The only problem is that the token has little to no utility. Traders don't have a reason to hold them. So as soon as they get free tokens, they sell them.

The chart speaks for itself:

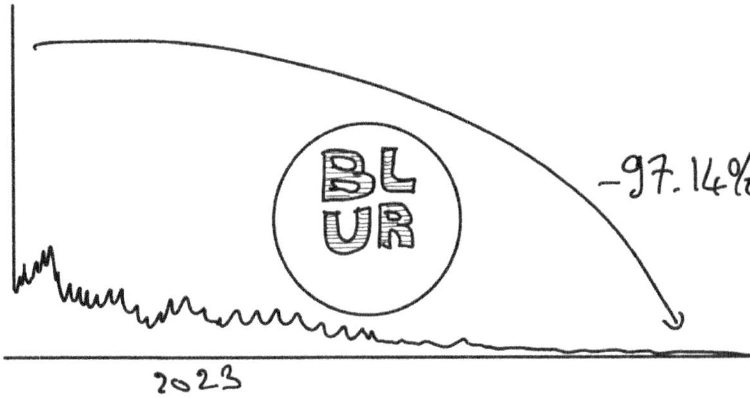

While the first bribe could make sense, the second one would need deeper and more comprehensive tokenomics and business models to *"make it."* The bribe of zero fees also creates the risk that traders will never be willing to pay fees again, which hurts the industry as a whole.

TERRA LUNA

Terra Luna was one of the most epic fails in crypto history. About $60 billion vanished almost overnight.

The Terra ecosystem consisted of two tokens:

- The Terra Luna token, used for governance and mining
- The UST, which was an algorithmic stablecoin designed for mass adoption

The Terra Luna token and UST *"stablecoin"* worked hand in hand. The peg of the stablecoin was maintained by the Terra Luna token. UST goes below $1, you sell Luna tokens to buy back UST. UST goes over $1, you sell UST against Luna token and take the price back to $1.

Now that you have this blockchain (Terra Luna) and the *"stablecoin"* (UST), you still need to attract builders, developers, holders, community members, liquidity, etc. So what do you do? You bribe it until you make it.

Terra Luna introduced the Anchor Protocol. Anchor was a lending-and-borrowing platform for UST, Luna, and other assets. Luna bribed the users with a crazy APY on their UST deposit that wasn't supported by a lending-and-borrowing equilibrium of UST.

Anyone could get a *"risk-free 19.5 percent APY on the US dollar."* That was the bribe.

Of course, we know afterward that it wasn't really the US dollar but UST, and it was extremely risky. People deposited around $20 billion in Anchor Protocol. The market capitalization of Terra Luna grew from $120 million to $40 billion in less than two years, and the UST reached $18.7 billion (70 percent of which was on Anchor Protocol).

Then everything collapsed abruptly in May 2022, taking the whole industry into a deep crypto winter. In retrospect, it's easy to say that it was all obvious and that Luna had no chance.

We're not here to judge them but to understand the *"bribe until you make it"* strategy (which failed). The **19.5 percent APY wasn't sustainable but brought millions of users and dozens of projects to the ecosystem.**

Our take on the strategy was to hope to bring with bribes enough developers, protocols, apps, and use cases to make the ecosystem truly sustainable and have all these people use UST and LUNA tokens. Basically to **pivot from a growth driven by bribes to a growth driven by utility.**

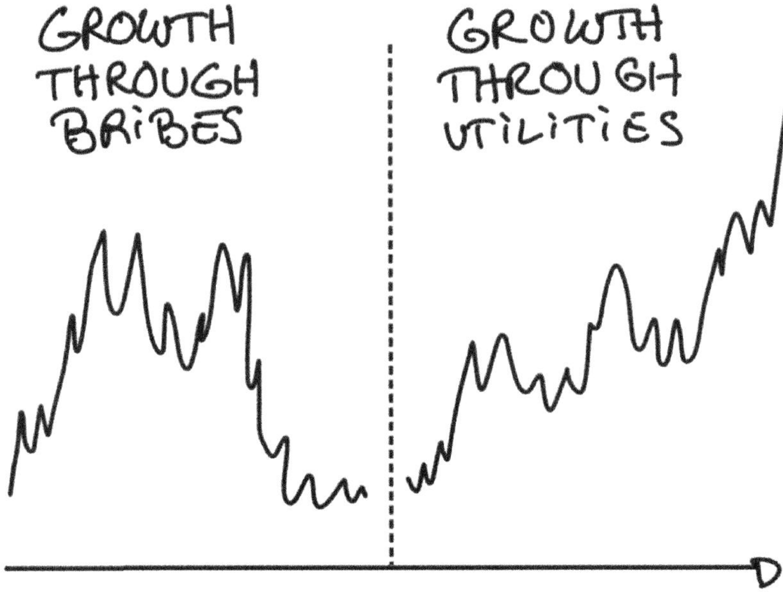

Would it have been possible? Was the project doomed anyway due to his tokenomics design? This we won't answer here.

But it leads us to our next point.

What's Missing Is Actually the *"Make It"* Part

No one cares that the start-up who made it faked it at the beginning. History is written by the winners. Only losers are judged and sentenced. That's unfair, but it's the sad truth of the human condition.

The *"bribe it until you make it"* strategy could work, but in small doses and if the **project is *more* than the bribe**. Blur is more than the bribe. Luna failed to be more than the bribe.

This point is of paramount importance. If the whole thing is a bribing scheme waiting to collapse, then you're navigating in muddy waters.

Bribing will bring traction, users, and attention to your project. That's almost guaranteed. But it's going to be a *"sword of Damocles."* It's the metaphor of a constant threat or danger that hangs over someone, much like the sword that hangs by a single hair over the head of Damocles in the ancient Greek tale.

The whole question is then, how fast can you build utility and real traction for the product itself—real demand and use cases for the NFT or token—to prevent people from simply farming or coming for the thrill of seeing Damocles's sword fall on the project? Notions about utilities, scarcity, loyalty, and tokenomics in the second section of the book are relevant to pursue here.

Key Takeaways

- Bribe people to switch from what they're currently using over to your solution, offering free token rewards, airdrops, or early-adopter rewards.
- Golden Rule: People that receive airdrops will sell immediately. No diamond hands in this part of Web3.
- Make sure that *"bribing"* is not the only interesting aspect of your business model. Most projects bribe too much and focus too little on building a functioning ecosystem.

The Apollo Juggernaut Method

I hired 500 Nigerians in the last 48 hours,
and we got 300 collaborations so far.

—Apollo in Slack, 2022

WIIFM

The Apollo Juggernaut Method requires some organization and focus, but it's one of the most powerful growth strategies.

The following is a solution that aims to answer the biggest question Web3:

"How the heck can I get people to notice my stuff?"

In Web2, that answer is relatively obvious: you make a Google or Facebook Ad account, enter the demographics of the person that you want to sell something to, click a button, and show them your ads long enough until they will eventually convert.

In Web3, that's a bit different.

Running ads doesn't perform very well. Tracking conversion is even harder because the buyer of the token will do the transaction on a platform you don't control (for instance, on Uniswap). Generally speaking, the crypto community doesn't react well to ads. Finally, ads on crypto networks and websites are extremely expensive to run.

That's why builders reach out to influencers and arrange promotional deals so they will shill you to their low-quality audience (more about that in the *"Working with Influencers"* chapter)

So things are not great.

The solution is a well-kept secret from the Web3 space.

It's a Trojan Horse Method but on a massive scale.

What was the Trojan horse again? You give people something that is covered as a gift. They open their walls for you and let you in. You enter the walls, are welcomed as a guest, and plunder the most valuable resources from them.

In Web3, this is slightly less violent. However, the basics still stay the same.

HOW PROJECTS IN THE NFT SPACE TEND TO GROW

You grow your project by offering whitelists to other NFT projects with the same target audience to promote your project.

Fair exchange (in theory).

Both communities get more eyeballs, and current holders are happy that they get new opportunities. Meanwhile, the upcoming project gets instant access to hundreds or thousands of potential qualified holders.

When we were working on Web3 advertising technology in 2022, we were struggling with the same old problem:

How do we get users?

We developed something that we call the Apollo Juggernaut Method, which is inspired by the NFT Trojan horse and goes in the following steps:

1. You come up with a gift.
2. You build a squad of promoters.
3. You start the scale.

You can use this approach for any project that is looking for more partnerships, impressions, and OG supporters.

Step 1—The Gift

To get the attention of the project or community owner, you need to offer them something good enough to get their attention and eventually open their doors to you.

Think about what is something that you could give away for free (no value to you) and that causes curiosity in the heart of the person that you're dealing with.

This could be one of the following:

- Whitelist to an NFT mint
- Exclusive access pass
- Invite link to a closed community
- Presale access for a token
- Free NFT
- X.com post announcing the partnership (if you have a big account)

An important note here is that whatever you give them **should have monetary value to them (*"if I mint this NFT, I will make 2 ETH"*) but little to no value to you (*"Here's $50 worth of my utility token*).**

But . . . there's no free lunch.

In exchange, you expect that the community owner would post about you in their Discord announcement channel, invite you to an AMA, or organize a giveaway with their community.

Since the group owners have the best interest of their community at heart, they will try to get as many gifts as possible but stick to their ground and keep your gift exclusive.

Anything that is easily given away holds no value.

Now that we've identified what to offer the community, we need soldiers that can help us to distribute it.

Step 2—The Squad

In the beginning, looking for projects and communities is something that you can do alone, and because you have the *"founder"* title on your X.com or Discord biography, some people might even lend you an ear.

At some point, this will become too time-consuming or impossible to scale.

That's why you get people to do the talking and selling for you. In old Greece, you called them messengers. In Web3, you call them collaboration managers.

They are a rare species whose sole job is to spend all day talking and connecting projects. They will arrange the deal, transfer the gift, and make sure that agreements are being held.

In exchange, they get paid in stablecoins.

Collab managers come in two shapes or forms.

THE UBER COLLAB MANAGER (A PROFESSIONAL)

He's been in the crypto space for years and knows all the OGs and high-floor-price communities. At some point, he might have started as a mod but climbed his way up the ladder and connected with hundreds of projects along the way. If there is a project that he cannot reach, he knows whom to bribe or talk to.

The saying *"Your network is your net worth"* couldn't be more accurate to describe them. A great *"uber collab manager"* can make all the difference for the success of your project.

- *Where to find them:* Referrals from founders of successful NFT projects or communities. They hang out in expensive alpha groups or private Discord channels or holders.
- *How much to pay:* Around $50–$500 per collab, or weekly retainer of around $200–$400, even though commissions usually work better.
- *Where they're from:* Tier 1 or 2 countries (China, North America, Europe).
- *How many you need:* One to five is usually more than enough.

THE DEGEN COLLAB MANAGER (THE AMATEUR)

In contrast to the *"uber collab manager,"* this individual can get stuff done because he works hard and because he has a lot of time. He has a phone, an internet connection, and eighteen hours per day to make money.

He's not connected or known, but it doesn't matter.

The degen collab manager is usually from a tier 3 or 4 country and has tons of time to work his way into the project. He will send messages to founders, join hundreds of Discords to open tickets, or go through dozens of projects just to close the deal.

They are usually nifty, creative, and extremely fast. They're, however, also the ones that will try all the shortcuts to fool you or take your money (more about how you can prevent this later).

- *Where to find them:* They hang out in technical analysis Telegram groups or DeFi educational groups. The easiest way to find them is probably to make a job posting in a really large but low-quality group, and you will attract the first dozens, then you talk to them and ask them to promote you in the other channels that they're in (Reddit, Telegram, private X.com).

- *Where they're from:* Nigeria, Philippines, Indonesia, and Vietnam.
- *How much to pay:* \$5–\$10 per successful collaboration.
- *How many you need:* Depending on the goal of the operation, you can consider getting hundreds of them, if you manage to remain quality.

Step 3—The Scale

By now you should have around **five to ten collab managers that support you** in your quest to connect with communities all across Web3.

To ensure the success of the attack, you need one thing:

Order.

Send all soldiers without instructions to the battlefield, and you will have guaranteed failure and a big headache.

Let's talk about the foundations.

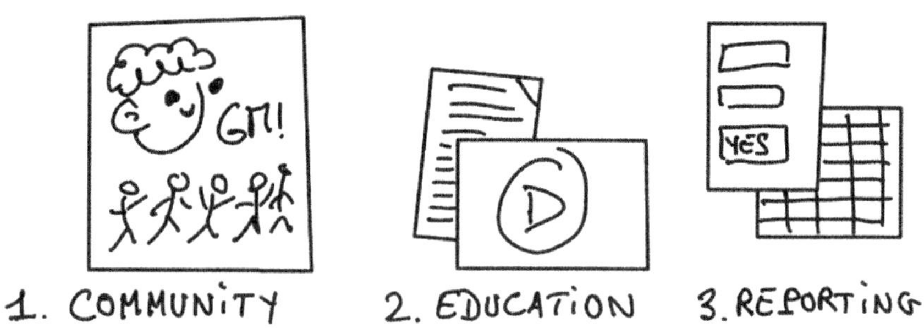

COMMUNITY

Gather your mods somewhere. You can host this group in either Telegram or Discord. One channel for announcements and one channel for communication should suffice.

EDUCATION

They should easily find a document and maybe video tutorials that **tell them exactly what they have to do—and how they get paid**.

The onboarding brief that you prepare for them should include the following points:

1. *Which projects are we looking for?* (List of ten to twenty ideal projects.)
2. *What do we offer them?* (Give a clear explanation of the gift.)
3. *How do you get in touch with them?* (Example workflow for X.com, Discord, research.)
4. *How do you talk to them and close the deal?* (Conversation examples, screenshots, which words to use and not to use.)
5. *What's the daily workflow?* (For example, "*Wake up, do this and this, get paid.*")
6. *How to get paid?* (Explain where to submit the proof and how to get paid.)

The size of your army can vary based on the number of impressions you would like to gather. We started with ten and ended up with over five hundred soldiers. Without structure, this would have been chaos.

Most of the people who will join this new opportunity (get paid for collabs) have done this before. You only need to implement clear lines of communication and reporting.

But . . . what could go wrong?

Most importantly, **you need a clear definition of what a successful deal is.** Is it you being with the founder of the community in a Discord channel? Is it them posting about you in their community? Is it an AMA with the project? Only if that milestone is achieved will they get paid. If that is not the case, you will have *"degen collab managers"* submitting everything that they can get their hands on.

Things you will encounter if you work with a large group:

- Multiple people reaching out to the same project
- Spelling errors in conversations
- Degens getting mad if the other project doesn't hold their part of the deal and starting to insult them
- Degens submitting a project, even if the deal isn't closed

That's why you should always go for quality over quantity. You're trying to close long-term relationships with long-term people.

To ensure additional order among your crowd, we recommend implementing *"sales team"* strategies:

- *Conduct daily ten-minute video calls* to motivate them and give them an image of a positive future.
- *Hire a cheap moderator* ($400 per month) to manage the community, block uninvited guests, and answer any questions that might arise during the collab process.
- *Facilitate extra giveaways* for the *"person with the most collabs"* per week or day.
- *Introduce levels for higher payments.* Get fifty collaborations, and then get $10 instead of $5.

All nice things to do, but **without structure, clear goals, and clear instructions, you won't be able to get it off the ground**. If you manage to organize your squad effectively, you will soon have dozens of partnership agreements flooding through your front gates.

REPORTING

Ask them to fill out an Airtable form once they close a deal. Then you (or your assistant) can go through the document once per day, confirm all successes, reject all failures, and pay the collab soldiers on a layer 2, low-gas-fee blockchain.

Fields in this form can be any of the following:

- Their Telegram name
- The project's name
- The project's X.com
- Screenshot of founder agreeing to collab
- Link/screenshot to *"milestone achieved"*
- Their wallet address

Key Takeaways

- Collab managers are your secret tool to get your first one hundred users.
- To gain access to the walls of neighboring communities, develop a gift or bribe that is attractive enough for them to open their walls to you.
- Your bribe must be cheap for you and valuable for the receiver.
- Always go for quality over quantity in the partnerships that you're closing.

Final Thoughts

Go build something before it's too late.

Friends, the world is at a crucial crossroads, offering two distinct paths.

PATH NO. 1—THE ELYSIUM SCENARIO AND THE GLOBAL FAVELA

If we continue on the current course, a tiny elite amasses all the power. As the French philosopher Montesquieu warned in his 1748 work *The Spirit of the Laws*, *"Power tends to corrupt, and absolute power corrupts absolutely."* This results in the concentration of power, resources, and essential goods in the hands of a select few. It's a world divided into the *"have yachts"* and the *"have nots."*

This scenario leads to increasing suffering, poverty, and violence, along with rising inflation, violence, and insecurity. Eventually, the privileged class separates from the rest of humanity.

It's the Elysium scenario.

In the 2013 movie *Elysium* starring Matt Damon, the wealthy choose to depart from Earth and attain immortality on a space station. Life on Elysium is perfect, with technology capable of solving all problems and diseases.

The remaining inhabitants of Earth endure a difficult existence marked by dust and violence. The residents of Elysium deploy robots resembling those from Boston Dynamics, armed with AR-15 rifles, to maintain control.

Life on Earth becomes a nightmarish experience.

Unfortunately for the people on Earth, reaching Elysium for a better life or to cure an illness is unattainable. Some attempt to build rockets for this purpose, only to face immediate suppression.

The movie serves as a metaphor for a world lacking social mobility and characterized by extreme inequality. In this not-so-distant future, if you're not born into the right group, prospects for an improved life are nonexistent. You're trapped in a global favela.

I'm sorry, but your birth into the wrong group means there's no way out. It's the end.

This serves as a metaphor, yet it reflects the potential trajectory of the world if we stay on the same path.

Nevertheless, there exists an alternative future.

PATH NO. 2: EMBRACING INCLUSIVE INSTITUTIONS THROUGH WEB3 ADOPTION

To understand path number 2, we must look back in time. Here's how it all unfolds:

Every time we witness a new technological innovation, humanity goes through the following phases:

- Phase 1: New and groundbreaking innovations appear, changing how value is created and shared.

- Phase 2: The economic landscape leads to increasing social inequality. The rich get richer, while the poor get poorer. These innovations create value but also provide ways for the wealthy to gather power and resources. These changes in society affect politics and how society functions. At the same time, we see a series of financial bubbles and crashes related to these new technologies. It's a time of upheaval, often accompanied by conflict and destruction.
- Phase 3: Then we see the introduction of what economists Acemoglu and Robinson in *Why Nations Fail* call *"inclusive institutions."*

Acemoglu and Robinson's idea of extractive and inclusive institutions lies at the core of their analysis of why some nations succeed while others fail.

Extractive institutions are characterized by a concentration of power and resources in the hands of a small elite, which often results in limited access to economic and political opportunities for the majority. This tends to hinder innovation, economic growth, and overall stability.

In contrast, inclusive institutions are designed to level the playing field, encourage broad participation in economic and political life, safeguard property rights, and foster competition.

Nations with inclusive institutions are more likely to achieve long-term success and prosperity. This difference emphasizes the vital role institutions play in shaping a country's path.

Here are examples of inclusive institutions:

- The formation of workers' unions in the nineteenth century was a way to slowly shift power to the working class, giving them bargaining power and better wages to support their families.

- The introduction of welfare programs after World War II aimed to distribute economic value and maintain peace in society.

Today we need new *"inclusive institutions."*

And our answer is . . . the blockchain and Web3.

Web3 will bring to humanity the following:

- **Decentralization and Equal Access**: Web3 technologies, such as blockchain, promote decentralization. They reduce the power of central authorities and provide equal access to information and resources for individuals and organizations. This can address issues of information control and inequality.
- **Transparency and Trust:** Blockchain's transparency and immutability make transactions and data trustworthy. This can enhance trust in economic and social interactions, reducing fraud, corruption, and the need for intermediaries.
- **Property Rights and Identity**: Blockchain can establish secure digital property rights and self-sovereign identities. This can empower individuals, particularly in areas where property rights are unclear or disputed.
- **Financial Inclusion**: Web3 can improve financial services, allowing those without access to traditional banking to participate in the global economy. This has the potential to reduce poverty and inequality.
- **Governance and Decision-Making**: Decentralized governance mechanisms enabled by blockchain can give individuals more say in decision-making processes, potentially addressing issues of political exclusion and corruption.
- **Innovation and Economic Growth**: Web3 fosters innovation by enabling new business models and decentralized applications. This can stimulate economic growth and create opportunities for a wider range of entrepreneurs.

- **Global Collaboration**: Web3 technologies facilitate global collaboration without relying on centralized intermediaries. This can help address global challenges such as climate change, pandemics, and poverty.

Blockchain will not solve everything, but it will solve enough things to make the world a better place for the majority of the population.

If Web3 fails, we go to Elysium.

And there is not enough room for everyone there.

That's why we wrote this book.

We're on a mission to make the best Web3 education available for anyone.

Because if Web3 fails, we're all doomed.

So . . . **go build something in Web3.**

PS. If you want to build this future with us, go to www.tokentitans.com/go, and apply to become a company that we work with or invest in. We love to scale and simplify early-stage Web3 ventures. The future is built through collaboration.

If you want us to invest in your venture or help you scale faster and simpler, scan this:

www.tuganapollo.com/go

LEXICON

100% rug rule. Hundred percent of people in Web3 and crypto have been called *"crooks"* and *"gangsters."* In the same way, 100 percent of projects that might see their price go down at some point have been accused of being *"rugs"* and *"scams."*

blacklisting. Similar to banning someone from a club. When a wallet is blacklisted, it's marked as unwelcome, and transactions from or to that wallet are blocked or restricted. It's a way to enforce rules and keep bad actors or unwanted activity out of your project.

burning. Similar to removing some coins from circulation and tossing them into a digital black hole, where they can't be used again. It's a deliberate act to make the remaining coins rarer, which can sometimes increase their value (if you burn a lot).

cash grab. A low-quality, low-effort project designed only to make money and offer little value to the buyer. This term is often used in relation to poor-quality NFT drops.

CryptoKitties. One of the first blockchain games involving NFTs. Players were able to collect, breed, and trade digital cats. One CryptoKitty sold for over $100,000 in ETH, bringing the first wave of attention to NFTs and blockchain gaming.

dApps. The applications that make up the decentralized Web. Most Web3 dApps look and feel just like regular websites and apps. The only difference is that you can access them by connecting your wallet and they run on a decentralized network.

diamond hands. A collector with diamond hands can resist panicking and hold on to an investment even when the price dips . . . believing that the price will rebound. Their hands are as strong and tough as diamonds and cannot be broken—the exact opposite of paper hands.

doxxing. To reveal your personal information (face, name, etc.) to the public. Doxxing can also be the act of disclosing private or personal information of an individual without their consent.

ERC-20. A token standard used on Ethereum and EVM-compatible networks that allows developers to build token applications that are interoperable with other products and services.

floor price. The lowest price of an NFT within a collection that's available to buy. It can be a good metric for the health of a project.

FOMO (fear of missing out). Causes people to make hasty emotional decisions, generally near the top of a speculative mania. FOMO is the force behind Ponzi schemes, stock promotions, and simple legit bubbles.

forking. "To copy and code." Usually, when a project is forking another project, they add more features to suit a specific utility or strategy.

FUD (fear, uncertainty, and doubt). Used to put downward pressure on the price of a coin or NFT. FUD is often spread about new NFT projects, often unfairly to tank the floor price. This can be done to sweep up bargains if successful or as an act of sabotage.

ghost chain. A blockchain that has nothing going on in its ecosystem.

governance token. Similar to a voting ticket in a digital democracy. It's a cryptocurrency token that gives its holder the right to participate in decision-making processes within a specific blockchain ecosystem or decentralized organization.

layers 1 and 2. Ethereum (ETH) is like the main road (layer 1), where all the action takes place directly. Arbitrum is like a faster side road (layer 2) connected to Ethereum, making transactions quicker and cheaper.

liquidity farmers. People who lend or stake cryptocurrencies into a liquidity pool to receive rewards.

litepaper. A concise, easy-to-digest version of a whitepaper that highlights the important information about your Web3 project. It's an effective way to capture the interest of potential investors and users and give them a better understanding of what your project is all about.

mint. Usually used to describe the launch of an NFT collection in which users interact with the smart contract and receive a random NFT. In the previous NFT bull market, NFT mints were highly anticipated since users who were whitelisted were able to sell their minted NFTs only minutes later for thousands of dollars in profit.

OGs. Referred to as *"original gangsters."* Being an OG means being there from the beginning.

ordinals (ordinal NFTs). New form of blockchain-based asset. They allow investors to create and purchase NFTs inscribed directly onto the Bitcoin blockchain. Ordinals enjoyed much attention in the spring of 2023 but quickly faded away due to high network costs.

OTC deals. Similar to a private table at a fancy restaurant. Instead of buying tokens on the public market, VCs prefer private deals with projects. It's like having a tailored menu and personal chef, allowing them to negotiate specific terms and prices without ordering from the menu.

presale. A limited-time sale before the official launch, where a project sells its tokens to a select group of early investors at a discounted price. It follows the same principles as an initial coin offering (ICO).

rug pull. Derived from the phrase *"pulling the rug out,"* it is a cryptocurrency scam in which fraudulent developers attract investors to what seems like a promising new opportunity, only to vanish with the invested money seconds later, leaving the investors with a valueless investment.

smart contracts. Similar to digital agreements or smart deals. It's a set of rules written in code that self-executes based on predefined conditions. Imagine a smart contract as a digital handshake, ensuring that specific actions occur automatically when certain conditions are met.

tokenomics. Derived from the words *"token"* and *"economics"*—the study of the supply, demand, distribution, and valuation of cryptocurrencies.

Tornado Cash. A decentralized privacy tool in the world of cryptocurrencies. It's like a mixer for digital money. When you put your digital coins (like Ethereum) into Tornado Cash, it shuffles them with coins from other people. When you withdraw, you get coins that are hard to trace back to your original ones. Yes—it's too good to be true. The founders are facing charges for laundering of over $1 billion worth of tokens.

utility token. Similar to a special coupon you can use within a specific ecosystem. It's a digital token issued by a project or platform that grants access to certain products, services, or features within that ecosystem.

vesting. A mechanism that allows Web3 companies to distribute tokens to their employees and other service providers over time, subject to certain conditions or milestones. This ensures that the team stays committed to the long-term future of the project, and it increases the trust of the investors.

wallet. Similar to a digital bank account for the decentralized internet. It's a secure tool that lets you store, manage, and use cryptocurrencies and other digital assets. Imagine it as your personal digital wallet but for the blockchain world.

Web3 law of gravity. The law states that things that go up in value often go down in value much faster than they go up.

whitelisting. Owning a whitelist is like having an exclusive guest list for a VIP event. It's a process where you register or get approval to participate in a specific activity, like a token sale or a restricted area. Only those on the list (whitelisted) are allowed access, adding an element of exclusivity and control to the event or platform.

Our Concepts

Apollo Juggernaut Method. Make a list of the ten communities that your target audience hangs out in. Come up with a bribe to offer the owner. Then have the owner talk about you to their community or on their socials.

Berlin Techno Club. Your job as a project owner is to make sure the music is always pumping in your community. Why? The ones inside the club should never leave, and the newcomers that just entered must feel the incredible vibes. Just like in a Berlin Techno Club.

Blockchain Aristocracy. OG opinion leaders and protocol or blockchain founders. They are here from the start and are very picky about whom they allow in their illustrious circle.

Blockchain Trilemma.

1. Scalability
2. Security
3. Decentralization

You can only have two, and you have to compromise on the third one.

Bribe it until you make it. What's the easiest way to attract hundreds of thousands of users to join your ecosystem? Bribe them with your utility token. This most often goes wrong, and most projects don't actually *"make it,"* so be weary of bribing too much.

FU Army. Have a crowd of holders, fans, or degens who support your project and mission so you can say FU and not depend on VCs, influencers, and other factors.

GB. We don't say *"GM,"* we say, *"Go build."*

MVG (Minimal Viable Guru). A semipublic figure who inspires to drive traction to a project.

Niche Monopolizer. Pick an ultraspecific niche, infiltrate the community, and become the *"go-to"* guy in that niche.

Orbiting Influencer. Every big project has them. It's a number of content creators that become big only thanks to the project. They start by commenting on the roadmap, summarizing AMAs, or giving opinions on new features. By doing that consistently, they become local heroes of the community, and since they get small token shares, usually also get very wealthy.

PayPal Mafia. A circle of powerful, like-minded builders with whom you will consistently build things.

Seal of Approval. Exit the technobabble. An easy method to see if your message is understandable enough is to answer the question:

Does a child or golden retriever understand it?

Yes? Here's your Seal of Approval.

The 300. Web3 is empty. It's a game of 300 builders.

Titan Slap. Every time you want to buy a shitcoin or pray for a 100x, we will give you a Titan Slap. You get rich by building, not investing.

Token Titan. Somebody that follows our trajectory of . . .

1. not investing but building,
2. not buying tokens but getting them in exchange for time,
3. understanding that crypto is not about when you can buy but how long you can stay,
4. building stuff every day, and
5. living a life outside what your old friends and parents think is a good career.

Tugan Method.

1. Target.
2. Understand.
3. Grow.
4. Advocate.
5. Negotiate.

This method was invented to show users how to contribute to a project by being early and making 10x on the coin without investing a penny. Or to show project owners how to crowdsource an army of content creators who are paid with a utility token.

VC Ponzi Farming. The Ponzi scheme way to raise funds if you're building for the *"have nots"*:

1. Launch product.
2. Publish a campaign on Zealy, Gleam, or Magic Store.

3. Get 500,000 users in 24 hours.
4. Raise funds.
5. Hope the high-quality users will follow.

Web2.5 Approach. It offers the benefits of the blockchain without the technical barrier—the best of both worlds.

Web3 Murphy's Law. "Anything that can go wrong will go wrong." And in Web3, that comes sooner than anticipated.

Web3 Perestroika Moment. The majority of people are afraid to get into Web3 because they think the government will make building in Web3 illegal. This won't happen because in every layer of society, many people benefit from Web3.

Web3 Power Triangle. This comes down to being a member of the PayPal Mafia, unlocking Web3 Aristocrat status, and owning an FU Army. If you manage to have two corners of the triangle, the third one comes for free. And if you own all three corners, you will be unstoppable.

Web3 Trilemma. Look at your Web3 project through the following three corners:

1. Attractive to holders
2. Profitable for the team
3. Long-lasting

About the Authors

Tugan Bara

Tugan Bara is one of the most renowned educators and contrarian thinkers in the French marketing space.

In recent years, he has taught his lessons and ideas to more than tens of thousands of entrepreneurs.

During that time, he has created many valuable tech startups together with members of his audience. Talk about a hidden motive . . .

Some of them are Tugan.ai, Frog.tech, and Bonzai.lol.

In 2020, he transitioned into building and distributing stuff in Web3.

Since then he has been involved in building many valuable community or tech-focused projects, among the recent ones being Side.xyz.

In his free time, he likes to ponder about philosophy, technology, and macroeconomics.

Niko Apollo

After graduating from business school, Apollo spent nine months working in one of the world's best hotels in Tokyo, Japan, where he honed the craft of creating beautiful experiences.

He left the hospitality industry shortly after and joined a wave of what some called *"internet cowboy entrepreneurs."* During this period, he became head of growth and operations in major e-commerce and education companies.

In late 2021, he received an offer from a friend who stated: *"Hey, bro, we're doing this NFT thing. Want to run it?"* The growth frameworks he designed are now being used by dozens of Web3 companies around the world.

When he's not coming up with process and growth hacks, he likes to sleep in 5-star hotels just for the sake of pondering about how you can create equally beautiful experiences online.

Legal Titans

All trademarks and service marks belong to their respective owners. Mentions of these trademarks are solely for editorial purposes, and no commercial claims are asserted for their use unless explicitly owned by the Author or the Publisher. The Author and Publisher have no affiliations with these marks, and their endorsement is not implied for any individuals or business entities mentioned in this book.

Limits of Liability

This book is intended as a general educational information product and is not a replacement for professional advice on the discussed topics. The materials are presented "as is" without any express or implied warranties, including, but not limited to, merchantability and fitness for a specific purpose. The Author and Publisher disavow all warranties, whether express or implied, including any assurance of defect corrections or virus-free websites or servers providing the book. The Author does not guarantee or make any representations about the correctness, accuracy, or reliability of the materials. Some jurisdictions may not permit the exclusion of implied warranties, and, thus, this exclusion may not apply to all readers.

The Author and Publisher are not responsible for any special or consequential damages arising from the use or inability to use this book, even if they were alerted to such potential damages. Some jurisdictions may not allow the limitation or exclusion of liability for incidental or consequential damages, and, therefore, this limitation or exclusion may not apply to all readers. In no case shall the total liability of the Author or Publisher exceed the amount paid for this book.

Readers agree to hold the Author, Publisher, and related parties harmless from any liability for claims due to injuries, including attorney fees and costs, except for claims of gross negligence or intentional tort, which will be settled through confidential binding arbitration.

The information in this book is believed to be accurate at the time of placement. It is for informational purposes only and should not be considered a source of specific legal, financial, tax, physical, or mental health advice. The described services are only offered where legally allowed. The information may not be all-inclusive and should not be relied upon as such.

Hyperlinks within this book may lead to external websites and information controlled by other individuals and organizations. The Author and Publisher do not guarantee the accuracy, completeness, relevance, or timeliness of the information or privacy policies on these linked websites.

The facts and information in this book are believed to be accurate at the time they were included for informational purposes. All data provided in this book is intended for information only. The information within is not meant to offer specific legal, financial, tax, physical, or mental health advice to individuals or companies and should not be depended upon as such. The described services are available only in jurisdictions where they are legally permitted. The information provided is not comprehensive and is limited to what is available; thus, it should not be considered all-encompassing or entirely accurate.

Recommendations are made in good faith, either based on personal experience or research into the Provider's reputation.

Earnings and Income Disclaimers

The Author and Publisher make no promises or guarantees about future earnings or financial success resulting from the purchase of this book. Any income statements or examples are estimates and do not assure the same results. Testimonials and examples in the book represent exceptional results and may not apply to the average person.

The state of the economy may affect your results, and success using the information in this book depends on various factors. The Author and Publisher do not guarantee or imply that readers will get rich or achieve any earnings. Business activities involve unknown risks.

Your success or lack thereof in using the information or strategies provided in this book depends on various factors. The Author and the Publisher cannot predict how well you will do because they have no knowledge of your background, work ethic, dedication, motivation, desire, or business skills and practices. Therefore, neither the Author nor the Publisher guarantees or implies that you will become wealthy, achieve success, or earn any income (or any sort of compensation)

Businesses and the earnings derived from them involve unknown risks and may not be suitable for everyone. You should not rely on any information presented in this book or provided by the Author or Publisher unless you understand that you may experience significant losses, including the money spent on purchasing this book and establishing, operating, and marketing your business activities, and further, that you may not earn any income.

Forward-Looking Statements

Any forward-looking statements in this book express opinions about earnings potential. Actual results may vary, and no guarantees are made regarding the achievement of similar results to the Author or others.

Purchase Price

The book's price is arbitrarily set by the Publisher and does not relate to objective standards.

Due Diligence

Readers are advised to conduct their own due diligence before making any decisions based on the book's content. Seek professional advice when necessary.

The Author and Publisher are not responsible for any losses or damages resulting from the use of links, information, or opportunities provided in the book. Readers should always perform their investigations before buying products or services offline or online, including those sold through hyperlinks in the book.

If you don't agree with these terms and conditions, don't read this book. By using this book, its products and services, or participating in any activities mentioned, you are legally agreeing to these terms.

Printed in Great Britain
by Amazon

55579706R00284